Advance praise í
Finding Francis, Followii

D0792451

"Francis lives! He walks right off the pages of this
violent world of America today. Michael Crosby has given us the opportunity to
meet Francis as if for the first time. A thoughtful and mature work from one of the
most prophetic writers in America today."

— Mary Jo Leddy, author, *Radical Gratitude*

"Only Michael Crosby could make so many creative and compelling connections!
As a follower of Christ and of Francis, I can only hope that this book receives the
readership it deserves. It is radical, personal, inspiring, and brilliant at the same time."

— Richard Rohr, O.F.M., Center for Action and Contemplation,
Albuquerque, New Mexico

"Readers of Michael Crosby's work know his passion for a new way of living Christian faith in our world. In *Finding Francis, Following Christ* he reveals the personal
roots of that passion through a retelling of the story of a hero's journey, that of
Francis of Assisi. The saint of thirteenth-century Umbria suggests an alternative to
our increasingly violent society, to an economics of global greed and dehumanizing
ideologies. Crosby's retrieval of early Franciscan stories will make readers stop and
think how much the world today could be different if the message of the Little Poor
Man of Assisi were taken seriously."

— William J. Short, O.F.M., Franciscan School of Theology, Berkeley

"Provocative as always, Michael Crosby offers in this exposition of the life of Francis
of Assisi a commentary on our own time and the radical requirements of the Gospel
of justice and peace. He most eloquently describes Francis' 'surrender' of the false
ways of power and possession and his 'capture' of the power and gift of God's love
in the Incarnation!"

— Joseph P. Chinnici, O.F.M., former provincial minister of the Franciscan Friars

"Michael Crosby's fresh approach to the Francis story attempts to engage the 'Franciscan imagination' as an effective means of negotiating the challenges of life in the
church and our world. He succeeds in doing what the early biographers of Francis
did — presenting the life of Francis as an effective model for Christian response to
the challenges of the gospel in their own culture and history. This is an important
book for all who seek the way of justice and peace as a way of life today!"

— Michael W. Blastic, O.F.M., The Franciscan Institute,
St. Bonaventure University

"Provocative, challenging, timely: Michael Crosby breathes new life into the enduring tale of Francis of Assisi. Leaning squarely on the best contemporary scholarship,
he reverently uses the example of Francis to point beyond himself to the mystery of
Christ in today's world. Reading *Finding Francis, Following Christ* is an enriching
experience for anyone eager to investigate the timeless character of Francis and to
discover, in the process, the eternal mystery of Christ."

— Regis J. Armstrong, O.F.M. Cap., editor,
Francis and Clare: The Complete Writings

"Once again, in *Finding Francis, Following Christ* we encounter the kind of honest, courageous, and heartfelt approach to his topic that many of us have come to expect from Michael Crosby's writings. His reflections are daring, insightful, and profoundly relevant for our time. This is not a simple hagiography for our edification. It is, instead, a passionate challenge to take on, in fact, to become the Christ as, indeed, Francis did."

— Barbara Fiand, SNDdeN, author, *From Religion Back to Faith*

"To wean ourselves from the web of personal, cultural, institutional, economic, military, and planetary violence is crucial to Christian conversion. Crosby draws from the best of Franciscan scholarship to present a Francis who shows the way. The 'Spirit of the Lord' leaps from every page!"

— J. A. Wayne Hellmann O.F.M. Conv., Saint Louis University

"This book provides a solid integration of Franciscan spirituality and history as it explores one of the greatest peacemakers of all times, Francis of Assisi. It shows the impact of his life to the burning question of the day — the pursuit of a just peace. Michael Crosby challenges us to reflect on authentic Christian discipleship in a world torn apart by violence, materialism, and ideologies. This is an important study for those who seek to live the Gospel of peace."

— Ilia Delio, O.S.F., Washington Theological Union

"Michael Crosby has not created yet another biography about Francis of Assisi. Rather, he uses the life of Francis to uncover his spiritual insights in fascinating ways. Creating the biography of a spirituality, Crosby has sketched a progression of spiritual insight seldom if ever found in a single glance. *Finding Francis, Following Christ* proves it is possible to construct a Franciscan spirituality that strongly challenges the Franciscan world without rejecting the official sources for Francis' life. . . . I know of no other Franciscan author so on top of the critical literature about joy! It's quite incredible." — William R. Hugo, O.F.M.Cap., author, *Studying the Life of Francis of Assisi: A Beginner's Handbook*

"Michael Crosby's book combines careful study of Franciscan historical and textual research of the last century, deliberate weaving of contemporary critics of the dominant culture, and the Capuchin's Order's collective and courageous effort to redefine Franciscan poverty for our times. The result is a study of themes that permeate the biographies of Francis and that provide a path of illumination for those who see in Francis an enchanting model of discipleship."

— Margaret Carney, O.S.F., S.T.D., President, St. Bonaventure University

"This is a thorough explanation and strong endorsement of the revolution in social and economic relations practiced and preached by St. Francis, following the example of the efforts of Jesus more than a millennium earlier. Both of them insisted on an equality and fraternity — with implied liberty from their inherited cultural structures — that was feared and resisted by secular and ecclesial authorities. These values continue to need and deserve our earnest and concerted defense wherever they are lacking or endangered."

— Beatrice Bruteau, author, *The Holy Thursday Revolution*

FINDING
FRANCIS,
FOLLOWING
CHRIST

MICHAEL H. CROSBY, OFMCAP

ORBIS BOOKS

Maryknoll, New York 10545

Founded in 1970, Orbis Books endeavors to publish works that enlighten the mind, nourish the spirit, and challenge the conscience. The publishing arm of the Maryknoll Fathers and Brothers, Orbis seeks to explore the global dimensions of the Christian faith and mission, to invite dialogue with diverse cultures and religious traditions, and to serve the cause of reconciliation and peace. The books published reflect the views of their authors and do not represent the official position of the Maryknoll Society. To learn more about Maryknoll and Orbis Books, please visit our website at www.maryknoll.com.

Nihil Obstat
Rev. Francis Dombrowski, OFMCap, STC
Provincial Censor of Books
June 17, 2007

Very Rev. Daniel Anholzer, OFMCap
Provincial Minister
Province of St. Joseph of the Capuchin Order
September 25, 2007

Library of Congress Cataloging-in-Publication Data

Crosby, Michael, 1940-
 Finding Francis, following Christ / Michael H. Crosby.
  p. cm.
 Includes bibliographical references (p.) and index.
 ISBN-13: 978-1-57075-729-7
 1. Francis, of Assisi, Saint, 1182-1226. 2. Christian life –
Catholic authors. I. Title.
BX4700.F6C783 2007
271'.302 – dc22

          2007032765

*As we celebrate the 800th Centenary
of the Founding of the Franciscan Order,
its approval by Rome and early movement,
I dedicate this book to all Franciscans
and others who have helped me understand more fully
the individual, communal, and institutional implications
of conversion to Jesus' Gospel of the Rule of God
in ways that convince me that God's Trinitarian Relations
must ground all our relationships.*

Contents

Preface

Some years ago I spoke at a suburban Milwaukee church on October 4, the feast of St. Francis. A wide range of people attended, including three or four Franciscan Sisters. I had chosen the occasion to share some of the ideas about Francis that will be found in this book.

When I finished my remarks, the Franciscan Sisters were the first to head for the door. Later, as people congregated near the refreshments, I sensed they were keeping their distance from me. Intrigued by their negative body language, I sought them out. It was then I discovered the cause of their disappointment. As one of them noted, "Father, you didn't say anything at all about the way he talked to the wolf."

While this pious sentiment is meaningful for some people, for many others such a "Francis-for-the-Birds" approach stands as an icon of irrelevance. Still others use Francis as an ideological battering ram to support their own pet peeves about our culture and the church.

Such a polarity of positions has challenged me to probe more deeply the meaning of the world's most popular saint. And this, in turn, has led me to a more profound study of the violent context of his times and the critical texts, including his own words and writings, that reveal a person struggling to be faithful to the Highest Authority he knew.

Francis' continued relevance can be found in the way he is invoked in relation to key issues in our society, such as poverty and violence; in relation to conflicts in our church around issues of equality and justice; and in contemporary spirituality, around the growing need for a cosmic consciousness that is centered in Christ. At the same time so many of the attitudes associated with Francis — enthusiasm, desire, intentionality, purposefulness, and, especially, joy — seem to be exactly the qualities that are widely sought; people pay huge sums to motivational speakers who can show how to incorporate these dynamics in their personal and professional lives. And so, believing that Francis offers such an intriguing and hopeful model, I am pleased to offer this reflection on his life and his message for the church and the world today.

Acknowledging that "where I stand" (as a white, male, Catholic cleric living in the United States) affects "how I see" Francis, I would like to offer a few points. First of all, my primary interpretive net for probing the life of Francis will be to assess his relevance for our times. I am particularly interested in what Francis reveals about the meaning of conversion and holiness. I desire to present Francis' evangelical model of imitating Jesus Christ in such a way (as Francis wrote) that we find in him a pattern that we ourselves might emulate in a way that gives "birth to [Christ] through a holy activity which must shine as an example before others."[1] Toward this goal, I will to try to interpret Francis in a manner that invites us to translate his mode of response to the violence in his world into a response to our own.

In writing any biography the wheat must be separated from the chaff. This is especially true in writing about someone so defined, debated, and dissected as Francis. Thus, I will refrain, as far as possible, from highlighting the popular stories about Francis (the "chaff") that have not survived the test of historical accuracy (the "wheat"). This approach has been made easier by the recently published three-volume work *Francis of Assisi*, edited by three friars, each representing one of the three main groups of the Franciscan "First Order": Regis J. Armstrong, O.F.M.Cap., J. A. Wayne Hellmann, O.F.M.Conv., and William J. Short, O.F.M.[2] Believing in the importance of limiting myself to the acknowledged Franciscan "sources,"[3] I will concentrate on those recognized texts that are considered more authentic, including the recognized words of Francis himself.[4]

I admit to feeling quite inferior to the many Franciscan scholars who have dedicated their lives to this study. Indeed as I read the popular works of authors like Sabatier, Jörgensen, and Chesterton, along with the works of those that represent the historical-critical method, such as Fortini, Esser, Englebert, and Manselli, I acknowledge that I can only stand on their shoulders. And yet I realize that the seeds of this work have been incubating for many decades. They go back at least to July 15, 1959, the day I consciously chose to become a Capuchin Franciscan. Although I may never have received a formal degree in Franciscan studies, I have been nurtured by works and studies on Francis for almost fifty years.

The actual decision to write this book took shape when I was asked to give a retreat to Franciscan friars of the Cincinnati province in 2005. I used the occasion to present Francis as a positive model for emulation in the midst of the political and ecclesiastical polarization of our day. When the friars affirmed my approach, I developed it further in a 2006 retreat at Villa Maria, Pennsylvania. I am deeply appreciative to those who helped me test these ideas, as well as those who later read the drafts of this book. These include Tom Plakut, the former director of our St. Benedict Meal Program, my cousin Suzanne Tamiesie, and my Capuchin brother, Dan Crosby. Their insights and connections, challenges, and support have enhanced the material presented herein. In particular I am thankful to my fellow Capuchin Franciscan Francis Dombrowski. For years he has acted as provincial censor of books, including my own. However, with this book, he went beyond the call of duty, continually urging me to make relevant to our current world the wisdom of Francis in ways that might be replicated. His gentle prodding has made the book much stronger as a result.

I have written quite a few books for Orbis over the years. I have never thanked its editorial staff for the varied ways they have "cleaned up my act." I want to thank Catherine Costello and John Eagleson for putting up with my recommended changes, sometimes (as with this book) until the very days of going to press. I especially want to thank Robert Ellsberg, now publisher at Orbis. Because I have had such an honest and helpful relationship with him over the years with my manuscripts, I asked him specifically to facilitate the editing of this book. I cajoled him not only because of his editorial expertise but also because, in his own books on the subject, he has become identified with the effort to make saints relevant to our lives today. Without his immense help and insights this book would be sorely lacking.

Finally, to all who read this book, I repeat the evangelical greeting of Jesus which Francis made his own, which he urged his followers to use, and which our violent world challenges us anew to make our own: "Peace be to your house."

CHRONOLOGY

The Life of Francis of Assisi in the Context of the Violence of His Times

632   Mohammed dies.

1098–99   First Crusade (called at Claremont, 1095). Kingdom of Jerusalem established.

1146–48   Second Crusade. Urban II. Promoted by Bernard of Clairvaux. Ends in humiliating failure. Bernard (1090–1153) praises rise of new military Orders: *De laudibus novae militiae*.

1160   Frederick Barbarossa (1152–90), Holy Roman Emperor, conquers Assisi.

1181   Francesco born as Giovanni (after John the Baptist) Bernardone in Assisi. Barbarossa visits Rocca Maggiore, ruled by his legate.

1187   October 2: Jerusalem falls to Saladin three weeks before Gregory VIII named pope.

            October 29: Gregory VIII calls for Third Crusade — the one thing that united pope and emperor.

1189–92   Third Crusade. Richard I, the Lion-Hearted. Modest success. Peace treaty.

1198   January 8: Innocent III elected pope (1198–1216). Orders the surrogate of Holy Roman Emperor, Philip (1198–1208), Duke Conrad di Lützenfeld, to transfer allegiance from the emperor to himself. On the way to surrender the entire duchy, including Assisi, to the pope, the townspeople (including Francis?) besiege and raze the Rocca Maggiore.

            August: Innocent III calls Fourth Crusade for 1202–4. Innocent's approach to Islam is diplomatic (via letters, effort to negotiate) and religious. Islam as evil: "Mohammed, that son of perdition. A disgrace the Sons of the slave-girl, the vile Moslems, should hold our mother captive."

1199–1200   Civil war in Assisi between feudal and merchant classes. Family of Clare Offreduccio moves to Perugia. Commune established.

1202   War between Perugia and Assisi. Assisi defeated at Colle-strada. Francis taken prisoner.

1202–4   Fourth Crusade.

1203   Francis ransomed by his father when taken ill in prison in Perugia. Long illness — until 1204.

1204   Signing of peace treaty between Perugia and Assisi. However, conflicts remain.

            April 12–15: Sack of Constantinople by Christian crusaders. They loot the city.

1205   Francis tries to join Walter of Brienne as knight in Apulia. Vision at Spoleto. Returns home. Wears hermit habit. San Damiano cross: "Francis, repair my house which is falling into ruin."

1206   Francis sells father's cloth. Tries to give proceeds to priest at San Damiano. Pietro charges him at the bishop's palace. Francis disrobes, transferring his loyalty from his father to his "Father in heaven."

1207   Spring: Experience of leper. Francis in Gubbio, nursing lepers off and on until 1208.

            Summer: Returns to Assisi. Gets hermit's habit from Guido. Begins work on San Damiano, St. Peter's, and St. Mary of the Angels (Portiuncula, "Little Portion"). Chalks "Tau" on back of habit.

1208   Hears Gospel (Luke 10:5–6) at Mass: (1) Take nothing for your journey; and (2) Proclaim "good news" of king-dom = peace. "This is what I want." Changes hermit habit to tunic of the poor. Around April Bernard and Peter of Cantanio join him (1C 23). They open Bible and read three passages: "Go, sell . . . ," "Take nothing," "If anyone wants to be a follower..." Bishops' concern about his poverty: "Let us not acquire...arms to protect it" (L3C, 33). Inquisition begins after papal legate killed in France. "Crusaders" kill seven thousand unresisting Cathari and Waldensians.

1209	With eleven followers and Rule, goes to Rome. Way of Life approved. Probably has peace plank contained in it: "Go, my brothers, pronouncing peace." "The Delegation of Peace." Learned greeting from "the Lord." People unaccustomed to the new greeting. Varied initial reactions. Francis: "As you announce with your mouth, make sure you have greater peace in your hearts" (AC, 8.38). Preaches to the birds. More conflict between Assisi and Perugia. Settlement at Rivo Torto. Emperor-elect Otto IV passes near Rivo Torto.
1210	Begins Third Order? Unlike Cathari and Waldensians, it was a joyful form of penance.
1211	November 9: Peace treaty between warring factions in Assisi. New majores/minores. First trip to Saracens. Dalmatia. Takes ship to Syria. Strong winds force a return (1C, 55).
1212	Children's Crusade. Victory leads Innocent to think Islam can be conquered militarily. Clare (b. 1193) runs way from home; enters at Portiuncula. When family comes, claims sanctuary.
1213	April 19: Innocent III issues encyclical (1) calling for Fourth Lateran Council to reform the church and retake the Holy Land; (2) calls for Fifth Crusade to take place (1217–21).
	May 8: Count Orlando offers Mt. La Verna to Francis for a hermitage.
1213–14	Francis' second trip to Saracens. Goes to convert the Caliph. Gets as far as Spain. Returns.
1215	Dominic gets approval for his Order from Innocent III. Francis preaches peace to birds. Fourth Lateran Council begins. Francis attends. Embraces "Tau" as Order's symbol. Meets Dominic?
1216	Francis' malaria forces him to accept care of Bishop Guido at his residence.
	July 16: Innocent III dies in Perugia. Honorius III elected. French Archbishop Jacques de Vitry at Perugia. He writes

about Order. Portiuncula Indulgence. First universal, then restricted.

1217   Pentecost Chapter decides to have eleven provinces, mission. Brothers go to Holy Land under Elias. Francis prays for peace in Arezzo, torn by civil war.

June: Fifth Crusade begins. Called by Innocent III; implemented by Honorius III.

1218   Malik al-Kamil succeeds his uncle Saladin as Sultan of Egypt, Palestine, and Syria.

1219   May 26. First missionaries to Morocco. Malik al-Kamil offers to make peace with crusaders; would give Jerusalem and the Holy Cross if they withdraw from Egypt. King of Jerusalem and some crusaders open to offer. Cardinal Pelagius, papal legate, rejects it; he heads crusade. Believed they could win. Cardinal Hugolino urges Francis to adopt Rule of Benedict, Augustine, or Basil. He rejects idea.

Pentecost Chapter. Beginning of dissent among friars between itinerants and conventuals. July to Spring: Francis' third trip to Islam. Sails to Acre and Damietta. Visits Sultan Malik al-Kamil.

August 29: Defeat of crusaders at Damietta.

November 5: Damietta retaken by crusaders.

1220   January 20: First martyrs killed in Morocco after insulting Islam. "The Saracens gladly listened to the Friars Minor preach as long as they explained Christ and the doctrine of the Gospel." Instead, they insult Islam; subsequently killed for blasphemy.

Francis goes to Acre and Holy Land; returns to find increasing divisions among brothers; goes to Honorius III: "Father Pope, God give you peace." Asks for "Protector." Cardinal Hugolino.

First Letter to the Custodians. Calls for bells to be rung every hour so "praise may be offered to almighty God by everyone all over the world" (Francis' *sâlat?*). Bologna incident; preaching brings peace. Francis resigns. Peter of Cantanio is vicar of the Order.

1221	General Chapter. *Regula non bullata* written (First, unapproved Rule). Includes c. 16 on how brothers should go about in world: not militarily but spiritually. Cantanio dies. Elias becomes vicar of the Order. Fifth Crusade fails.
1223	November 29: *Regula bullata* approved by Honorius III. Midnight Mass at Greccio; Francis as deacon.
1224	At La Verna, Francis allegedly receives stigmata around September 14. First Franciscans to England.
1225	On a visit to Clare his eye sickness turns worse.
	April and May: Writes Canticle of Creation.
	June: Adds to Canticle reconciliation verse concerning feud between Bishop Guido II and Oportulo, *podestà* of Assisi (AC, 84). They reconcile. Dispute also resolved with peace agreement.
	Francis was cauterized with a hot poker along his temple from his eyebrows to his ears. For health reasons, he stays at the bishop's residence.
1226	May/June: Composes the *Testament*. Francis' health declining, he insists on returning to Portiuncula. Dies there October 3 or 4.
1227	March 19. Cardinal Hugolino of Ostia becomes Gregory IX (1227–41).
	Frederick II (1220–50) negotiates with Sultan Malik al-Kamil to give Jerusalem, Bethlehem, and some other holy places in exchange for Saracens to be able to visit Dome of the Rock and al-Aqsa mosque. Gregory IX is upset because he saw crusade as way of salvation for crusaders. Gregory IX issues a bull to build a basilica to honor the impending saint, Francis of Assisi, July 16, 1228.
1228	Francis declared a saint by Gregory IX in Assisi. Gregory IX authorizes Thomas of Celano to write the first biography of Francis.
1229	February 25: Celano presents completed biography to Gregory IX.
1230	Transfer of Francis' body to the basilica.

Abbreviations

Writings of St. Francis

Adm	The Admonitions
BlL	A Blessing for Brother Leo
CtC	The Canticle of Creation
CTExh	The Canticle of Exhortation
ER	The Earlier Rule (*Regula non bullata*)
ExhP	Exhortation to the Praise of God
LR	The Later Rule (*Regula bullata*)
LtAnt	A Letter to Brother Anthony of Padua
1LtCl	First Letter to the Clergy (earlier ed.)
2LtCl	Second Letter to the Clergy (later ed.)
1LtCus	The First Letter to the Custodians
2LtCus	The Second Letter to the Custodians
1LtF	The First Letter to the Faithful
2LtF	The Second Letter to the Faithful
LtL	A Letter to Brother Leo
LtMin	A Letter to a Minister
LtOrd	A Letter to the Entire Order
LtR	A Letter to the Rulers of the People
OfP	The Office of the Passion
PrCr	The Prayer before the Crucifix
PrOF	A Prayer Inspired by the Our Father
PrsG	The Praises of God
RH	A Rule for Hermitages
SalBVM	A Salutation of the Blessed Virgin Mary
SalV	A Salutation of the Virtues
Test	The Testament
TPJ	True and Perfect Joy

Franciscan Sources

AC	*The Assisi Compilation*
AP	*The Anonymous of Perugia*
1C	*The Life of St. Francis* by Thomas of Celano
2C	*The Remembrance of the Desire of a Soul* (Celano's Second Life of Francis)
3C	*The Treatise on the Miracles* by Thomas of Celano
L3C	*The Legend of the Three Companions*
LFl	*The Little Flowers of St. Francis*
LJS	*The Life of St. Francis* by Julian of Speyer
LMj	*The Major Legend* by Bonaventure
LMn	*The Minor Legend* by Bonaventure
1MP	*The Mirror of Perfection,* Smaller Version
2MP	*The Mirror of Perfection,* Larger Version
ScEx	*The Sacred Exchange between St. Francis and Lady Poverty*
TL	*Tree of Life* by Ubertino da Casale
VL	*The Versified Life of St. Francis* by Henri D'Avranches

Scripture abbreviations are from the New Revised Standard Version of the Bible, with Apocrypha. Some passages from the Writings of St. Francis and Franciscan Sources have italicized words. These italics indicate references to the Sacred Scriptures. For the scriptural source, confer the actual text.

The Necessity of Having the Gospel Fulfilled in Our Lives

For it had to be that the Gospel call be fulfilled in the one who was to be in faith and in truth a minister of the Gospel.[1]
— Brother Thomas of Celano, *Life of St. Francis,* 3.7

The Journey Pattern of the Mythic Hero

In his many books on heroes, heroines, and the myths that survive them, Joseph Campbell showed that great cultures define their character through individuals whose lives are held up as models of the heroic. When the story of such a hero or heroine is told in a way that the "person becomes a model for other people's lives, he has moved into the sphere of being mythologized."[2] In other words, when a people not only regard the hero as one to be elevated but emulated, the hero or heroine has reached a level of mythic proportions.

Stories of the hero use mythic images and language according to a predictable pattern. Often that pattern articulates a journey of some kind. Sometimes this involves an inner quest; at other times it involves an extended voyage. Most often the journey is initiated by some crisis or conflict in the person's life. It may arise from an internal sense of not feeling complete, a sense of being overwhelmed by forces beyond one's power or a desire to escape from cultural or social dynamics that have begun to debilitate the person's life and sap his or her energy. Given this alienating experience, such people withdraw from the situation, consciously or unconsciously seeking an alternative way to address or redress the critical situation. The time of withdrawal can be short or long. However, in the mythic story, what occurs during the departure from one's "world" involves an experience of something that empowers the person to return to the previous situation in a new way. The crisis/withdrawal/empowerment pattern is outlined well by Campbell:

1

You leave the world that you're in and go into a depth or into a distance or up to a height. There you come to what was missing in your
consciousness in the world you formerly inhabited. Then comes the
problem either of staying with that, and letting the world drop off, or
returning with that boon and trying to hold to it as you move back
into your social world again.[3]

Campbell found this mythic pattern of crisis/withdrawal/empowerment
replicated in many religious founders who offered their world "a new way
of life." In order to found something that would be considered authentically
new, they had to leave the old. In their consequent withdrawal they began
their quest. In the process they came upon an insight; a germinal idea was
discovered. This new discovery contained the "potentiality of bringing forth
that new thing."[4] According to Campbell's perspective, classic examples of
such universal heroes are the Buddha, Jesus, and Mohammed. From my own
understanding, another example of such a hero — a source of inspiration
as well as emulation — is Francis of Assisi (1181–1226). As the Brazilian
theologian Leonardo Boff noted so well:

He is the purest figure (gestalt) of Western history, of the dreams,
the utopias, and of the way of relating panfraternally that we are all
searching for today. He speaks to the most archaic depths of the modern soul, because there is a Francis of Assisi hidden within each one
of us, struggling to emerge and expand freely among the moles of the
modern age.[5]

Before examining how the mythic journey or vision quest was fulfilled in
Francis in the way he envisioned the seed of the Gospel as that "new thing"
that could change people's lives, it will be good to begin by examining its
initial embrace and proclamation in the life of Jesus himself, especially as it
is portrayed in the good news of Jesus according to Matthew.

The Pattern of Violence/Withdrawal/ Scriptural Fulfillment in Jesus

The Gospel attributed to "Matthew"[6] evidences a highly developed structure, including many and varied uses of "triads." Some of these triads are
simply a threesome such as references to almsgiving, prayer, and fasting
(Matt. 6:2, 5, 16); teaching, preaching, and curing (Matt. 4:23; 9:35); the
three temptations (Matt. 4:1–11); and "the name of the Father and of the
Son and of the Holy Spirit" (Matt. 28:19). Other Matthean triads appear

in dyadic form: "Ask, and it will be given you; search, and you will find; knock, and the door will be opened for you" (Matt. 7:7) or the narrow gate and wide gate, the good fruit and bad fruit, and the house built on rock compared to the one built on sand (Matt. 7:15–27).

Still other triads appear in the way Matthew structures important stories. For instance, one of these structured triads is found in two places (Matt. 14:22–33; 27:51–54). It involves a divine epiphany (Jesus walking on water; his death evoking the quaking of the earth). The human feeling of being overwhelmed by dread and fear follows this. The triad ends with a confession of Jesus as "Son of God" (Matt. 14:33; 27:54). Other structured triads appear with people being blessed or authorized to share in Jesus' power, then given a name because of this grace and, finally, being commissioned to be witnesses of this grace to others (Matt. 5:11–16; 10:1–7; 16:17–19; and 28:18–20). Still another structural triad relates to the topic of the mythic hero.

In the midst of some kind of crisis or conflictive situation, someone "withdraws" (*anachorein*). In the process of withdrawing from the overwhelming situation, some sort of empowerment takes place: the scriptures find their fulfillment in the person going through this journey. While this pattern is revealed in the infancy narrative of Matthew (Matt. 2:13–15, 22–23), a critical triad is found after Jesus goes through what Campbell calls his mythic experience in the desert after being baptized by John the Baptist,[7] only to be forced immediately to undergo an even more traumatic experience, which Campbell never deciphered, but which Matthew makes quite clear: "Now when Jesus heard that John had been arrested, he withdrew (*anachorein*) to Galilee. He left Nazareth and made his home in Capernaum by the sea, in the territory of Zebulun and Naphtali, so that what had been spoken through the prophet Isaiah might be fulfilled:

Land of Zebulun, land of Naphtali,
on the road by the sea, across the Jordan, Galilee of the Gentiles —
the people who sat in darkness have seen a great light,
and for those who sat in the region and shadow of death light has
     dawned.

"From that time," Matthew concludes: "Jesus began to proclaim, 'Repent, for the kingdom of heaven has come near' " (Matt. 4:12–17).

The triadic, mythical pattern is clear: the crisis begins with the realization of the violent arrest of John. This leads Jesus to withdraw from the violence. In the process he is empowered in order that the scriptures might be fulfilled in him. This is accomplished through his preaching of another "kingdom" than Caesar's.

As he began his ministry of preaching the Gospel and inviting the people to change their hearts as well as their allegiance to those powers that were inimical to God's rule, Jesus became an increasing threat to the religious authorities. When he cured a man in the synagogue with a withered hand on the Sabbath, the Pharisees went out and conspired against him, seeking "how to destroy him" (Matt. 12:9–14). However, their decision to kill Jesus, according to Matthew, represents another crisis that he structured in another triadic, mythic form: "When Jesus became aware of this [decision to do violence to him], he departed [*anachorein*]. Many crowds followed him, and he cured all of them, and he ordered them not to make him known. This was to fulfill what had been spoken through the prophet Isaiah:

> "Here is my servant, whom I have chosen,
> my beloved, with whom my soul is well pleased.
> I will put my Spirit upon him, and he will proclaim justice to the
>   Gentiles.
> He will not wrangle or cry aloud, nor will anyone hear his voice
>   in the streets.
> He will not break a bruised reed or quench a smoldering wick
>   until he brings justice to victory.
> And in his name the Gentiles will hope." (Matt. 12:15–21)

If this triad was used by Matthew to highlight a key way conflict was addressed in that Gospel, it is little wonder that the same pattern would be found in Francis of Assisi's conversion, especially since the purpose of his "leaving the world" was to have "the Gospel" fulfilled in his life — a life that was surrounded by the dynamics of conflict and violence.

The Pattern of Violence/Withdrawal/ Scriptural Fulfillment in Francis

Francis lived in a world defined by violence; conflicts could be found everywhere. Cruelty and aggression defined life at all levels, from the top of society to its lowest members. According to R. I. Moore, "deliberate and socially sanctioned violence began to be directed, *through established governmental, juridical and social institutions,* against groups of people" that were scapegoated to such a degree that "membership of such groups in itself came to be regarded as justifying those attacks."[8] This culturally sanctioned violence reached its apogee in the conflict between the pope and the Holy Roman Emperor.

Shortly upon being elected pope, Alexander III (1159–81) repudiated some of the territorial claims made by the emperor, Frederick I (Barbarossa) Hohenstaufen. When Frederick resisted, the pope excommunicated him. In the ensuing struggle, the Holy Roman Emperor installed two anti-popes. In his goal of having Assisi submit to his hegemony he issued a decree on November 21, 1160, declaring: "Be it noted by all the faithful of our Empire, both future and present, that the city of Assisi, with all its *comitato* especially and freely belongs to our imperial jurisdiction."[9]

From the battles between the pope and emperor and their united persecution against various out-groups, conflicts extended throughout the lands under their rule. Its spiral sucked in the peoples of Perugia and Assisi, the bishop and *podestà* (mayor) of Assisi, the nobles and merchants, including the Bernardone family. It totally enveloped the young Francis Bernardone. According to Arnoldo Fortini, the late twentieth-century mayor of Assisi who wrote a historical biography of Assisi's most-noted citizen: "St. Francis ... took part in this incredible violence." He then clearly states: "It destroyed his youth."[10]

The most immediate and blatant manifestation of this violence and its eroding effects on Assisians like Francis can be found in the ongoing cultural hostility that characterized relations between Assisi and its neighbor and archenemy, Perugia. Fortini explains:

> In order to understand this essential point about his life, we must recall the implacable rivalry during the Middle ages that divided Assisi and Perugia, the two cities on opposite sides of the Tiber, facing each other from the hills enclosing the sweet valley of the Porziuncola. Probably in the history of the wars of Italian communes where was no hatred so tenacious as this one. It began at the dawn of communal life and was extinguished only with the diminution of city autonomy at the time of the harsh papal restoration [1540].[11]

When soldiers and others from enemy communes were taken prisoner, they could expect only the roughest of treatment. Fortini writes: "There was no pity for prisoners, enemies from birth, killers of one's own people." He explains further:

> In the time of St. Francis, the people laughed at the agonies of enemies who were tortured and killed. They bragged with crude vulgarity about the things they had done to the women of the conquered cities. They made games of inflicting slow tormenting agonies. They shed blood

now in arrogant wholesale slaughter, now with delicacy. Revenge —
the vendetta — became a fixed idea.[12]

He adds that the violence perpetrated among the people in their warring ways was even extended to their animals: "All the municipal chronicles
abound with accounts of cruel and vulgar crowing and jeering over the hu-
miliations inflicted on enemy cities. Here, an ass is hurled with the trabuch
over walls under siege. There, horses are led to drink in the moats around
city walls. Annual festivals are held in which pigs and asses represent people
of the conquered cities."[13] All this hate and inhumanity was sustained, if
not officially sanctioned, by religious justification. In effect, violence became religiously sanctioned; the people could not imagine any other way of
relating.

What Fortini notes of the attitude justifying the continued warfare between Assisi and Perugia could be said of the conflicts at the other levels
as well:

> Each oppression of a stronger state by a weaker one, each unjust vio-
> lence, each odious conquest, always must be draped in a mantle of
> apparent legitimacy and given moral and juridical justification, so that
> the aggressor, who in reality relies only on superiority of arms and acts
> solely from pride and greed, can proclaim that he is motivated only
> by the cause of human and divine law. It is a ridiculous hypocrisy of
> the wicked masquerading as the righteous. It fools no one; but for all
> that, in every march of invading armies, it is repeated with exasperat-
> ing monotony. So through the centuries there has been a series of these
> dismal comedies, enacted on scenes of fearful tragedy, so that the most
> brutal tyrant can present himself in the guise of a celestial messenger,
> an avenging angel brandishing a sword of righteousness.[14]

All this culturally conditioned violence had a corrosive effect on the
morality of good people like Francis of Assisi. In the process it had begun to destroy his body as well as his spirit. As Brother Thomas of Celano,
the first to write a biography of Francis (completed less than two and a half
years after his death), writes: "a fatal disease had spread everywhere and
infected the limbs of so many that, were the doctor to delay just a little, it
would stifle breath and snatch life away."[15]

This culture of violence generated a crisis in the life of Francis of Assisi. In
the process, he found himself withdrawing from the violence around him in a
way that would eventually become a story of mythic proportions. However,

as we will see in the paragraphs below, the process of Francis' weaning himself from the way of violence began slowly and haltingly.

Although he had been taken prisoner in 1202 in one of the battles between Assisi and its archrival, Perugia, Francis still found no problem in making plans in 1205 to become a knight in the army of Walter of Brienne. As will be explained more fully later, it was while he was on his way to join Walter that he stopped at Spoleto. There he had a dream in which he was asked which "Lord" was most fitting for service, the "Master," i.e., God, or the "Servant," i.e., Walter of Brienne. When he answered, "The Master," he was told to return home, that is, to withdraw from that way of living his vocation. Here Thomas of Celano outlines how the triadic dynamic began to take place in Francis himself. In the face of the violence of the world around him, sustained by armaments and great tales of chivalry, he felt a call to withdrew from it so that he might find "Jesus Christ in his inmost self."[16] In his withdrawal from the world, Francis embarked upon the journey of the mythic hero. In effect he "surrendered" one view of the world and began the process of embracing another worldview. This experience not only evidenced the beginning of a change in him; it served as the founding experience of the "surrender and catch" process, as described by Kurt H. Wolff.

Wolff developed this secular theory of conversion as a kind of sociology of knowledge. His approach helps in our understanding of that kind of spirituality which evidences an alternative way of thinking and feeling about our life and relationships, society's structures as well as their worldview (which will be used in the successive chapters of this book). This includes the embrace of another form of life by which one decides to be present in the world. This evidences the possibility of a countercultural worldview, including the lived-articulation of "an alternative society."[17] He observes:

> Just as the heroic cycle is incomplete without the return, the surrender experience should actually be more properly called "surrender-and-catch" as a single, continuous experience. Descent without return is simple physical death; surrender without end may be psychosis, or some form of "going native." Descent and return without elixir seem meaningless; surrender without catch is either meaningless or in-complete. Thus we begin to understand part of the moral imperative implied in the expression "exemplary model" — here it is a demand for completion of the experience. In order for the culture to accord validity to the adventurer's — or the surrenderer's — experience, the full round must be made, the cycle must be completed, and some con-clusion or evaluation put forth. In this sense, catch becomes the social

component of what otherwise seems a purely individual experience; and just as it seems difficult to separate the individual from the social, it seems that surrender is not a whole without the catch which places the experience into the individual's social-historical context.[18]

Instead of withdrawing from the world by following the most dominant form then available, which involved a departure into a monastery, Francis chose a different path for his conversion from his culture of violence: a new way to live the evangelical life. In withdrawing from the world, he became empowered in his body and person, Celano notes, to lay the foundation of a building wherein he could discover the indwelling of the Christ in him. Later, in his *Life of St. Francis,* Celano notes that the triad of conflict/violence leading to "withdrawal" or departure from "the world" in order to let the scriptures/Christ be realized in his life, characterized the way Francis patterned his life: "More than anything else he desired *to be set free and to be with Christ.* Thus his chief object of concern was to live free from all things *that are of this world,* so that his inner serenity would not be disturbed even for a moment."[19]

As Celano describes it, the Spoleto experience served as the launch from which Francis embarked on an entirely new way to live in the world. In his withdrawal from the violence of society that had infected his own members, he gradually became empowered to have the Gospel itself become incarnated in his own life. As Celano concludes: "For it had to be that the Gospel call be fulfilled in the one who was to be *in faith and truth a minister of the Gospel.*"[20] This same triadic, evangelical way is open to us as we face the current crises in our church and society that too often are characterized by control, abuse, and violence, especially for those of us living as Roman Catholics in the United States.

Assisi's Violence Writ Large in the "American Way"

September 11, 2001, will be marked in the collective psyche of people throughout the world, but especially for U.S. citizens. It has also been said that this day of violence violated our national innocence. While this is the "story" we tell ourselves as victims, those who perpetrated this heinous act have justified their behavior by telling themselves another story. In this narrative, their act of violence was religiously sanctioned under the rubric of *jihad.* As interpreted by those who plowed planes into the World Trade Center, the Pentagon, and a Pennsylvania field it represented a divinely sanctioned, just action against an unjust and corrupt nation of infidels or unbelievers. In their way of thinking, *we* were the perpetrators of a sinful way of life. It had to be stopped from its expansionistic efforts in fidelity to a god who not only tolerated blood sacrifice but recognized as martyrs those who would do Allah's avenging. From their perspective this violence was religiously sanctioned. It was a reaction to the violence they felt had invaded their cultures: the godless "American Way." However, it was perpetrated among a people who told themselves that this "American Way" was blessed by God and that their nation had a mission to evangelize the world with its vision of freedom, including free markets and free elections.

The American story began in 1492. The United States of America came into being as a nation through military force; indeed it was conceived in violence — at least for those who saw the strange people coming in huge boats to their land. Later violence would be deemed necessary to be free of an institutionalized kind of violence being perpetrated by a foreign colonizer.

As the founders considered how their new nation might be governed, it became clear that the people would be empowered only if they were granted certain rights, especially the right to property. However, in order to create a new kind of polity based on the right to property, they realized that one of the main purposes of any government would be the task of arbitrating disputes arising from conflicts related to competing property claims. From the beginning the founders knew that the ownership of property does not always make good neighbors; its protection demands eternal vigilance. This responsibility justified another right: the right to bear arms in order to protect, not just the property itself, but the owners who linked their lives as well as their sacred honor to it.

The desire for ever more property found the settlers moving west. Believing God missioned them, they forcibly took over the lands of less powerful people who had lived on them for centuries. Later this sense of domestic mission got expanded via a foreign policy called "Manifest Destiny." In effect the United States determined, by itself, that, to ensure its political and economic interests (at least within this hemisphere), it had the right to intervene anywhere any other power became perceived as a threat to the nation's "interests."

After going through various wars to protect the American way and even though the nation's main "enemy" fell with the breakup of the Soviet system, our militarization continued as the umbrella under which the nation would promote its economic interests in the name of political freedom ("democracy") and economic freedom (the U.S. form of "free markets"). Unfortunately, too often the ever more globalized U.S. form of capitalism came to be experienced by others as meeting the wants of U.S. interests to the detriment of their own needs. The U.S. need to ensure its own "rights," now combined with appeals to "national security" (whether for oil or safety), was used to justify the eclipse of unique cultural patterns that may have had different priorities and expressions. A consequence of this ever increasing effort to globalize the economy to ensure that these "values" be realized for ourselves came to be expressed in an ever increasing militarization of the nation. This had its effect on our collective psyche as a people.

The fact that this way of exploitation, domination, and coercion might be perceived by others as violent was beyond our comprehension. Violence was something found in others, not ourselves. Indeed, as I wrote this book, the Pew Global Attitudes Project for 2006 noted that, while non-Muslim Westerners, including most of us in the United States, view Muslims around the world as violent, the Muslims who were polled characterized us as violent ourselves.[21] It was also shown that seven in ten people in a poll of more than twenty-six thousand people in twenty-five countries, not just Islamic ones, said the U.S. military presence in the Middle East provoked more violence than it prevented.[22]

Violence can be defined as any human force that inflicts unjustified injury. Given this definition, the effort we are making to ensure the realization of our American lifestyle is considered as violent by others because it exploits people and the planet. Without realizing the impact of our way of life on other people and the planet itself (such as continuing our existing consumption patterns that contribute so much to global warming), a kind of culturally justified, but formally unrecognized, systemic violence has become endemic to our culture. In the process we have become immunized to its eroding effect on our own psyches as well as the soul of our nation. This institutionalized, yet ideologically justified and religiously sanctioned violence reached its unfortunate apogee in a concrete witness of dramatic violence that shocked the nation from its stated innocence: the school shootings at Columbine High School, in an upscale, pleasant suburb of Denver populated mainly by professional, upper-class white people.

Shocked like the rest of us, the conservative Catholic Peggy Noonan attempted to explain what led two supposedly normal white teenagers to implement a plan to kill their innocent classmates. The former speech writer for President Ronald Reagan and, later, for Vice President Dick Cheney opined in the *Wall Street Journal*: "People have had it. Something is different about this story. We've been through it before but the reaction this time suggests some critical mass has been reached." She argued that, with this critical mass, people seemed more willing to honestly seek an answer for why such violence would be done by seemingly assimilated young men from successful families. Noonan began by offering her own answer: "Here's mine. The kids who did this are responsible. They did it. They killed," she wrote, as would many whose worldview is of a more conservative perspective. But then she added a critical qualifier that reflected the perspective of people like myself who believe culture also has a significant effect on our individual and social psyches: "But they came from a place and a time, and were yielded forth by a culture."

While acknowledging, as the recognized Republican thinker that she is (enough to have a weekly column in the *Wall Street Journal*), that the boys were personally responsible for their violent behavior, Noonan moved into a sphere of the "why" behind it all and asked a question that some commentators are now daring to raise: was there anything in their world that may have contributed to their violence? This probe revealed to her a powerful contributor to the boys' violence. In an analysis I had never seen before from someone with her philosophical viewpoint I read: "What walked into Columbine High School Tuesday was the culture of death. This time it wore black trench coats. Last time it was children's hunting gear. Next time it will be some other costume, but it will still be the culture of death. That is the Pope's [John Paul II] phrase; it is how he describes the world we live in."[23]

Having described our U.S. culture around the same metaphor of violence that Matthew characterizes as giving rise to Jesus, that Thomas of Celano and, later, Arnoldo Fortini, used to describe the destructive dynamics that infected Assisi's psyche, including the life and spirituality of one of its own teenagers named Francis Bernardone, Noonan describes the violence which has inundated our culture as the "waters in that we swim." She writes: "The boys who did the killing, the famous Trench Coat Mafia, inhaled too deep the ocean in which they swam." Then, before the mass acceptance of violent video games, rap music that denigrates women and gays, and talk radio that is filled with violence and vindictives against anyone who might differ, she stated:

> Think of it this way. Your child is an intelligent little fish. He swims in deep water. Waves of sound and sight, of thought and fact, come invisibly through that water, like radar; they go through him again and again, from this direction and that. The sound from the television is a wave, and the sound from the radio; the headlines on the newsstand, on the magazines, on the ad on the bus as it whizzes by — all are waves. The fish — your child — is bombarded and barely knows it. But the waves contain words like this, which I'll limit to only one source, the news:

*...was found strangled and is believed to have been sexually mo-
lested...had her breast implants removed...took the stand to say
the killer was smiling the day the show aired...said the procedure
is, in fact, legal infanticide...is thought to be connected to earlier
sexual activity among teens...court battle over who owns the frozen
sperm...contains songs that call for dominating and even imprisoning
women...died of lethal injection...had threatened to kill her children
...said that he turned and said, "You better put some ice on that"...
had asked Kevorkian for help in killing himself...protested the game,
which they said has gone beyond violence to sadism...showed no re-
morse...which is about a wager over whether he could sleep with
another student...which is about her attempts to balance three lovers
and a watchful fiancé ...*

What seemed to have escaped Noonan's otherwise insightful analysis regarding the consequence of our culture's media violence, is the fact that,
ultimately, all such words and images in our media are "brought to you
by..." In other words, almost all the ways we come to know about our
violence-laden culture of death in the media are corporately sponsored and
promoted by corporate interests. All of this is done in the name of free markets. The violence of the "free market" as it plays itself out among us as a
people is not just the media violence that she speaks about: it's about deeper
realities that bespeak violence and the pain it brings to so many. These we
also read in our headlines: "A Culture of Corruption,"[24] "Developing World
Afflicted by 'Diseases of Affluence,' "[25] "In a Culture of Greed, How Bad Is
an Affair?"[26] and "Income Inequality, and Its Cost,"[27] "The Tyranny of the
Market,"[28] to mention just a few.

Peggy Noonan goes on to note that our world today and the culture in
which we find ourselves are far different from the experience of those of
us who are older. Consequently, she writes, "We think our children will
be OK too. But they never had a normal culture against which to balance
the newer, sicker one. They have no reference points to the old, boring
normality. We assume they know what we know: 'This is not right.' But
why would they know that? The water in which they swim is the only water
they've known."[29]

As an antidote to the violence, Noonan suggests that, quite possibly,
things could have been different for Eric Harris, eighteen, and Dylan Kle-
bold, seventeen, if one teacher had enabled them to search for an alternative
way to deal with life's conflicts. This would have involved what I call "withdrawal" from the violence and an opening to a higher power (for us, the

scriptures) that could have dissuaded them from their killing. However, "if that teacher had intervened that way, he would have been hauled into court."

Without commenting on her point regarding the separation of church and state, her ultimate point is what matters here. This is what makes me resonate with her concluding insight about the two ways we can approach the violence in our culture: with a gun, which only exacerbates the violence, or with the scriptures, which may offer an alternative: "It occurs to me at the moment that a gun and a Bible have a few things in common," she declared: "Both are small, black, have an immediate heft and are dangerous — the first to life, the second to the culture of death"[30] that goes by the name of violence.

Seven years later, commenting on the death of Coretta Scott King, widow of the civil rights leader who himself died violently as a result of gunfire, Bob Herbert wrote a column on violence in our culture entitled: "An American Obsession." Noting that Dr. King had a message (biblically inspired, I would add) that offered a nonviolent alternative to our divisions and conflicts as a nation, Herbert observes that we never listened because "our addiction to the joy of violence is far too strong."

In discussing Vietnam and Iraq as well as violence in his own black community, Herbert found himself agreeing with Peggy Noonan about the media's contribution to this violence, but also disagreeing with both Martin Luther and Coretta Scott King about a way out of its all-pervasive influence. He concluded his tribute to her: "Coretta Scott King has been called home. Like her husband, she always believed that America's addiction to violence could be brought under control." Then he writes: "They were wrong. We love it too much."[31]

Embracing the Quest of the Hero

I always thought that violence was something outside myself; it was located in the ways of relating found in the kind of cultural and social dynamics in the structures and systems noted above. Then, in 2002 I read a definition of violence from the U.S. Catholic Bishops. It said that violence is any kind of behavior used to control another through fear and intimidation.[32] They also said two things about violence that challenged me to look at my own way of relating rather than to limit myself to pointing fingers at the violence beyond myself. "Violence," they said, "is *never* justified." Next they declared: "Violence in any form — physical, sexual, psychological or verbal — is sinful; often it is a crime as well."[33]

When I read this statement, with its definition and application to violence in "any form," it became clear to me that the forms of violence detailed by the bishops — those ways of relating that are found more at the one-on-one level (physical, sexual, psychological, or verbal) also have their institutionalized expressions in those forms of violence found in political, economic, and ecclesiastical constructs as well. After all, they say, "Violence in any form...is sinful."

While many Catholics in the United States might be open to recognize some forms of violence in their economic structures (especially when they lose their jobs to outsourcing in sweatshops) or political processes (which are critically influenced by corporate lobbyists), it is not easy for them to admit that violence can exist institutionally in their own religion. To equate key ecclesiastical constructs in the Roman Church with violence might seem, to many Catholics, to border on the heretical or, as Camilo Macisse, O.C.D., has written, "nonsensical."

Until recently Macisse was superior general of the Discalced Carmelites and also served, during his term, as president of the Union of Superior Generals in Rome. So his position offered a unique perspective on the operation of the church in the Eternal City. Defining violence as "the application of physical, moral, or psychological force to impose or coerce," he concluded that this way of operating "should be unthinkable in the community founded by Jesus."[34] As he then considered how violence was expressed in the centralizing tendencies of the existing dynamics in the Church of Rome, he came to identify violence itself with that kind of centralism "which seeks to concentrate decision-making powers in a church bureaucracy distant from the life of believers in different circumstances."[35]

The realization that violence can neither be justified nor defined in any way that does not call it sin became very powerful to me as I looked at my world and its violence, the church defined as "holy," as well as my own ways of relating. I concluded that, if the definition is accurate, then our society, our church, and my life are a lot more violent than I want to admit. Furthermore, if I were going to be free of the "sin" of violence in myself and in my "world," I would have to withdraw as far as possible (at least in my own mind if not my membership) from this violence in a way that would separate me from its sinful ways. While I have chosen to remain within such systems of violence, this demanded that I free my mind from any form of intellectual support or justification for its sinful expressions. This demanded another kind of engagement that I found most helpful: the withdrawal, or *anachorein,* of the scriptures.

Anachorein in the face of the conflicts, the destructive patterns and violence in, among, and around us that characterize the heart of the "sin of the world," is not what happens when people "drop out" or "give up." It involves what Wolff writes about in his notion of surrender: it represents a kind of a military notion. He writes: "The term 'surrender' itself, with its ironical military connotation, polemicizes against the official Western and potentially worldwide consciousness of the relation to the world, both nature and man's world and even man himself, which is not surrender but mastery, control, efficiency, handling, manipulating."[36] Indeed, it "is the opposite of violence."[37]

The notion of withdrawal or surrender (following Wolff) arises from a crisis: the realization that, to remain in the situation of violence (with its overwhelming power), will only suck us into its clutches more surely. Unable to turn around this violence using the present ways of engagement, I disengage for a while. This disengagement is found in withdrawal; it constitutes a strategic action that is meant to free us from being caught up in the cycle of violence even more. For me, as a person very committed to social transformation in the structures of our political economy as well as the church, it's a form of disarmament.

After trying to bring about an attitude of *anachorein* in the way I addressed issues of (in)justice and (non)violence, I found that, unknowingly, I had begun to move to the third level of the Matthean triad outlined above. The realization came to me when I had taken some time to be away with my priest friend, Joseph Juknialis.

Joe and I were in his canoe on the Rock River in Wisconsin. We had paddled upstream for an hour and now were making our way back, going with the current, enjoying our wine and cheese and talking about things of importance to us.

"I was with that group of couples that you met some time ago," Joe told me. "The women in the couples' group also belong to a group of women that began years ago at Christ the King Parish [in Wauwatosa, Wisconsin, a suburb of Milwaukee] when I was a new priest and young like them." Joe recalled one of the women sharing with the couples' group a conversation that had taken place in the women's group not long before.

It seemed that the women were facing a new conflict in their heretofore sedentary lives. For years they had found their role fulfilled as wives and mothers and even as grandmothers. But now their husbands had retired and were under their feet at home; their children had moved from the Milwaukee area so there were no grandchildren to care for on a regular basis.

Consequently the question arose as to what "their purpose" in life might now be.

"The women said that not one of the women in the group was able to say what their purpose in life now entailed," Joe recalled. Then, in almost the same breath, he said to me: "So, Mike, you're retirement age. You've written your books and you've made your mark in life. Given all this, what would you say your purpose in life is now for you?"

The question, coming out of nowhere, surprised me. I had never thought of asking myself quite so clearly about the purpose in my life as I looked to my future. I found myself wanting to think a bit more about how I would respond. So in order to stall I thought I'd bring a little levity to Joe's question. "The purpose of my life," I said with all seriousness, "is to 'know, love and serve God in this life and to be happy with *him* [stressing the male image for God] in the next."

After we both laughed at how easily the *Baltimore Catechism* definition came to me, Joe said, "No, Mike. That's not good enough. Seriously, tell me what you think your purpose in life at this time really is."

Startling myself, I found myself saying simply: "I want to be the Christ."

What had happened within my heart on my spiritual journey that found this surprising statement to come from my lips? In a way wanting to "become the Christ" should be the goal of every Christian if Paul's dream for the followers of Jesus in Galatia would be realized: that "Christ is formed [*morphein*] in you" (Gal. 4:16). However, perhaps because we have not thought that this is actually the purpose of baptism itself nor have been formed to think that this is the ultimate goal of Christian discipleship, the notion deserves some expansion. Toward this end, perhaps a brief narration of a critical part of my story will shed some light on why I would find myself saying: "I want to be the Christ." However, the fact that I could make such a statement would only be the result of much stumbling.

For years I fought a powerful sense that I was "supposed" to be a priest; I thought, "God willed it."[38] But I did not will it. So, to "lose my vocation," I decided I would date, drink, and be delinquent well before most other teenagers. Despite doing my best to forget about becoming a priest, the idea persisted. Finally, I felt that, if I didn't give into this sense, I would be displeasing to God. So I went to a seminary.

Once in the seminary, the idea of being a priest grew on me; in fact, I found myself not resisting my "call" at all. While not embracing the idea, I felt comfortable with this way of life. At the same time, I determined I wanted to combine priesthood with belonging to a community. That meant I would join a religious congregation.

Two finally rose to the top of my list. The first group I'll call the Jovenists, based in the East. I visit them and was immediately drawn to their work with young boys (which appealed to me because I now had developed a messianic sense of being called to save other teenagers from the "wicked" ways I had once embraced). The second group was the Midwest Capuchins (who strictly followed the Rule of St. Francis). One of my siblings, Dan, had already left our home in Fond du Lac, Wisconsin, to join them. He was in their college in Crown Point, Indiana. I liked them, but was not particularly drawn to them. On the way home after visiting the Jovenists, I stopped in Crown Point to visit my brother. In passing he had mentioned that he had been reading a book that noted the stated "purpose" of various religious congregations of men. Some said they were founded to teach, others to preach, and still others to be missionaries of one kind or another. The Capuchin Franciscans, he noted, said that their purpose was "to live the Gospel."

One day, with one month left before I would have to enter a novitiate (the initial formation period of a year and a day), something in me made it clear that it would be the day I would make my decision. So in the afternoon I drove to our parish church, St. Patrick's in Fond du Lac (now closed, due to the priest shortage). There I created a chart on a piece of paper. On the top left I wrote "Jovenists"; on the top right it was "Capuchins." Beneath, on the far left, I wrote "work," "spirit," and "purpose."

As I filled in the first two boxes, it was becoming clear to me that the Jovenists were getting much higher marks than the Capuchins. However, when I came to write in my thoughts about what each group said its purpose was, a blank came to me as to why the Jovenists had made it so important to work with teenage boys. In other words, I liked the fact that they were doing this ministry, but did not know "why" they were so involved; what did they want to accomplish by their presence among youngsters at this critical age?

Unable to fill in the box, I moved to the Capuchins and what they said their purpose for existing involved. There and then I remembered my brother Dan telling me that, following Francis of Assisi, the Capuchins embraced a way of life whose purpose was "to live the Gospel." Immediately I found myself saying: "This is what I want. I don't know if they are doing this, but I want to be part of a group of people who at least say that this is their purpose in life." I had made my choice; to live the Gospel would become the goal in my life. I would join the Capuchins, not the Jovenists.

For me, as it had become for Francis of Assisi, my life now would be set in the direction of living the Gospel. However, I realized that this Gospel way of life could never be lived as it was in the time of Jesus nor of Francis. It would have to make sense to the world of the second half of the twentieth century and be relevant for the twenty-first century I anticipated being part of. In effect, what Thomas of Celano said of Francis Bernardone of Assisi had to find its translation in Michael Crosby of Fond du Lac: the Gospel had to be fulfilled in me.

Now, sitting with Joe Juknialis in the canoe, after decades of being challenged to allow the scriptures to be fulfilled in me, I found myself saying: "I want to be the Christ." Surprised at such a brash statement, which also sounded quite Buddhist to me (as in "I want to be the Buddha"), it did make sense. It dawned on me that, if "the Christ" is the one in whom the scriptures were to be fulfilled, then, to the degree I allowed this to happen in me, empowered by the one and only "Christ," I too am called to become "the Christ." With Paul, I too must groan, as in childbirth, until Christ be formed in me (Gal. 4:19).

With this understanding, I have come to believe that this is the call of every baptized person: the words that Celano used to describe Francis' whole life and what I discovered must be the core purpose of my life, I now believe must find its unique echo in the life of all serious disciples of Jesus Christ: it has "to be that the Gospel call be fulfilled"[39] in them.

Using the Francis story in the context of the other stories struggling to be told in the culture of Assisi and the church of his time, the following chapters will suggest a way Francis' story — which was an embrace of the Gospel story within the context of his culture's story and the church's story — became so compelling that it still serves as a model for us today. This model has become one meant not only for inspiration but imitation as well.

Truly, all of us are called in the Spirit to "become the Christ." In each of us, the Gospel must be fulfilled. Francis of Assisi offers us a model for how this can be realized in our lives, our society, and our church today. The next chapters will offer a way this might be done.

ONE

Francis of Assisi

A Saint for All, a Saint for All Times

It seems to me that, were we only to correspond to God's graces, continually being showered down on every one of us, we would be able to pass from being great sinners one day to be great saints the next. — Solanus Casey, O.F.M.Cap.[1]

A Society of Hero-Worshipers

One need only look at a newsstand to realize we are a people who are very influenced by the cult of personality. Not counting the "in" movie star or sports hero whose escapades and feats are chronicled by the paparazzi, we have the gurus of business and hi-tech. Seminars bring motivational speakers to our cities promising success for those willing to pay hundreds of dollars as an entrance fee. Once in a while someone comes among us, like a Grace Kelly or a Princess Diana, who captures our imagination by their looks and intriguing ways. We have our Dalai Lamas and our popes. Who can forget the adulation that surrounded the death of John Paul II?

From reading the news, listening to the radio, or watching MTV, one might think certain musicians have totally captured the psyches of our youth. However, a study done of Generation Y indicates that many young people have more nuanced understandings about what it means to be a hero. Disgusted with pop culture's preoccupation with celebrities, Gary Hale, a lobbyist and former state senator in Connecticut, decided to create an ad-free website asking people twenty-five and younger to describe "your true hero." In just two months in 2001 the site drew more than 18,400 stories. Rather than choosing anti-heroes such as certain rap stars or athlete-pitchmen like Michael Jordan on the basis of wealth, achievement, athletic prowess, or rebellion, some 38 percent chose heroes from their own families. An article in the *Wall Street Journal* about the results stated: "While their heroes had plenty of triumphs, students tended to focus on their attitudes: the ability under pressure to maintain humility, humor, compassion, respect, and a focus on serving others. Many writers also showed a remarkably keen eye for how well their heroes balanced work, family, and community." The author concludes: "Based on my reading of dozens of entries and interviews with several writers, the stories on *yourtruehero.org* say much about what memories children carry forward into adulthood."[2]

Kurt H. Wolff, whose theory of surrender and catch will be developed later in this book, notes that the hero represents something larger than regular life in two ways: "first, as a celebration of a level of consciousness achieved by the society, and second, as the exemplary model (paradigm) of further change... The hero is a composite of all that the society deems important, in order that he may properly represent the importance of the societal achievement which is being celebrated — the synthesis of the old forms into new." He asks: "Is this formulation of the hero as exemplary or paradigmatic not another, more historical and sociological formulation of the surrenderer venturing forth as a transcendental subject?"[3]

When I was studying theology in Berkeley I took a course entitled "Saints and Holiness." It was fascinating, very insightful and illuminating, as well as highly instructive. Team-taught by a sociologist, a theologian, and a historian, we considered the phenomenon of the saint or hero from a whole host of disciplines. This ranged from reading a comic book on Mother Teresa to watching a film on Sufi saints.

It quickly became clear to me, a Roman Catholic priest involved in the work for the beatification of a member of my province, that the official recognition of saints is not confined to Catholicism. The Orthodox Churches have all sorts of saints; one of them, the fourteenth-century abbot Sergius of Radonezh, is often described as another Francis of Assisi. The Protestants have officially recognized and liturgically celebrated their holy men and women as well, such as the seventeenth-century priest-poets George Herbert and John Donne. Other great figures among the Protestants are their founders, such as Martin Luther, John Calvin, and John Knox. A more recent Protestant model of holiness, Dietrich Bonhoeffer, who was killed by the Nazis just before the end of World War II, is widely considered a saint — and not just by Protestants.[4]

Neither are saints confined to Christianity. Hinduism is replete with them. Buddhist monks in Russia regularly attend to the uncorrupted body of Dashi-Dorzho Itigilov, the twelfth Pandito Hambo Lama, who died in 1927. Islam has many holy sites dedicated to the memory of the saints who embodied the teachings of The Prophet. The rituals surrounding visits to such sites fascinate us; we are intrigued (and shamed?) by the fasts that constitute celebration of such religions' high holy days. Even their conflicts often revolve around one group's claims for the legitimacy of a saint who is not recognized by another group.

But if the category of "saint" is universal, it can be said quite surely, at least for Christians, that Francis is the Saint among Saints. The Franciscan friar Richard Rohr notes: "He has been written about so frequently that in the library of international languages he has the single longest bibliography."[5] It is apparently the case that, next to Jesus Christ, more articles and books have been written on St. Francis of Assisi than any person who has ever lived.

Reverence for St. Francis is not confined to Christians. Francis, who made at least three trips to the heart of Islam and, in the process, came to a deep respect for its teachings and leaders, is also revered in that religion. Consequently, he is recognized by many Islamic scholars as a holy person, worthy of emulation. As the Islamic scholar Fareed Munir notes:

> St. Francis demonstrated his unique understanding of Christianity and his sincerity to it by his tolerance and appreciation of Islamic beliefs and virtues, though the public opinion of his day promoted the Islamic religion to be detestable in every respect. St. Francis, although a devout Christian, could still appreciate the Muslim point of view. For that reason, from the Islamic perspective, St. Francis was a Muslim at heart.[6]

Many others think Francis was "at heart" one of their own. In a fitting tribute to Francis by a bishop who took to heart so many of Francis' characteristics, the late Raymond A. Lucker suggested that Francis be declared "Person of the Millennium."[7] He has been declared patron of his native Italy (along with another Franciscan, Bernardine of Siena, and Catherine of Siena). Long before the word "ecology" became widely known, Francis was proposed as a patron of the earth itself.[8] However, as we shall see in the chapters that follow, Francis is not just a "nature saint"; he is, as Franciscan Michael D. Guinan insists, a saint of creation. "Creation and Creator go together, as they certainly did for Francis. He saw, in and through creatures, the hand of their Creator God."[9] If any saint can be regarded as a "protector" or "patron" it is this man. Indeed, as the first biographer of Francis, Brother Thomas of Celano, noted of him: "He helps everyone, everywhere. He is near to everyone, everywhere."[10]

Addressing the plethora of materials on Francis that have appeared in recent years, the Franciscan scholar Leonhard Lehmann writes:

However uneven their quality may be from a historical point of view, they show clearly that Francis found the answer to many of our own contemporary problems. He has been portrayed as "the prophet and brother of our times," as "the future come to life," and even "an ecumenical and ecological revolutionary." All these titles stem from a conviction that Francis, the medieval man, has a message for us, too.[11]

This message is not meant only to inspire us intellectually, as we will see later in this chapter. It is intended to inspire emulation. As we read at the very beginning of one of the earliest biographies of Francis: "Servants of the Lord should not be ignorant of the lives and teachings of saints through which they can come to God."[12]

Before considering more specifically the relevance of Francis' message for our culture, our church, and our lives, it might be good to place his unique holiness in the context of what it means to be a saint.

Moving beyond Past Notions of "Saints"

In many ways, for most of the past two thousand years, the notion of a "saint" remained virtually the same — at least in the Roman Catholic Church. The meaning of "saint" during that time was understood within a structured hierarchy of people of higher and lower rank — with God ruling on top. These relationships were defined by the dynamics of patronage that ruled in the Roman Empire at the time of Jesus, colored the subsequent writing of the Gospels, and achieved canonical status insofar as the existing world was ordained by God to represent the "perfect society." Within this worldview the saints functioned as heavenly patrons, bestowing favors and providing access to the Ultimate Patron, God *Himself*. Theologian Elizabeth A. Johnson describes this dynamic with great clarity: "The imagination of this construal sees God like a monarch ruling in splendor, with hosts of courtiers ranked in descending order of importance. Being far from the throne, people need intercessors who will plead their cause and obtain spiritual and material favors that would otherwise not be forthcoming."[13]

Francis himself came out of a culture of patronage. However, precisely because of the violence he experienced within this way of life, he undertook to withdraw from it. This countercultural movement away from the existing power relations of control that lead to violence, is in part, I believe, what accounts for his wide popular appeal. Born into a culture of hierarchy and patronage, he was led by God to find a deeper reality, which speaks to our times: not the "kingdom" of God, but the "kin-dom" of God at the heart of all relationships. This perspective involved a breaking down of hierarchical relationships of domination and inequality to regard everyone as equal members of one family. In this approach, Francis echoed Johnson's vision of the role of true saints today: to reveal to all of us the profound relationship into which we all are invited, to be part of a "circle of companions by the power of Spirit-Sophia."[14] The saints are those who serve as inspiration and emulation for people who seek to be part of that circle. In many ways, this notion of a saint as one who is not apart from us or higher than us is what I find represented in the Los Angeles Cathedral of Our Lady of the Angels.

Visiting the cathedral in 2004 I was overwhelmed by the huge tapestries that appear on the interior walls, flanking the worshipers within. These twenty-foot-high pieces portray the saints of the past; however, their faces are based on real, contemporary people of different races, ages and backgrounds. Gazing on these images, one cannot help but feel that sanctity is within our reach. The traditional otherworldly portrayals of saints in other churches pale in comparison to this portrayal of what a saint might mean today: the embodiment in the neighbor of a pattern of life that is meant not just for inspiration but identification, not just adulation but emulation.

Who Defines What It Means to Be Holy?

In every religion, not just Catholicism, saints, heroes, and gurus have been recognized for their holiness and have been promoted for various reasons (often political and commercial, besides the obvious religious ones) as examples to be followed. Simply put, they are recognized for being godly or, as we read in the Hebrew scriptures: "You shall be holy, for I the Lord your God am holy." From this perspective everyone among the children of Israel was called to be a saint.

This idea was adopted by the early church. In the Letters of St. Paul, the word "saint" was synonymous with discipleship; it was the name he gave those baptized into Christ Jesus. However, despite this broader notion, the word "saint" has generally been applied to those who stood out among their contemporaries in some unique way. It was this observable difference from others in Antioch that led the early disciples of Jesus to be "called Christians" (Acts 11:26).

No religious institution has so thorough a process as the Roman Catholic Church for determining who will be publicly recognized as a saint. Kenneth Woodward has studied this process in his book *Making Saints,* which has the subtitle, *How the Catholic Church Determines Who Becomes a Saint, Who Doesn't, and Why.*[15] It is a highly readable behind-the-scenes account of the process by which the Vatican "canonizes" a holy person, a certification that makes it possible for that person's name to be cited in the church's official liturgy.

For two years I was involved in the most demanding part of this process: the writing of two of the three volumes required before a holy person can be considered "venerable" (the final stage in the process before "beatification" and "canonization"). The proposed saint was a Capuchin Franciscan, Solanus Casey (whom someone has called the "Forrest Gump of Saints"[16]). Basing my work on a volume of collected testimonies by people who knew him (including their answers to twenty-seven pages of questions prepared by the Congregation for the Causes of the Beatification of Saints) I wrote his official biography. I followed this with another, shorter required volume, which documented the "heroicity" of fifteen characteristics or virtues manifested in the life of the saint: faith, hope, love of God, love of neighbor, prudence, justice toward God, justice toward neighbor, fortitude, temperance, the spiritual and corporal works of mercy, poverty, chastity, obedience, and humility. I was struck by a statement by Solanus Casey that has special reference to the universal appeal of a Francis of Assisi: "As manifested in the lives of the saints, if we strive and use the means God has given us, we too can ascend to great sanctity and to astonishing familiarity with God."[17]

In Catholicism there are four main kinds of "official" saints. I would call these provincial, personal, period, and perennial saints. The first are the "provincial" or local saints. These are not well known beyond the territories in which they functioned; Solanus Casey is an example of this type. While he is becoming increasingly popular throughout North America and beyond, he is mainly revered by the people of Detroit.

Then there are what I call the "personal" saints — those who have a personal significance to a particular religious community. In the Roman Catholic Church, these constitute the majority of those officially canonized, probably because they were bishops and priests from certain dioceses and founders of religious orders who can afford to dedicate the personnel and financial resources to go through the process of canonization.

"Period" saints are promoted at certain times to address particular concerns. For instance, in the 1950s, there was the canonization of Maria Goretti, an Italian peasant girl who was killed while resisting the sexual advances of an older neighbor. She was held up as a beacon of purity, challenging the cultural climate of sexual permissiveness. Another example of a "period" saint (who is also clearly a "provincial" saint) is Juan Diego of Mexico, who was canonized by Pope John Paul II, even though a number of historians maintain that he never existed. This was done, in part, to stem the defection of Mexican Catholics to the proliferating number of Protestant sects.

Finally we have "perennial" saints. One example, in our lifetime, is Mother Teresa of Calcutta, whose reputation for holiness is so widespread that the official rule, which stipulates a period of five years after the death of the person before initiating the process of canonization, was lifted to facilitate her cause. As a result she was beatified in 2003, a mere six years after her death.

Here, as in many other ways, Francis of Assisi set his own standard. He was canonized by Pope Gregory IX only two years after his death.

Why the Appeal of Saints Today?

In *The Meaning of Saints*, Lawrence Cunningham offers a description of a "saint" that I find particularly helpful: "A saint is a person so grasped by a religious vision that it becomes central to his or her life in a way that radically changes the person and leads others to glimpse the value of that vision."[18] In other words, a saint is someone whose life is not only grounded in a powerful experience or conviction, but one who opens a new path for others to follow.

In her critically acclaimed book *Saints and Postmodernism: Revisioning Moral Philosophy*, Edith Wyschogrod argues that the stories of saints, or hagiography (to use the academic term), "is to be preferred to moral theory" as a guide for how we conduct our lives. She argues that, in a world of relativism, a "postmodern ethic" must look to "life narratives, specifically those of saints" in order to make sense to people today.[19] The main contentions of her argument can be constellated into eight insights that show the relevance of saints, and of Francis of Assisi in particular, to our world today:

1. Moral theory is an unsatisfactory way of addressing matters that require action in contemporary life.

2. Saints' lives should not be imagined as emanating from some specific religious community but as found across a broad spectrum of belief systems and institutional practices.

3. The role of hagiography is not in recounting the life of the saint without sharing what this means as well as how it invites the audience to be "swept up by its imperative force."

4. The saint's body "is accorded special meaning" in the telling of the story.

5. The saint's life is doubly coded regarding his or her existence in time. On the one hand saints' lives express a time that belongs to their work and achievement, but on the other hand, saints also live time as pure flux or passage.

6. Although saints are embodied creatures and, thus, gender-identified, "because saintly generosity consists in the abnegation of her/his own being, the saint speaks, as it were, with the voice of the Other." Consequently the saint "becomes a nongendered body."

7. Agreeing with some postmodernists but going beyond their meaning of "desire," Wyschogrod says that the saint is the one driven by desire. As such, desire not only constitutes the underpinning of culture and history; it must be seen not as a lack but as pure positivity.

8. Building on this notion, contemporary saintliness, says Wyschogrod, "is not a nostalgic return to premodern hagiography but a postmodern expression of excessive desire, a desire on behalf of the Other that seeks the cessation of another's suffering and the birth of another's joy."[20]

Benedictine Sister Joan Chittister has embraced Wyschogrod's insight, suggesting that St. Benedict, the ultimate founder and source of inspiration for her community, offers an appeal to what she calls the "monk in all of us."[21]

Chittister points to the violent world that provided the context for Benedict's life. The church, at the time, was more temporal power than spiritual leader; power had become "the drug of choice." All of society's little people were ground up, ground down, ground to dust by the competition for it. Change in the system was impossible, she writes: "Because the very people who were oppressed by it, appalled by it, or destroyed by it supported it. The very people who had the most to gain by its reform sustained it. How? Simply by assuming that nothing else was possible and nothing could be done." She notes that in the fifth century, seven hundred years before Francis,

one person, a young man, resolved to change the system not by confronting it, but by eroding its credibility. He simply decided to change people's opinions about what life had to be by himself living otherwise, by refusing to accept the moral standards around him, by forming people into organized communities, . . . by the sharing of goods, by caring for the earth, by teaching a new perspective on our place in the universe.[22]

Reading these reflections made me think of Francis. It also made me reflect, sadly, that the ongoing relevance of Benedict and Francis is a reflection of how little the milieu of violence has changed from their time to our own.

The Universal Appeal of a Threshold Figure Like St. Francis

In *The Inner Reaches of Outer* Space, Joseph Campbell writes about what he calls "threshold figures." These are those [a]historical figures that reach mythic proportions. They embody in their lives (or, at least, in the way their lives have been narrated) "two worlds at once: temporal in the human appeal of their pictured denotations, while by connotation opening to eternity."[23] As I noted in the introduction, I believe Francis of Assisi not only represents one of these figures; he has become a kind of archetype, at least in the Christian tradition, of all those who have tried to model their lives on Jesus Christ — particularly on his withdrawal from the violence of the world.

Traditional hagiography ("narrations about holy people" from *hagios* [holy] + *graphein* [to write]) was meant, first of all, to edify audiences. It had a second purpose as well: to help promote a cult around the person whose story was being narrated. However, because the purpose of hagiography in the Christian tradition was meant to show how a person embodied the pattern of Jesus, it was ultimately based on Christ, whose "story" in the scriptures was to be replicated in the person's life. Consequently, the goal of hagiography was not to provide "truth" in the sense of a strict narration of facts; rather, the "facts" were adapted and sculpted in ways meant to show how "the divine project" revealed in Christ had been "realized in the saint's life."[24]

Many hagiographies of Francis written in the first century after his death are highly suspect to academics today, simply because they were trying so hard to be faithful to the literary pattern of "truth" in their times. Consequently, I have chosen to concentrate on the authenticated writings of Francis himself and on only three of his early biographies, especially the first one, *Life of St. Francis,* by Brother Thomas of Celano.

This officially authorized story of Francis was published shortly after his canonization in 1228. Thomas patterned his book along the lines of traditional hagiography, trying to show how Francis became an embodiment of the scriptures and how he exemplified in his life the time-honored patterns of holiness. In the way he portrayed Francis' life and the origins of the Order, modern hagiographers have found that Thomas of Celano's portrayal is probably more accurate than the biographies that followed, including his own follow-up biography, which is popularly known as Celano's *Second Life of St. Francis.*[25] Indeed, Emanuela Prinzivalli writes: "In his renewal of an ancient form of holiness, Francis tends to assume the form of a very special saint, one who is 'new.'" Despite its overlay of myth, Prinzivalli concludes, "the First Life shows a concern for historical reality that is more in accord with modern tastes."[26] According to Prinzivalli, Celano viewed "a saint as one who restores the world to a state of paradise," in a way that replicated the "Jesus Story."[27] This approach, which I tend to share, has special resonance with the ecological concerns of our age.

Throughout this book I will be relating the story of Francis to the challenge of contemporary discipleship. However, before attempting to do this, I believe it is necessary to be aware of the obstacles to translating Francis' story into our story by examining the shadow side of the competing stories around us.

Our Stories and Other Stories

Returning to my opening remarks about the course I took on "Saints and Holiness," at its end we were left with one question: after all this study of what allows one to be considered a saint, what had we learned? We concluded that saints are those who have found a way to *intentionally* fulfill in the story of their lives the great command of loving God, their neighbor, and themselves, or, as Francis himself would write: "How happy and blessed are those who love God and do as the Lord Himself says in the Gospel: *You shall love the Lord your God with all your heart and all your mind,* and *your neighbor as yourself.*"[28]

The very intentionality in the way they set out to accomplish this in "the story of their lives" put them in conflict with the competing and dominant stories or narratives of their culture. In thinking about how I might write this story of Francis I realized that his own story was influenced for good or harm by the other stories being told by the world around him. To isolate the story of Francis from the influence of these competing narratives would not only be dishonest; it would also keep the power of his story from offering the moral influence that might have an impact on the mores of our time.

I first learned how important it is to distinguish between a "story" and its "ideology" in 1985, while sitting in a classroom at the University of California in Berkeley. There I listened to Robert Bellah teach from his highly acclaimed and recently published book, *Habits of the Heart: Individualism and Commitment in American Life.*[29] In summary, Bellah and his associates tried to describe the outline of the story we all tell ourselves in the U.S. culture.

As they discovered, the primary "language" being taught in the home, in schools, in the media, and in the churches is *individualism*. At the same time they found its adherents talking as though they longed to live by another "language": *community*. As long as individualism defined us as a people our talk about being committed to community would be a struggle, if not impossible. In other words, the ideology of individualism trumps the narrative of community. The latter ideal is compromised because of the prevailing, all-embracing, monolithic ideology of the former.

This dynamic of believing we are living out a certain truth or being faithful to one story, while being captured by an alternative "truth" or all-pervasive ideology, can undermine our authenticity. What is more, as Kurt H. Wolff attests, "we make common cause" with forces that actually militate against our best interests. As an alternative, he suggests that our various narratives are best served when we suspend or bracket them in a form he calls "surrender."[30] I will show how this happened with Francis when he called into question both his culture's story and his church's story. The new reality that emerges from this surrender is what Wolff calls "catch." It is "a new, more trustworthy, more believable, more warranted catching or conceiving than could even be expected before the experience of surrender or the desire for it."[31]

If we are not aware of those uncritiqued stories with which we make "common cause," they can take control over our lives. The forms of control found in the various ideologies that undermine the core stories that have been told to us, I call "the ideology of the 'isms.'" When ideology is absolutized in any narrative, the authenticity of the story is distorted (i.e., "de-storied"). These absolutizing tendencies found in the key stories affect how we see ourselves in ways that do not represent the core story. They become echoed in the "super-ego" or outside collective or cultural voice that tries to dominate our thinking, feeling, and action. When we come under the sway of these "isms," our story gets skewed; our freedom to be our unique "I am" is compromised. The more monolithic this ideologizing tendency becomes, the more destructive the underlying dynamic in that story will be.

Conversion, as reflected in the life of Francis, invites us to be free of the "isms" or ideologies that can control our mind and corporate psyches. Unless we find a way to such freedom, we cannot find the healthy interplay of the various narratives that must come together in the critical narration of the story of our lives. In the life of Francis, particularly as it relates to the challenges of our time, we shall be particularly interested in the the culture's story and the church's story.

The culture's story is what we tell ourselves as a people regarding our difference and superiority over other peoples. In the case of the United States, this often gets expressed in such phrases as "We are the greatest nation on the face of the earth," and other attitudes that fall under the heading Americanism. I believe "Americanism" is the key "ism" that keeps us from being our best selves as a people.

A good definition of "Americanism" can be found in the neo-conservative journal *Commentary*. In addressing the widespread anti-Americanism in the world, David Gelernter defines its opposite: "By Americanism," he writes, "I mean the set of beliefs that are thought to constitute America's essence and to set it apart; the beliefs that make Americans positive that their nation is superior to all others — morally superior, closer to God."[32]

I would say that Americanism represents the way of thinking that uncritically accepts other "isms" as well, such as the classism that justifies the ever increasing divide between rich and poor, the materialism and consumerism that justify our right to control the key resources of the earth for our own interests, the militarism that eats more and more into the federal budget.

Americanism has become so ideologically engrained in the corporate psyche of many citizens of the United States that it has become almost absolutized as the ultimate story around which other stories are told and interpreted. The result is what Richard John Neuhaus calls "Our American Babylon," wherein America "is the church."[33] When this occurs, a kind of cultural captivity of Christianity and a domestication of the radicalness of the scriptures ends up replicating what happened in Israel when it became assimilated under Solomon. The result is what Old Testament scholar Walter Brueggemann calls the "royal consciousness": *"the establishment of a controlled, static religion* in which God and his temple have become part of the royal landscape, in which the sovereignty of God is fully subordinated to the purpose of the king."[34]

The Roman Catholic Church has its own story, an understanding of itself as the only vehicle of salvation, superior to all other ways. In the Catholic Church, this "Romanism" is grounded in a deeper "ism," which is ideologically nurtured day in and day out: patriarchal clericalism. Clericalism connotes the conscious or unconscious concern to promote the particular interests of the priesthood (with its power, perks, and prestige) over all others in the church who are merely baptized. The patriarchal form of this clericalism limits all such power, perks, and prestige to males alone. This is justified by the ideologically grounded conviction that this divide is divinely sanctioned. It is further expressed in rituals and rubrics that sanction the divide canonically (all of which have been written by the clerics themselves). "Among its chief manifestations," Donald Cozzens writes, "are an authoritarian style of ministerial leadership, a rigidly hierarchical worldview, and virtual identification of the holiness and grace of the church with the clerical state and thereby with the cleric himself."[35]

As we now turn in the following chapters to interpret Francis' story, we need to unmask the ideologies of culture and church that skew it. If Francis was able, in his "surrender," to rise above the absolutizing power of these ideologies, we are invited to do the same in the way we surrender to another way of living in the world and relating to each other. Consequently, as we try to understand Francis' story, free of the social and ideological "isms" in our own culture and religion, each of us must return to our own unique story as the filter through which we do our interpretation. In the narration that reveals the story of our lives, as in the case of the other stories, we have our own "isms," each seeking hegemony in order to become the dominant way we order our lives. Highly influenced by our cultural story in the United States, we find the individualism we have already described. Unless we understand how its filter can do violence to the other narratives, we will not be able to move into the countercultural conversion that Francis' story demands of us. The result can be the kind of exaggerated relativism that is increasingly recognized as a debilitating force in society.

In his sermon at the conclave that elected him as Pope Benedict XVI, Cardinal Joseph Ratzinger spoke of "the dictatorship of relativism" as a controlling ideology of our time.[36] This ideology recognizes no authority outside one's self; it reflects the subjectivism that is characteristic of our time; it also results in the violence that invites us to "surrender." Our postmodern world is characterized by this attitude, especially in the West.

If we can find a way of balancing the core message of each of the stories around us in a way that is integrative rather than divisive through being seduced by their ideological "isms," we will have come to discover the Reign of God ruling our lives. We will discover, as Peter A. Campbell and Edwin M. McMahon write, that "the Kingdom of Heaven is within!" This will be discovered when we find our "individual stories, which are integral to the entire Cosmic narrative," being "written in our bodies." The process by which we can be led to our true story, that which we actually share in common with all other humans, Wolff calls the "bracketing of our received ideas."[37] Peter Campbell and Edwin McMahon call it "focusing."

This focusing is at the heart of spirituality. The more I know about it and use it in my own prayer, I have found that, along with Wolff's notion of "surrendering," it seems to reflect a way Francis came to discover his story at the heart of creation's story. This grounded him in God and empowered him to speak with such force vis-à-vis the other stories around him.[38]

With this as background, I now can move to explain more fully the relevance of Francis' story and how it might be applied to our lives today.

TWO

Assisi and Francis
Faith-Stances in Contrast

"...a man like St. Francis of Assisi, for instance. What does he really mean?...A complete break with the pattern of history...A man born out of due time. A sudden, unexplained revival of the primitive spirit of Christianity. The work he began still continues...But it is not the same. The revolution is over. The revolutionaries have become conformists. The little brothers of the Little Poor Man are rattling alms boxes in the railway square or dealing in real estate to the profit of the order." He laughed quietly. *"Of course, that isn't the whole story. They teach, they preach, they do the work of God as best they know, but it is no longer a revolution."*[1]

— "Pope Kiril," in Morris L. West, *Shoes of the Fisherman*

The Crisis of Faith as
Traditional Stories Are Challenged

At the time of Francis of Assisi's birth, central Italy was moving from the Dark Ages to what we now describe as the dawn of the Middle Ages. While northern Italy had already witnessed the beginning of the intense commercial activity that would finally evolve into full-blown capitalism, Assisi was rapidly catching up. As in other urban areas, merchants, bankers, industrial entrepreneurs, and other professionals were replacing feudal lords as society's dominant force. While the people involved in such commerce did not constitute the majority of the townspeople, they commanded the new market economy and consequently grew in wealth as well as political power.[2]

The gradual breakdown of feudalism in the late twelfth and early thirteenth centuries was accompanied by increasing movement from rural areas to cities in a way that brought about the rise of the city-states. The merchants in these city-states were able to make money, which became the key medium of exchange. Where once business relationships in feudalism were

33

defined by trust and trustworthiness between lord and vassal in patron/client relationships, money could be exchanged quickly. This had psychological as well as economic implications, fostering mental habits that would become increasingly central to the church and society.

What were these mental habits? According to Alexander Murray: "One was the habit of desiring more and more money, a habit which medieval theologians usually called avarice. The other was the habit of desire for that power and dignity which society concentrates in its institutions. Despite some confusion, this usually went under the name of ambition."[3]

The cultural changes connected to the rising market economy created strains on people's previously held meaning systems of faith and religious identity. Traditional religion was rapidly losing its force in their lives. The Capuchin Franciscan Lázaro Iriarte describes this "loss of faith" very well:

> Autonomous crafts workers, merchants and other educated common-
> ers were claiming a role, not only in public administration, but also
> in the life of the Church. Religious structures, whether pastoral or
> monastic-liturgical, could not satisfy their needs. What was needed
> were expressions that were more authentic, more responsive to people's
> moral and spiritual beliefs, more in harmony with the new communal
> dynamic.[4]

Within this setting, Francis of Assisi was born and bred. However, having had his own crisis of faith in the cultural and ecclesiastical patterns of violence, Francis' withdrawal found him empowered by the Gospel in a way that would revitalize the faith of his compatriots (in sharing their culture's story) and his co-religionists (in sharing their "church's story"). He did this by an appeal to the "life of penance" — a countercultural stance, no longer defined by the violent narratives as they were lived in his society and church, but reinterpreting everyone's life according to the perennial values of the Gospel. His way of withdrawal became a way of surrender, which, as Wolff notes, "says No to the establishment."[5]

In a similar way today, given the loss of national innocence with regard to the culture's story (with the events surrounding September 11, 2001) and the church's story (as represented by scandals in the Roman Catholic Church), more and more people find themselves alienated within the political economy of corporate capitalism and institutionalized religion. They have grown weary of the rhetoric of the dominant political and ecclesiastical authorities, with their emphasis on a clear, rigid, and monolithic worldview. Alienated by their leaders' ideologies and unable or unwilling to explain why they feel so overpowered by such rhetoric and intensity, they simply drop out from the shouting. They give up; no longer able to identify their core values with such "beliefs," they "lose faith."

The way of religious faith involves a triangle. On one side there is the element of *prescription* (creeds, catechisms, and codes); on another there is *proclamation* (the word and witness of others, including the authors of scripture); and finally, the *personal* experience of the divine "Other" that creates a relationship of trust and intimacy, grounding the other two parts of the triad. When a religion's story is limited to the one element of prescription, to the detriment of the other two elements, many "beliefs" touted as objective truths trump a faith that is always, by definition, uncertain. The result is often religious ideology, with idolatry not far behind. When this occurs, as Karen Armstrong notes, "the institution becomes more important than justice. That has often been the besetting sin of the Catholic Church."[6]

When cultural patterns and religious tradition trump divine revelation, it's no wonder sincere "believers" can become confused. As Richard Rohr explains it, this leads people to "confuse the maintenance" of the religious container (i.e., the "system") "with the contents themselves. They confuse the rituals with the reality that they point to."[7] Consequently the "truths of the faith" become a matter of certitude rather than that faith which always demands a leap. The leap of faith and trust in God alone enables us to be open to the process of authentic surrender — which includes suspending my received notions about God that may be wrong or wanting upon a deeper examination. Such a faith, according to Wolff, invites us to be open to "distrust . . . everything less than God."[8]

While "faith" represents what is ultimate in our culture's and church's stories, oftentimes those narratives get compromised because of what Robert Schreiter calls "the narrative of the lie." He notes that, while "we humans cannot survive without a narrative of identity," when a few get control of the group narrative to serve their own self-interests rather than the good of the people, they seek to impose their own narrative, which becomes the official ideology, and which everyone must believe as a matter of "faith," as the way to redemption and salvation.[9]

The consequence of letting ideology trump the core message of the story is that the story becomes less and less believable. The result is a crisis of faith in ever increasing numbers of people who cannot intellectually submit their minds nor their consciences to such a group or many of its beliefs, even when they seem grounded in what is called "tradition." Indeed, as Kurt H. Wolff has shown so well, it is often the historical aberrations found within a religious tradition itself that contribute to people's crisis of faith in a way that invites them into the process of surrender and catch (which we will discuss at greater length in chapter 5). He notes that surrender involves the breakdown of that which is false within a tradition; it reveals a deeper, truer "faith that is the prerequisite of surrender." He notes that, "if life is to be saved, it must be lost to a cause." Indeed, building on Wolff, I would note that only "the person who surrenders to this cause [of Christ and the Gospel] moves on to the faith in surrender."[10] He adds:

> it must be said that surrender is of relevance only to the person for whom "tradition" (or a given, once important tradition) has become meaningless: surrender is an *answer* to discontinuity, an effort to come to terms with discontinuity, rather than its advocacy. If, and to the extent that, I accept "the group" as my guide, I have no reason, no motivation to entertain the idea of surrender or to be interested in the experience. The discussion of surrender is based on the assumption that I can *not* trust the group any more than I can trust tradition.[11]

As I've noted earlier and will explore in chapter 5, much of tradition and its beliefs lock people into certain givens that can easily serve ideologically to justify inequity and to discourage the leap of faith. Whether we speak of politics, economics, or religion, it seems increasingly important to distinguish "beliefs" in the forms of dogmas and decrees, fear and fatwas, from faith as it is expressed in ways of meaning that energize people like Francis of Assisi into deeper expressions of care and compassion. In this effort I believe an insight proffered by Sharon Parks is crucial. She writes that "if we are to recover a more adequate understanding of human faith in the context of present cultural experience, we must be clear that when we use the word *faith* we are speaking of something quite other than *belief* in its dominant contemporary usage."[12]

Faith, according to Sharon Parks, is not about belief as much as it is about meaning. From her clinical work she has discovered that it "is in the activity of finding and being found by meaning that we as modern persons come closest to recognizing our participation in the life of faith. It is the activity of composing and being composed by meaning, then, that I invite the reader to associate with the word *faith*."[13]

In terms of the culture's story, many find lacking what anthropologist Clifford Geertz has called a "politics of meaning." As Michael Lerner writes:

> Americans hunger for a framework of meaning and purpose to their lives that transcends their own individual success and connects them to a community based on transcendent and enduring values. For a significant number of Americans, the major crisis in life is not lack of

money but lack of meaning — and that is what I mean when I say we face a spiritual crisis.[14]

This spiritual crisis is echoed in many parts of Western Catholicism. Even Pope Benedict XVI has acknowledged this, speaking to the Swiss bishops in November 2006 about the "crisis the Church is facing, especially in the West."[15] It reaches the ears of countless concerned parents who regularly hear their children's complaint: "But it doesn't mean anything any more." Its reality is found in the fact that 40 percent of the Catholics in the United States are lapsed or inactive (not just "withdrawn"). Its evidence is found in the two "major findings" of a study on Australian Catholicism commissioned by the Australian Catholic Bishops' Conference as to why so many Catholics have stopped "going to Mass":

1. A large majority of participants believe that the Church is out of touch with the current world and is not relevant to their own lives.

2. In general, participants' alienation from the Church has been a gradual process in which changing attitudes to Church teaching have interacted with negative personal experiences of Church personnel and regulation.[16]

Given the above, it is little wonder that Francis Quinn, the former bishop of Sacramento, California, would indicate that the "overarching crisis in today's church," for many Catholics, involves "not faith in God, not faith in Jesus Christ, but a crisis of faith in the institutional church."[17]

In light of these crises of faith, these experiences of meaninglessness that so many experience in the way the various stories of our faith are told, it seems that the example of Francis might offer a way to rediscover a faith that is believable and meaningful for our times. In this hope, we turn to his story.

The Context of Francis' Story

The advent of the second millennium, especially from the latter part of the eleventh century, brought significant changes to European society, including Italy. Population growth was supported by better methods of farming, the development of new crafts and trades, and, especially, expanded commercial opportunities and products. At the same time, time-honored social patterns prevailed. The most entrenched of these, structurally and ideologically, was the system of feudalism, or the seigniorial economy. Although the most blatant forms of feudalism were not present in Assisi, this system still had a powerful impact in creating, sustaining, and justifying, the class structure.

As a result of clericalism and the abuse it generated, R. I. Moore contends that "it is...probable that the period between the Third Lateran Council of 1179 [two years before Francis' birth]...and the Fourth in 1215, saw the most rapid diffusion of popular heresy that Western Europe had yet experienced."[18]

At the lowest and most populated rung of life were people living in rural areas who were indentured to a *signore* economically and socially. In turn, the *signori* were answerable to a higher authority, making every human being the virtual if not real property of another. This hierarchy was considered to be of divine origin.

A key characteristic of the feudal pattern of society was the division of all peoples, at all levels, and even among groups, into *ordines* or structured orders or classes. This resulted in the emergence of what Moore calls "the bureaucratic regime, or the professionalization of the exercise of power,"[19] which maintained its hegemony through fear, intimidation, and persecution. Where at first persecution may have been a weapon in the competition for political influence, it "was turned by the victors into an instrument for consolidating their power over society at large."[20]

The greatest division in society was constituted by those defined as the *potentes* (the powerful) and the *pauperes* (the poor). Despite those who were of the nobility and, therefore, the *majores,* the world was basically composed of the poor, the *minores.* Arnoldo Fortini, who served as mayor of Assisi in the late twentieth century, described how these structured relationships were expressed in his city seven centuries before:

> The two Latin adjectives *maiores* and *minores* were used by the medieval Italian to measure and classify power, virtue, nobility, authority. There were *maggiori militi,* greater fighting men, and *minori militi,* lesser warriors, *magiori* and *minori* townsmen. Even the merchants are by now divided into three grades: *maiores, sequentes, et minores,* according to their wealth. In battle, the *mercanti maggiori* fight on horseback with cuirass, lance, and sword, the *sequentes* also fight on horseback with lance and sword but without the cuirass, the *minori,* on foot with bows and arrows.[21]

Over time, the dynamics of structured unequal power relationships, with their particular impact on the urban poor, took their toll. According to Prospero Rivi,

There was violence and injustice everywhere, few marriages were made for love, there was no lay culture, almost no technical or scientific progress. From this point of view the *contemptus mundi* [contempt for the world] basically meant the refusal to descend to compromising with a political society probably less Christian than the most secular of our present nations.[22]

Assisi was a microcosm of the unequal power relationships in the wider society, with all the attending poverty, decadence, and violence. It was frequently referred to as a new Babylon. As such women were demeaned and abused; orgies of various kinds were commonplace. Its streets were filled with merchants trying to exploit and gangs who were willing to kill. As in all cultures highly characterized by dynamics of honor and shame, revenge was a right, vendetta was a sacred duty, and violence itself was sanctioned as God's will.

This violence was expressed in a particularly vicious way in the form of persecution. This persecution was directed at specific targets: lepers, Jews, heretics, and male homosexuals.

In his groundbreaking book *The Formation of a Persecuting Society: Power and Deviance in Western Europe, 950–1250* R. I. Moore contends that religious persecution "faded away with the Roman Empire" but reappeared during this time. Such a system of violence would have to be justified via the creation of "scapegoats." Key among the scapegoats that incurred the wrath of society during the entire life of Francis were members of the four groups noted above.[23]

Moore notes that during the 950–1250 period, the last quarter constituting the entire lifespan of Francis, "persecution became habitual." He explains:

That is to say not simply that individuals were subject to violence, but that deliberate and socially sanctioned violence began to be directed, *through established governmental, judicial and social institutions,* against groups of people defined by general characteristics such as race, religion or way of life; and that membership of such groups in itself came to be regarded as justifying these attacks.[24]

Any form of social deviation was labeled "deviancy," which justified exclusion from the community, including the church and its religious celebrations.

The Sapping of Faith in Assisi's Culture of Violence

Such cultural norms were inevitably expressed in religious life. And yet God had little effective meaning in daily life. If "faith" existed, it was something connected to another world, not the world of the everyday.

Even when Francis looked at those monastic communities whose members had "fled the world," he did not find that much difference when it came to faith. As he observed the main religious orders around him, such as those following the way of Bernard of Clairvaux and, especially, the many Benedictine monasteries in and around Assisi, he found society's violence replicated. Fortini notes that monasteries operated in the public "very much on the feudal pattern." Great patrimonies were accumulated through donations, legacies, and personal contributions of the monks. Consequently Benedictine abbeys became true castles "with vast jurisdictions, serfs, men-at-arms." The result was a situation wherein abbots were "more often warriors than men of the church." Their faith seemed to be grounded in armaments rather than the "ground of all being."

The Benedictine Order that had once been founded to be a beacon of peace had become more of an obstacle to it. As Fortini writes (using the present tense):

> Even monastery life is not a peaceful one. Often enough even the high towers of monasteries are shaken by the storms of these turbulent times; and the monks do not hesitate to put on a cuirass, buckle on a sword, and ride out on horseback, like other fighting men.
>
> Records show the Benedictine monasteries for women, governed by abbesses, are also not oases of peace. They engage in quarrels with the bishop and neighbouring feudal lords. Sometimes they are not even places of sanctity. The capitulary of Arechi (or Arichi) of Benevento accused nuns of being too interested in such things as a good complexion and soft white hands, of seeking ways to meet men, and of worse things yet.[25]

The Benedictines weren't the only ones who lived lives of violence under the mantle of religion. It seemed to characterize the pattern of behavior of one of the local parish priests whom Francis knew. Furthermore, these divisions, with their parallel forms of animosity, found their way into the canons who prayed the divine office in the major churches. By the time of Francis, "the canons of the church of San Rufino were vaunting the title of *maggiori,* in contrast to those of Santa Maria Maggiore, who had become *minori.*"[26]

Probably nobody knew better how to exploit these conflicts, especially between the popes and emperors, than the bishops themselves. Indeed, by "the end of the twelfth century, the bishop of Assisi, shrewdly steering a course between popes and emperors, comes to acquire an enormous holding. By the time of St. Francis he was apparently the owner of half the property in the commune."[27] All this was confirmed in a papal bull by Pope Innocent III on May 12, 1198.

In fine, whether in economics or politics or even the church, what Fortini wrote of Gubbio could be said of Assisi and every commune in Italy: "It was a city dedicated to warfare, trade, and government, to the building of towers and palaces, the making and unmaking of treaties with popes and emperors." The people at every level in such a situation, including religious leaders, "could not even imagine a faith that was not sustained by military skill."

It could be added that, if the people could "not even imagine a faith that was not sustained by military skill," neither could they imagine human relationships not defined by structured inequality — even slavery, as well as wealth concentrated in the hands of the very few. Into this reality, not unlike our own, Francis of Assisi appeared. He came with an alternative imagination that inspired people from his day down to our own, generating in them a renewed sense of God, the holy, and of faith itself.

The relevance of this point was made abundantly clear by Ronald Rolheiser, O.M.I., reflecting on the crisis in contemporary Catholicism, which he attributes to a lack of imagination, which in turn contributes to a "loss" of faith.

> What needs to be inflamed today inside religion is its romantic imagination, and this is not so much the job of the theologian as it is the job of the artist and the saint. We need great artists and great saints, ideally in the same person.
>
> We see this, for instance, in Francis of Assisi ... As a great artist and a great saint he was able to inflame the romantic imagination of the church and the world.[28]

Francis' Story: An Alternative Faith

There were no atheists in Assisi at the time of Francis. However, Assisi reflected culturally conditioned, religiously sanctioned violence and, to that degree, was de facto a city filled with theoretical belief but controlled by practical atheism. In other words, the culture's story as well as the church's story defined people's faith; this way of belief was far from faith in the story that revealed Jesus Christ and his Gospel of the Reign of the Trinitarian God.

All of this, especially Assisi's internal and external wars, had a powerful impact on Francis' story and thus on the origins of the new Franciscan movement. Fortini writes: "The war accompanied Francis's spiritual crisis, as well as that of his first companions, who were his fellow citizens. It continued until the approbation of the rule and may well have been the factor that determined its coming into existence."[29] In the same vein, Thomas of Celano writes that, in such a milieu, where his fellow citizens displayed "nothing of the Christian religion in their own lives and conduct," but contented themselves "with just the name of Christian,"[30] Francis, "strengthened by the Holy Spirit . . . followed that blessed impulse of his soul."[31]

Francis' spiritual awakening began with a dream that brought about a crisis in his life. According to *The Legend of the Three Companions*, it began with "a vision" one night on his way to Apulia. Francis found himself led into "a beautiful bride's elegant palace." Its walls were hung with glittering coats of mail, shining bucklers, and all the weapons and armor of warriors. These, he was told by the one who had led him into the room, "belonged to him [Francis] and his knights."[32]

However, things changed in a follow-up experience once Francis arrived at Spoleto. Half awake, half asleep,

> He heard someone asking him where he wanted to go. When Francis revealed to him his entire plan, the other said: "Who can do more good for you? The lord or the servant?" When [Francis] answered him: "The lord," he again said to him: "Then why are you abandoning the lord for the servant, the patron for the client?" And Francis said: "Lord, what do you want me to do?" "Go back to your land," he said, "and what you are to do will be told to you. You must understand in another way the vision which you saw."[33]

This "understanding in another way" would represent the beginning of Francis' "surrender," his liberation from the received tradition of religiously grounded knighthood. This involved a conversion from a militaristic approach to life and a faith that would justify violence in the name of God to another approach constituted by a novel way of disarmament. In this way he would experience himself becoming a knight of another kind.

Francis' dream, as Julio Micó writes, was the beginning of his transformation in faith itself:

Behind the traditional image of God which Francis had formed was hidden the living God who utterly changed and broadened his spiritual horizons. Thomas of Celano (1C 5) describes this disconcerting experience in the well-known dream at Spoleto. In a typically feudal setting, it shows us the change in values that God wrought in Francis. Up to this point his one aim in life had been to win knighthood on the field of honor. But now all his thoughts were turned towards his Lord, who had given him life and for whom he would henceforth live.

The God of Francis's conventional background, who had remained unchanged and perfectly compatible with his other values, now gave place to the living and life-giving God who conquers and takes over, who broadens and even tears apart the accustomed horizons of one's life. Francis's consent to the evidence of God's lordship would mean that from then on he would live in a kind of continual ecstasy, a permanent leaving of self behind to go out to the God of fulfillment. After this experience, he would no longer be able to go on cultivating his own personality but would set forth along new roads as a pilgrim of the Absolute, searching for the well spring at which he could quench his thirst for God.[34]

Francis' faith now moved from a cultural faith that canonized the status quo to a personal faith that critiqued not only the status quo, but also his own former participation in it. It invited him to embark on an ever deepening process that would move from a faith defined by creeds and canons to one that was personal and transformative. In fine, as Micó summarizes the Spoleto experience, it "changed his image of God from the conventional God who scarcely mattered in life's options to the living and true God who had won his heart so completely that he could never again disregard Him . . . Hitherto, he had confused God with the idols which society held up before him, but now it was the one true God Himself who became the sole purpose and support of his life."[35]

Francis was convinced that the Spoleto experience which began his calling — as well as his response to that calling — was totally the work of God. He called this being led by "divine inspiration." He was convinced that it was God who had spoken to him in his dream; it was God who invited him to "withdraw" from the might and militarism around him; it was God who would lead him where he would go. This conviction of God's power-at-work in him via the life of grace would continue for the rest of his life. Toward the end of his life it would be summarized in his *Testament,* wherein he gave total credit to God alone for anything of good that had occurred in him and led him to do what he did. Whether it was in the embrace of the leper, or his way of dealing with priests known to be public sinners, or in what brought about his commitment to the Gospel and the very community of brothers that was created around that vision: everything good that happened to him came about because of God. He called this the "Lord's inspiration." Convinced that everything had begun in God, he spent his life trying to remain grounded in that same inspiration or Spirit-source. Nothing, he said, should get in the way of this Spirit of the Lord and its "holy operation." Nothing should extinguish this Spirit of prayer and devotedness or groundedness. All was grace. From this experience or inspiration, his faith now found him viewing the world differently than he had before. This form of faith, which led him to be consciously connected to everyone in the universe, found him increasingly alienated from the surrounding world, with its distinctions and distortions, with its resulting forms of divisions and discrimination. In my mind, Francis' willingness to recognize how far his traditional religion had kept him from authentic faith can be found in the prayer he offered before the cross in San Damiano not long before his leper experience and his resulting conversion. I believe it represents the prayer of all who find themselves alienated from the ideology of society and church, and who long to be grounded in God alone:

> Most High, glorious God,
> enlighten the darkness of my heart
> and give me true faith, certain hope, and perfect charity,
> sense and knowledge, Lord,
> that I may carry out Your holy and true command.[36]

From Religiously Sanctioned Violence to Gospel-Based Faith

Francis' time was characterized by class divisions maintained through military might. These divisions were justified, by their beneficiaries, as God-ordained. I believe the same dynamics can be seen all around us. In a recent column in the business section of the *New York Times*, Anna Bernasek wrote: "Inequality has always been part of the American economy, but the gap between the rich and poor has recently been widening at an alarming rate." Yet I have heard few "alarms" sounded from the leaders of my church or other denominations, who seem preoccupied by other threats to "moral values." No alarm was rung when Bernasek stated, "Today, more than 40 percent of total income is going to the wealthiest 10 percent, their biggest share of the nation's pie in at least 65 years."[37] Instead, this ever increasing disparity between the rich and the poor is justified in the corporate world as necessary for the economy, and it goes largely uncriticized from the pulpits in our churches.

One of the reasons why such disparity continues can be found in the fact that politicians in power write the rules that benefit them and their financial supporters. Or, worse yet, as Bernasek notes in her article,[38] they actually pass laws written for them by corporate lobbyists. Matthew Continetti has illustrated this process in *The K Street Gang*. As an enthusiastic and idealistic young Republican Continetti came to Washington only to discover that "a small cadre of conservative activists, steeped in free-market ideology and antigovernment rhetoric, systematically looted tens of millions of dollars from public and private entities, encouraging wasteful federal subsidies and keeping vast fortunes for themselves."[39]

Another recent book, *Polarized America: The Dance of Ideology and Unequal Riches,* shows that the increasing political polarization being experienced in the United States in recent years not only mirrors, but is caused by increasing economic inequality. This in turn is fueled, in good part, by policies that favor the super-rich, such as tax breaks for the wealthy and efforts to repeal the estate tax. However, to keep the people at large from recognizing how much more this disparity rests on the backs of the middle class than the poor, divisive diversions must be percolated. While the governing party promotes economic policies favoring a narrow elite it must focus people's attention elsewhere. The best way to do this is to accuse the other party of undermining the culture's story by being unpatriotic and godless.[40]

This power was particularly evident until 2006, the period of Republican control of Congress. Recently, at the very same time that members of the U.S. Congress voted to give themselves a cost of living increase, they refused to raise the minimum wage of the poorest workers in the land. Throughout the same period these members of Congress were intent on repealing any tax on the estates of the wealthiest people in the country.

The federal minimum wage, $5.15, had remained the same since 1997. Since then its purchasing power had decreased by 20 percent. The consequence was that a single wage-earner making the minimum wage, working for 52 weeks, earned $10,700 a year — more than $5,000 below the federal poverty line for a family of three. However, during that ten-year period the members of Congress, who already made $165,200, a year, raised their salary by $31,600, more than 20 percent. Workers earning the minimum wage at that time would need to work forty hours a week for sixteen weeks to earn the $3,300 which the members of Congress voted for their annual pay increase in 2006.[41] Only in 2007 did Congress increase the minimum wage.

Unlike the rich and the poor of Francis' day who believed that economic divisions were divinely sanctioned, a different dynamic prevents the middle class in the United States from challenging "the system." This is the hope that one day they will be its beneficiaries. This is clear from an article in the *Chicago Tribune*.

In response to a reader's question: "How do you define 'rich,' anyway?" Clarence Page responded: "People who are at the opposite end of the income scale are 'poor.'" However, having said that, Page continued: "Americans don't like to talk about class, yet they like to think that they are experts about it anyway. A *Time* magazine survey found that 19 percent of Americans believe they have incomes within the top 1 percent. (Hello? The critics must be right about the state of American education)." He continues with an even more revealing statistic: "Another 20 percent believe they will be within the top 1 percent one day. No wonder Americans are awash in credit card debt — and show so little concern for the deficit that our national budget is slipping back into."[42]

The consequence of such a mind-set reflects an attitude of entitlement that is part of our individualism as a people: we have the right to the resources we want at the cheapest possible price. What happens to other people and the environment is not of great concern, as long as our lifestyle can be maintained. Even when some of us might proudly say we do not shop at Wal-Mart because of its sins against workers and small businesses in the towns it "invades," this isolated countercultural stance numbs us from realizing Wal-Mart itself is just a microcosm of the "Wal-Martization" of our national psyche. The result, as Robert B. Reich, former U.S. secretary of labor wrote, is that the violence that is endemic in our political economy has created for us a "Faustian bargain: it can give consumers deals largely because it hammers workers and communities." He explains:

> We can blame big corporations, but we're mostly making this bargain with ourselves. The easier it is for us to get great deals, the stronger the downward pressure on wages and benefits. Last year [2004], the real wages of hourly workers, who make up about 80 percent of the work force, actually dropped for the first time in more than a decade; hourly workers' health and pension benefits are in free fall. The easier it is for us to find better professional services, the harder professionals have to hustle to attract and keep clients. The more efficiently we can

summon products from anywhere on the globe, the more stress we put on our own communities.[43]

As we saw in the previous chapter, for the most part, there has been a cultural captivity of the churches in the United States. Consequently you will find, not only among evangelicals, but in my own Catholic tradition as well, almost a mirror image of its members with mainline thinking on almost every social issue, except that Catholics are less likely to support the death penalty.[44] In our cultural captivity, we have created for ourselves the same metaphor Celano used to describe the Assisi of Francis Bernardone's day: "Babylon."[45] Its deadly ways have infected our national soul in such a way that we are being destroyed in the process.

Like the Jews at the time of Solomon, we have been seduced into a kind of "royal consciousness" that isolates us from the destructive patterns of our way of life. As a result we have become blinded and deaf to understanding its impact on the poor and on the planet. This phenomenon has a devastating impact on the souls of those of us who claim to be followers of Jesus Christ. Living amid a "culture of death," we not only become immunized to violence; we have become its unconscious carriers. According to the authors of a popular book on St. Francis, "The image of God in us — the image of our true humanity — is scarred because we have learned to coexist with the violence of injustice. Neither we nor the poor can be whole persons as long as [such] injustice goes unchallenged."[46]

Can Francis' Story Impact Our Culture's Story and Religion's Story Today?

In my early years as a Franciscan, I believed that Francis had set in motion a process leading to the steady demilitarization of society after his death. I noted how the lay group he founded, now known as the Secular Franciscans, followed a way of life he outlined in his *First Letter to the Faithful*. This way of life, or the "Life of Penance," involved a turning away from the patterns of the world that vitiated against the Gospel. Included in this "Rule" was the prohibition to bear arms. As a result of this prohibition and because so many lay people joined the movement founded by Franciscans, I argued that fewer and fewer people were available to fight wars; thus his teachings about not bearing arms brought about a more rapid dissolution of feudalism.

Now I am less sanguine about his effect on social change, especially since I have not been able to find that passage in his *Letter*!

Nonetheless, despite the fact that Francis never seems to have consciously considered himself a change agent, nor did he ever declare his goal was consciously to change unjust structures in the Roman Church and wider political economy, there is no doubt that he did have a great impact on history. His uniquely Gospel-based effort had definite economic, political, and religious implications. Consequently, as Stanislaus da Campagnola writes, by "inserting himself into the very heart of his own society, Francis helped to accelerate the progress of society." To buttress this conviction he argues:

> It cannot be denied that Francis with his movement shook up, marked, and impregnated the entire society of his age. When we say that by inserting himself into the heart of his society he helped accelerate the progress of human society, we are of course speaking in modern scientific terms...
>
> In an era of underdevelopment and progress, of senseless violence and efforts towards peace, his religious activity contributed to the breakup (*disgregazione*) of old privileged social classes and the building up of the newly emerging social classes.[47]

Today, many features of our U.S. brand of capitalism manifest the very things that Francis of Assisi rejected. One of these is the great divide between the rich and poor. Another is the way our society, like Assisi of long ago, is convinced that only military might can effectively ensure the preservation of our increasingly materialistic lifestyle. Francis could no longer believe in such a system. Therefore what Fortini writes seems abundantly clear: "The Franciscan movement came into being as a reaction to that class war and to the conditions prevailing in Assisi at the time of Francis's youth."[48] If conflicts related to property were the source of violence, Francis realized, neither he nor any of the brothers could claim property or, as the Earlier Rule states, defend it if they were challenged to give it up. Thus Francis' unique approach to poverty was really his effort to keep the violence of his society at bay within his fraternity.

I believe it is time for another St. Francis. The "revolution" need not be over. We need to find in Francis' story that heroic or mythic pattern that speaks to the deepest part of our dissatisfactions and disillusions with the world in which we live, and so rekindles our capacity for joy and hope. We need also to find in his story a way that invites those of us of the Western spiritual tradition, as Fenton Johnson suggests, to "return to its authentic, egalitarian, faith-based roots as articulated in all the Gospels, stripped of the institutionalized Church's obsession with temporal power and prestige."[49] If we can move in this direction, perhaps we will have found a way that will invite courageous youth, eight hundred years after the founding of Francis' Order, wanting to explore contemporary ways of probing the heart of his vision, nuancing the core of his message, and embracing the Gospel again in a way that will make the reign of God revealed in Jesus Christ as compelling for our age as it was in Francis' time.

THREE

Francis' Approach to Change

Point Out the Ruin or Repair It?

Francis, don't you see that my house is falling into ruin? Go, then, and repair it for me.[1]　　　　　 —Words from the cross at San Damiano
to Francis of Assisi, circa 1205

The Experience of Francis
at the Cross of San Damiano

The Spoleto experience of the dream launched Francis' spiritual journey. However, although he came to realize what he would *not do,* i.e., fulfill his long desire to achieve honor via knighthood, he had no clarity about where his dream would direct him.

Despite his uncertainty, as he returned to his home in Assisi, he seemed to intuit that he had found something that would take him beyond the path of his earthly father, the businessman Peter Bernardone. Thomas of Celano, describing this time in his life, draws on the image of another commercial enterprise that he was beginning to transact: "Like an experienced merchant, he concealed *the pearl he had found* [Matt. 13:46] from the eyes of mockers and *selling all he* had, he tried to buy it secretly."[2]

The image of finding the pearl refers, of course, to the parable told by Jesus in Matthew's Gospel about entering the kingdom of heaven, or the reign of God. Finding this treasure brings about great joy. In Francis' case, he could hardly contain his joy. Thomas of Celano writes that he had confided to a friend about his newly found "treasure." He spoke of his find in figures of speech to others, yet his excitement was such that it made them think he had found "the woman of his dreams," as the saying goes. Still not fully aware of what was happening, he could only respond: "I will take a bride more noble and more beautiful than you have ever seen, and she will surpass the rest in beauty and excel all others in wisdom."[3]

50

It was not long after saying this that Francis had a transforming experience when he went into the little church of San Damiano. The church had been abandoned and left in much disrepair. Above the altar hung a large crucifix, which stands almost seven feet high and over three feet wide. It had been painted in the twelfth century, first on linen and then glued to a walnut cross. The various figures, such as the Mother of Jesus and the Beloved Disciple, who surround the Crucified Christ, reflecting the passion narrative from the Gospel of John (19:25–26), have definite Syrian and Byzantine characteristics. Instead of a crown of thorns, Jesus' head is surrounded by a glorious halo of light. From the cross, the Crucified One ponders the world quite peacefully. Above the inscription "INRI" ("Jesus of Nazareth, King of the Jews") is another image of Jesus ascending into heaven surrounded by angels. This follows the pattern of John's Gospel, which conflates Jesus' death and resurrection, ascension, and Pentecost (the extension of the body of Christ into the world by the Spirit for all ages).

At the time of Francis and, indeed, until the present generation of scripture scholars, the "Beloved Disciple" was equated with John the Evangelist, who in turn was linked to the Apostle John, one of the first twelve disciples of Jesus. However, as I have shown elsewhere, this can no longer be supported by an unbiased reading of the text itself. Instead, in a church that was gradually moving to an almost-eclipse of Jesus by the figure of Peter and the Apostles, the Beloved Disciple seems to represent every disciple of Jesus for all ages who, united with the Mother of Jesus, makes a new house for God to dwell in on earth as in heaven.[4] I find that Francis himself may have intuited this somewhat in his Earlier Rule in the way he placed the figure of John the Evangelist before that of the two great apostles of the church — Peter and Paul[5] — and talked about our need to "make a house" for God to dwell in.

Even if this was not his intent, my approach to Francis' understanding of his community being created as a new household under God the Father in heaven resonates with what the Franciscan biblical scholar Michael Guinan writes of Francis' vision of the world and its links to John's Gospel: "We will not argue that Francis understood the Gospel passage explicitly in the way we propose, but rather that his relationship to creation is perfectly at home in the Johannine sacramental vision of the world."[6] In this world, the household of God, the Word had "made home." Even if the "world" would destroy the physical temple or house of his body, Jesus declared in John's Gospel, it would be rebuilt via his resurrected body, the church and, indeed, all creation itself.

As Francis prayed before the crucifix he heard a voice ask: " 'Francis, don't you see that my house is being destroyed? Go, then, and rebuild it for me.' Stunned and trembling, he said: 'I will do so gladly, Lord.' "[7] *The Legend of the Three Companions,* which narrates the above experience, notes that Francis originally "understood that it was speaking about that church, which was near collapse because of its age." This led him to leave the church and find the "priest sitting nearby and, putting his hands into [his] pouch, he offered him a handful of coins. 'My Lord,' he said, 'I beg you, buy some oil and keep the light before the Crucified burning continually. When this money runs out, I will again give you as much as you need.' "[8]

As Francis' original interpretation of the words from the cross matured, he would be led to a much deeper understanding of "the house" that needed such repair. It would be an invitation for him to enter more deeply into the process of reconstruction and conversion with implications much broader than any ruined building that stood outside Assisi's gates. As Michael Blastic notes, the words eventually would lead him "to understand that the mission was rather one of repairing a space in which the lives of men and women who have been broken and destroyed as human beings can be rebuilt and flourish."[9] It would be this, but even more. Since the "house" was the basic unit of the political economy at that time, its repair involved something much more than a building; it would involve a systemic transformation.

What Is the "House" in Ruins That Needs Repair?

Traditionally the experience of Francis before the cross of San Damiano has been interpreted first, as Francis initially acted upon it — physically repairing this and other churches in the area — but also in the sense of a larger call to repair the ruination of the universal church of Christ. However, this notion itself, I believe, has been too limited and isolated from the context within which the words came to Francis. Unless we understand this historical context, we will fail to grasp the wider implications of the message and how it also contributes to the universal appeal of Francis.

With the ascendancy of Innocent III to the papacy (1198–1216), there came about the reign of Rome in a way never before known in "the world" as the people of Italy knew it. Assisi itself was a witness to this phenomenon.

During Francis' early years, Assisi had been part of the Holy Roman Empire, controlled by Frederick I Barbarossa (1152–90), Henry VI (1190–97), and Philip (1198–1208) through their surrogates who lived in the Rocca Maggiore, a fortress on top of the hill overlooking Assisi. However, when he was elected pope, Innocent III began an effort to restore papal rule in central Italy. He threatened the then-ruling imperial surrogate (and kinsman to Philip), Duke Conrad di Lützenfeld, to transfer allegiance from the emperor to Rome. While he was on his way to settle with the papal legates, the townspeople of Assisi, sensing their chance to take control of their own town, besieged and razed the Rocca Maggiore. The nobles fled to Perugia, effectively setting in motion the rise of Assisi as a city-state.

Given this broader understanding of the "house" of the papacy, which ultimately ruled central Italy, including Assisi (even in its newly found freedom), it seems a case can be made for a "broader" interpretation of this text that parallels what Sandra Schneiders writes about the way we might broaden our interpretation of the scriptures themselves. She writes in *The Revelatory Text:* "There is no such thing as the one correct interpretation of a text. Texts are susceptible of endless new interpretations as different interpreters, with different questions and different backgrounds, interrogate the text about its subject matter. There is also no one correct method or constellation of methods for interpreting a text."[10]

The same holds for the way we approach the Franciscan texts today, such as this passage about the need to repair the house falling into ruin. As the Franciscan historian Joseph Chinnici makes clear, the retrieval of the original tradition must be done "in such a way that it might become available to disciples of Christ and members of his Body in the twenty-first century." This demands, he insists, a process by which "the intellectual forms of the scholastic heritage give way to modern interpretive categories inherited from linguistic philosophy, sociology, psychology, feminist studies, ritual analysis, and recent historical interpretation." While remaining "faithful to key intuitions and insights" both in the spiritual experience of Francis and in the tradition that interpreted his phenomenon in philosophical and theological expressions of one era, the goal of those trying to articulate any contemporary relevance of Francis must be to "bridge the past and the present" in a way that uncovers the "historical resonance between two distinct eras. Such a dialogue and exchange," he concludes, "can only illuminate both the understanding of the tradition and its contemporary deepening and application."[11]

Consequently, recalling these insights, I have come to regard Francis' San Damiano experience as about something much more than the need to initiate church reform. Since the metaphor of the "house" is embedded in the entire political economy, I will argue that the house that always needs to be restored from its ruination applies everywhere — including the "house" of one's self, our transactions with each other, our way of relating to others, and, indeed, to creation itself. Such kinds of house are truly forms of business.

Repairing the House by Building a New Kind of Homemaking

In the previous chapter I discussed the theory of Sharon Parks relating to the crisis of faith experienced today by many with regard to their culture's story and their religion's story, and what happens when they no longer find these stories speaking to their deepest longings. I noted that she calls this crisis of faith, a "crisis in meaning." As she has probed the implications of this crisis, she has discovered that any "theory of faith development must necessarily, therefore, be attentive to the transcendent and covenant images and symbols — the deep, culturally confirmed metaphors — by which meaning is given form and upon which moral-ethical being and becoming depends."[12] "The primary task before us, both women and men, is not that of becoming a fulfilled *self* (or a fulfilled nation)," which only reinforces individualism and narcissism, "but rather to become a faithful *people,* members of a whole human family, dwelling together in our small planet home, guests to each other in the 'household of God.'" We will never find the meaning we seek and the faith that brings us peace until the fullness of meaning is found. A help in doing so is the metaphor of the house, as I have described it above, or what she calls "the imagery of home, homesteading, dwelling, and abiding is restored to a place of centrality in the contemporary imagination."[13]

Furthermore, in an effort to reclaim the heroic images found in the notion of the mythic journey, which we described earlier, Parks goes even further when she writes that the future will find the themes — journey and house — being (re)united in a way that becomes transformative for all. Just as we "have learned much about the transforming power of pilgrimage," she writes, so we "need also to recover the transforming power of the art of home-making. The soul's discipline is shaped both by venturing and by abiding."[14]

This way of thinking received its own kind of confirmation, especially regarding the need to stress the "repair" needed in the house rather than just concentrate on its "ruination," as I was writing this book. One day I was presiding at the Catholic liturgy of the Eucharist. It was the end of a retreat, and I had chosen special readings that would fit the themes we had discussed. I had told the coordinator of the liturgy which readings they would be, and she agreed they would fit well. However, all my efforts came to naught as a reader retreatant approached the podium. Rather than reading the selection

I had chosen, the person began to read the "first reading" for the day's liturgy.

In this, the "official" reading from Amos, I had never heard so many references to the need for a "house" in "ruins" to be "repaired." This reading confirmed my conviction that the metaphor of "house" that Francis learned to be in need of repair could never be limited to the church alone. The reading from the very end of Amos declared:

> For lo, I will command, and shake the house of Israel among
> all the nations ...
> On that day I will raise up the booth of David that is fallen,
> and repair its breaches, and raise up its ruins, and rebuild it as
> in the days of old;
> in order that they may possess the remnant of Edom
> and all the nations who are called by my name, says the Lord
> who does this.
> The time is surely coming, says the Lord,
> when the one who plows shall overtake the one who reaps,
> and the treader of grapes the one who sows the seed;
> The mountains shall drip sweet wine, and all the hills shall flow
> with it.
> I will restore the fortunes of my people Israel,
> and they shall rebuild the ruined cities and inhabit them;
> they shall plant vineyards and drink their wine,
> and they shall make gardens and bear their fruit.
> I will plant them upon their land,
> and they shall never again be plucked up out of the land that I
> have given them,
> says the Lord your God. (Amos 9:9, 11–15)

Whether Israel's "house" was standing on solid ground or in need of repair in the form of conversion was critical in the eyes of prophets like Amos. In a similar way, in the "Gospel Story" that Francis would embrace as the guidepost for his life, we hear Jesus telling his followers to "proclaim the good news, 'the kingdom of heaven has come near'" (Matt. 10:7). The way they were to do this involved going from one town or village to another, finding a *house* that would be "worthy" and greeting it with "peace" (Matt. 10:13). The health of the house would be defined by the reception offered to those who came with the greeting of peace.

Francis took this "apostolic commission" seriously. In both his earlier and later rules, in the section outlining how the brothers were to "go about in the world," he said: "Into whatever house they enter, let them first say: 'Peace be to this house!' "[15] He was absolutely convinced, he wrote in his *Testament,* that this greeting was to be used when he and the brothers went from house to house.[16]

While chapter 10 will discuss Francis' unique "peace platform" and its implications for the world at all its levels, for the rest of this chapter I would like to place my emphasis on the metaphor of "house" spoken from the cross at San Damiano.

Moving to a Fuller Understanding of the "House" in Ruins That Needs Repair

In both the Hebrew and Greek scriptures found in the Old and New Testaments, there is no word for "family" such as we have it. Instead the word for the house — *bet*[*h*] in Hebrew and *oikía/oikos* in Greek — might mean the physical place, as well as the whole set of relationships and their structuring within the building that took place among its members and their resources. In other words, persons, their relations, and their resources defined the "house." How persons ordered (*nomos*) their relationships vis-à-vis the resources in the house (*oikía/oikos*) resulted in an economic reality: *oikonomía* (=*oikía/oikos* + *nomos*). Thus we have the core ingredients that constitute every definition of economics: persons, relationships, and resources. Economics, of whatever form, revolves around the ordering of resources among persons. In this sense the "house" involves "business."

Since the house was the basic economic unit of the entire imperial household that ruled the world at the time of Jesus, the evangelical way of peace he proclaimed "to the house" (which will be discussed in greater detail in chapter 11) would offer a countercultural stance toward that of a Pax Romana designed to maintain Caesar's control throughout the world. Also, because at the time of Jesus, the same *oikía/oikos* that constituted the basic religious unit of the empire also defined, for those in the house-churches, their *ekklesía,* it is not surprising that Francis' embrace of the evangelical greeting of peace to each house would have economic and ecclesiastical implications and consequences.

In my writings, I have taken the notion of *oikia/oikos* and applied it to every level of the world. I call the individual level of the world — that which constitutes our selves or our intrapersonal reality — the *oikía.* The second level is the world of our regular relationships or interpersonal commerce. This is the *oikonomía;* it defines how we as persons relate to other persons, each with our resources that will be ordered in various ways. The *oikouméne,* as it did at the time of the writing of the scriptures (i.e., Matt. 24:14), represents the whole inhabited world of persons, their relationships, and their resources. The fourth level is the universe itself. This I term the *oikología,* the underlying reality that sustains the other three forms of *oikía/oikos.*

All of this has been made by, through, and for the *oikía ton theon,* that "household of God" that is constituted in what theologians call the "economic trinity." Herein the three persons are each fully divine in their unique "I am," which is such only because the "I am" of the one does not exist without the "I am" of the other. In the relationship between the "I am" of the one and the "Thou art" of the other, a "We are" is constituted wherein all the resources of the one are fully available for the others. Francis understood that, if all things, spiritual and corporal, have been made to image this God,[17] they do so most fully when they become equal to each other in their relationships, ensuring the fullness of freedom for all as well as total equity in the way the resources of their commonwealth are shared. This "special 'I-You' relationship," Leonhard Lehmann writes, gave birth to a "worldview that can rightly be called affirmation" of everything that constitutes creation.[18]

Francis saw creation and everyone and everything in it part of God's domain or household. All became revelatory to him of the Trinitarian God relating to us in a way that energizes us with a divine connectedness as brothers and sisters in a common household. This included the brothers, wherever they may be; it included all Christians and, indeed, everyone on earth; to serve them was his call. In fact, all creatures were members of a common household; as such they were his brothers and sisters as well. All of them were gifts of God.

I believe that the words Francis heard from the cross of San Damiano offer us a way of personal, group, and social (political, economic, and ecclesiastical) analysis that can be used with comparative simplicity. It begins with simple observation of what is wrong in our own lives, in our relationships, and in our structures: "Don't you *see* that my house is being destroyed?" This refers to the traditional first step in the Jocist "see, judge, and act" model of social analysis.[19] The conclusion that something is being destroyed is based on a prior sense of what is healthy about those relationships. This involves judgment. However, here, the judgment can be based only on the very household of God, the "Economic Trinity," which, as we will discuss later, involves right relationships among equal persons fully sharing all resources in their "household." With this critical awareness of what undermines those relationships at any level of life, one is willing to risk trying to act in a way that will bring about "right relationships," or justice within the household in a way that reflects moral or Trinitarian living. This effort involves being led by the Crucified Christ to "rebuild" the house in a way that reflects the Trinitarian Reign of God.

In the past, in my effort to bring about change in the world, I have concentrated on bringing about right relationships among people and their resources (i.e., "justice") by concentrating especially on the *oikouméne* with its institutions, their "isms," and their ideology, as well as on that of the *oikología*. In the way I went about my efforts to bring about social change and more justice in the world, I was much better, I must admit, at pointing out where there were "ruins" than how to "repair" those ruins.

At the same time, I have also discovered that, as I worked to bring about change in the *oikouméne,* I may have neglected to repair broken and fragile relationships with others, especially those with whom and among whom I lived and worked (the interpersonal level of the *oikonomía*). Even more, I discovered — hopefully not too late — that, in the process "my own house" was not in order. I had "unfinished business." Therefore I also needed to work on repairing it as I tried to reorder relationships at the other levels of life. This demanded my own conversion, working on my own spirituality.

From the message of the Crucified One, Francis was invited to repair "the house." How he chose to do this would have tremendous consequences. He had one of two ways to approach his task: pointing out where it was "falling into ruin" or working to "repair it." If he concentrated on exposing its sins, he could easily go the heretical way of many reformers before him. If he could find a way to "repair" it that would attract others to join him in this reconstruction project, it could have a powerful effect.

In the study of spirituality, there are two main ways that have been shown to inspire change in people's lives. One stresses the need to let go of those things that hinder growth, while the other emphasizes what must be done after "letting go." The "letting go" is technically called the *kenotic* approach (after the Greek word *kenosis*); more popularly it is called the *via negativa.* It constitutes what Kurt H. Wolff calls "surrender." The other approach that concentrates on what should be done rather than avoiding what should not be done is technically called the *apophatic* way; in popular language we know it as the *via positiva.* This constitutes what Wolff calls "catch."

I find both approaches important as we realize where our houses are headed to ruin and how they can be repaired. Maybe it has been because of my personality, but I know that my approach toward change — especially outside the "house" of myself — too often concentrated on the negative, on pointing out where the "ruins" could be found. I was much less good at approaching the ruins with a recipe for repair.

The more I have probed the uniqueness of Francis's nonviolent approach to life, especially in face of the ruins that were so apparent all around him, I find that what attracted people to him was that he did not follow the path of those reformers before him who harped on the ruins; instead he offered a way of repair based on positive relationships and leading to joy.

With this as background, I want to discuss an approach to conversion at all four levels, inspired by Francis of Assisi, that will emphasize constructive dynamics for repairing relationships rather than adding to the destructive dynamics that merely add more to what is already being ruined.

1. Repairing the Oikía/Oikos of the Self

Kurt H. Wolff notes that perhaps "the 'home' of surrender is the body" itself.[20] Indeed, as we will see in chapter 5, Francis considered his body itself changed when he went through the process of embracing the leper, which Wolff would call an experience of "surrender and catch." If the body is home to the self and if the process of conversion involves a surrender of the ego to give rise to the true self, then the body itself, along with all its senses, becomes the dwelling place for the divine activity.

Many psychiatrists and psychologists believe that dreams contain important teachings for those who want to probe their meaning. At the heart of any interpretation of such dreams, the image of "house" has powerful implications. For instance, Carl Jung taught that recurring images in dreams are really root metaphors that reveal much about us. A key metaphor recurring in many people's dreams is that of the "house." The house and what happens in the house when we dream, at least from the perspective of therapists like Jung,[21] offer much to help us understand ourselves. Indeed, building on this notion, people like Clare Cooper Marcus wrote her *House as a Mirror of Self: Exploring the Deeper Meaning of Home*.[22] A similar theme is explored in a 2001 movie starring Kevin Kline, *Life as a House*.

Dream research shows that what happens to the dreamer in a closed space such as "the house" often can reveal something not only happening in our bodies but in our very selves. Thus the need to be aware of this "house" as we consider its implications for us in our own lives. Indeed, this notion is buttressed by a common saying referring to the need for conversion in our personal lives when we say that we need to get our "house in order."

When we consider the "house" as our body-selves and consider the way Francis, by his own admission, treated his own body, Francis was not particularly good about taking care of himself. Because he abused it with many fasts and scourgings, many sleepless nights in shiver-producing caves, he had to apologize to what he called "brother body" toward the end of his life. He had to find a way to be reconciled with the violence he did to himself, to repent, and have his body forgive him.

Despite the fact that legends are told about the hardships he imposed as negative penance on his body, it is very clear that he took the necessary time to make sure his "house was in order" with regard to making a home for his God in the way he sought to have God "remain" with him, as the Gospel of John describes discipleship, in prayer. Thus he urged his brothers in the Earlier Rule: "Let us always make a home and a dwelling place there for Him Who is the Lord God Almighty, Father, Son and Holy Spirit."[23]

In many ways, the "house" that Francis tried to make of his body that it might be a fit dwelling place for God was cultivated in prayer, especially when he entered the many different remote caves and caverns. He could spend days upon end in such places without having to seek distractions because he was continually distancing his heart from whatever might be an obstacle to his sense of God's abiding presence in and around him. In effect the caves became external witnesses to the interior cave he had made for his God to be at home within him.

I have not been able to find myself "making home" for God when I visit the caves around Assisi because I find them too damp and cold. However, when I consider the need to quiet myself in a way that "makes room in my house" for the stillness that can sense the presence of the Other, I must admit that, beside my own Franciscan tradition, I also draw much inspiration from some of the key Carmelite writers. For instance, in her classic on the spiritual life, *The Interior Castle,* St. Teresa of Avila built on the image of the "dwelling place" or mansion being prepared in heaven for us by Jesus as noted in John's Gospel (John 14:2). "In order to have some foundation on which to build," she structured an approach to the spiritual journey: "I began to think of the soul as if it were a castle made of a single diamond or of very clear crystal, in which there are many rooms, just as in Heaven there are many mansions."[24]

For his part, St. John of the Cross used the image of a house to open his famous canticle *The Dark Night:*

> One dark night
> Fired with love's urgent longings
> — Ah, the sheer grace! —
> I went out unseen,
> My house being now all stilled.[25]

In a wonderful poem built around this opening stanza of *The Dark Night*, the Carmelite poet Jessica Powers wrote her own now-classic poem: "A House in Order":

> How does one hush one's house,
> each proud possessive wall, each sighing rafter,
> The rooms made restless with remembered laughter
> or wounding echoes, the permissive doors,
> The stairs that vacillate from up to down,
> windows that bring in color and event
> from countryside or town,
> oppressive ceilings and complaining floors?
>
> The house must first of all accept the night.
> Let it erase the walls and their display,
> impoverish the rooms till they are filled
> with humble silences; let clocks be stilled
> and all the selfish urgencies of day.
>
> Midnight is not the time to greet a guest.
> Caution the doors against both foes and friends,
> and try to make the windows understand
> their unimportance when the daylight ends.
> Persuade the stairs to patience, and deny
> the passages their aimless to and fro.
>
> Virtue it is that puts a house at rest.
> How well repaid the tenant is, how blest
> who, when the call is heard,
> is free to take his kindled heart and go.[26]

If Jesus promised he would make "home" for us with the one he called "Father," that home begins in our conscious contact with the Trinitarian God. In the depths of our hearts, we must continually "clean our house" so that we might always make home for that God or be about our Father's business.

2. Repairing the Oikonomía

Nowhere in the writings of Francis do we find a condemnation of the political economy (*oikonomía*) of his day, even though it seems the underlying "sins" of power and greed found in feudalism merely changed external faces with the rise of mercantilism or the market that came more to the fore in urban centers like Assisi during his lifetime. His vision of economic life inspired by the Gospel, however, offered an alternative to its destructive dynamics. In the process it would stand witness to counter any economy based in selfishness and greed.

As noted earlier, all definitions of economics involve three realities: persons, relations, and resources. Consequently, when persons take priority in the way an economy is ordered, the preservation of community or fraternal relationships also will take priority in the allocation of the available resources. Freedom will be ordered to meeting basic needs in a way that engenders trust among the participants. However, when the relationships take priority over the persons involved as well as the resources allocated, you will have a command-type economy; any freedom of persons is subservient to the preservation of the structures of dominance (usually defined by the political group ultimately in control). When the resources take priority over persons involved and affected, including how they relate to each other and make transactions, the market takes priority. Consequently "freedom" will be defined as access to the market. When this happens the freedom of the market takes precedence over authentic individual freedom.

Against a political economy that was experiencing the rapid rise of a market economy based on the exchange of money, Francis of Assisi adamantly refused to define his brotherhood in any way by money; thus, he de facto rejected the market economy. The brothers were to appropriate to themselves neither house, nor place, nor anything at all. Because they committed themselves to be free from the desire to own anything, they were able to be "at home" with everyone of all classes and with everything.

Francis outlined a way of economic and ecclesial life called "fraternal," which would be based on exchanges among the brothers on the basis of their needs. Thus, in one of the most-quoted passages in his Later Rule, Francis declared that his economy would be based on households defined more by a certain way of relating than on being in a certain place:

> Wherever the brothers may be and meet one another, let them show that they are members of the same family [i.e., "household"]. Let each one confidently make known his need to the other, for if a mother loves and cares for her son according to the flesh, how much more diligently must someone love and care for his brother according to the Spirit![27]

First of all, the quality of life for the brothers would define them as loving and caring for each other as friends. This was a unique approach to religious life, and it is wonderfully described in the story told by Julian of Speyer in his biography of Francis. It seems that a certain Brother Riccerio deeply desired to be recognized as a friend of Francis not so much because of the notoriety this might bring him, but because he was scrupulous and thought that friendship with Francis would assure him friendship with God. However he told this to no one.

One day, Francis, who knew his state of mind, called him to his side and said: "My son, from now on let no fear or temptation disturb you, because you are most dear to me, and among those especially dear to me, I love you with a special charity. Come to me confidently whenever it pleases you, and leave whenever you like."[28] In fine, confidence should characterize the way the brothers should relate to each other, just as confidence should characterize the way they made known to each other their basic needs. This brings us to the second way Francis sought to create a new kind of fraternal economy.

Second, in outlining an economic way of life for his brothers based on their needs rather than their wants Francis gave the world a new understanding of economic development that began with what he called the "grace of working." In the Benedictine world, physical work was the domain of the lay brothers; in his classless world, Francis prescribed work for everyone. Work would be the great equalizer. Indeed, not even work itself would be good enough; the desire to work had to find the brothers eager to ground all their relationships with each other and those around them, in that way of living that made them commoners. As such work would ground all relationships among the brothers, wherever they might be. This kind of work would define the new fraternal *oikonomía*. He elaborated on what he meant by this image in his Final Rule: "Those brothers to whom the lord has given the grace of working may work faithfully and devotedly so that, while avoiding idleness, the enemy of the soul, they do not extinguish the spirit of holy prayer and devotion to which all temporal things must contribute." Then he added: "In payment for their work they may receive whatever is necessary for the bodily support of themselves and their brothers, excepting coin or money."[29]

Since the mid-1990s, we Capuchin Franciscans have been trying to develop an alternative economy, at least among ourselves whenever we "come together." We do not want it to be based on the present forms associated with the existing market economy that stress resources over persons. Rather we envision a "fraternal economy" that places the priority on persons over resources. The development of women and men, not wealth creation or its (re)distribution, comes first. How this might develop — at least among the eleven thousand of us spread over more than one hundred countries — is the source of much discussion.

3. Repairing the Oikouméne

Only if the brothers were unable to be "homemakers" themselves, taking care of each other by their work, Francis said, should they go asking for alms. However, by asking for alms, when their own economic efforts would fail, they would have recourse to the next level of life: the systemic. By asking alms to help their local *oikonomía* the brothers would be extending to the systemic level an invitation to be part of a new social order defined by justice in the household of society, the whole inhabited world, the *oikouméne* (Matt. 24:14). This may also be a way that Francis could make up for his failure as a youth to reorder his wealth toward the poor in a way that would make him rich "in the works of justice."[30]

A key passage in the Sermon on the Mount, used to begin every Lenten season, stresses the need to perform *dikaiosūne,* or justice, in a triadic way. The first concrete way of bringing about this justice begins with the giving of alms (Matt. 6:1–4). True to this evangelical way of bringing about conversion within and among the house churches, Francis said the brothers should not be ashamed to ask for alms, especially if their work had not produced "enough" for their households. Stanislaus da Campagnola thus writes in his "Francis of Assisi and the Social Problems of His Time":

> He was so strongly convinced of the socio-religious value of begging that he defended the *mendicare* [begging] as corresponding to the *mercede* [wages] or *stipendio* of one's labor. A passage related by the so-called *Legenda antiqua perusina* reflects his true thinking: "Francis regarded the seeking of alms for the love of God as an act of nobility, dignity, and courtliness in the eyes of God and the world, for he used to say that what the heavenly Father created for our benefit, after the fall he lavished freely as alms on both the worthy and the unworthy for love of his beloved Son."[31]

Asking others in the "household of faith," who had more than enough to give of their excess to those who were in need, actually enabled the latter to be faithful to Jesus' mandate. In a beautiful passage, Thomas of Celano narrates:

> This richest poor man, moved by a great feeling of pity, in order to help the poor in some way, used to approach the rich people of this world during the coldest times of the year, asking them to loan him their cloaks or furs. As they responded even more gladly than the blessed father asked, he used to say to them, "I shall accept this from you only on the condition that you never expect to have it returned." The

first poor man who happened to meet him, he would then clothe with whatever he had received, exulting and rejoicing.[32]

However, if when they begged, the brothers would ask for more than enough, Francis considered that to be a violation of justice. Indeed, an early document shows that Francis believed that, if the brothers asked "for more alms than necessary," this "would have been to commit a theft against other poor" who had a right to it.

In the ideal *oikonomía*, nobody should have less than enough. Conversely, in a limited goods situation, such as was envisioned at that time, neither should anyone have more than enough. By their almsgiving the brothers would be helping to bring about a reordering of relationships and restructuring of society in a way that would empower the poor and, in the process, restore justice where it had not been found. The ideal of the reign of God would thus find "good news" brought to the poor. Da Campagnola insists that for Francis to have recourse to alms "in case of necessity" was actually "the indication of a *haereditas* (legacy), *iustitia* (just right), something due to all who were *pauperes Christi* (Christ's poor)."[33]

During the journey that began when I realized that "it was extremely necessary that the Gospel message be fulfilled in me," I began my public ministry as a Capuchin Franciscan during the days of the "Great Society," almost forty years ago. I believed that structures were being put into place that would end poverty in my lifetime. I have since learned that that won't happen. It won't happen, in good part, because of the "great divide" in our society regarding the ways poverty is approached. These polarized positions say, on the one hand: "If the poor are primarily responsible for their plight, then government ought to prod them to change their ways," while the other states: "If poverty is primarily the consequence of economic and social forces largely beyond their control, then government ought to give them money and change the rules of the economy."[34]

The reality of poverty was very different at the time of Jesus and when the Gospels were written. Indeed, while the phrase "the poor" is found at least sixteen times in the Gospels, the word "poverty" appears but twice and then it is contrasted with the miserly contribution of one who is rich (Mark 12:44; par. Luke 21:4). Furthermore, when we consider the time of Francis (which was closer to the economic reality of Jesus' day than ours), the kind of "poverty" we experience locally and globally today did not exist.

The economy of Jesus' time was a patronage system and almost everyone was poor or indebted. While this system was declining in Francis' day, patronage still existed, the majority of people were indentured on farms, and the system recognized those with resources as responsible to make sure the poor were not absolutely miserable.

While one position today simply says the way to overcome poverty is for the poor to "get a job," at a time when jobs are unavailable or moving offshore, this mantra can be quite irrelevant. However, while half of the people of the world still live on less than $2 a day, it seems quite obscene when, in the United States, those with at least $1 million in net worth increased 6.8 percent from 2004 to 2005. Worldwide, the number of wealthy individuals climbed to 8.7 million, a 6.5 percent increase from 2004. In that same period the combined wealth of high-net-worth individuals worldwide increased to $33.3 trillion, an increase of 8.5 percent.[35]

However, this does echo Francis of Assisi's approach to what we Capuchin Franciscans have begun to call the "Fraternal Economy." At a meeting I attended in spring 2006 in Porto Alegre, Brazil, we Capuchin Franciscans committed ourselves to take the learnings from our efforts at the level of our own *oikonomía* and try to apply them in our ministries and places where we live. We see in this wisdom a viable alternative, at least at the micro-level, to the present form of U.S. capitalism, in which we can see the rich getting the biggest share of the pie in at least sixty-five years.[36] In a "Letter from Porto Alegre," we wrote our brothers about our desire to take our learnings about creating a fraternal *oikonomía* among ourselves and to offer it to the *oikouméne.*

We began from the realization that socialism has "all but totally collapsed"; what is left is "the neo-liberal system, with its concept of the free market." This economic system "has extended its 'globalization' throughout the world. It is a system that creates much wealth but concentrates and secures this wealth in the hands of the very few." The consequence, we declared, found "the rich become richer" in ways that result in the fact that "hundreds of millions of people are systematically excluded from participating in those goods."

Rather than point fingers at others, we realized that we too have become seduced by the system with devastating consequences to our personal, communal, and collective souls: "We ourselves have often been desensitized to the tragic proportions of poverty. We have been lulled into believing it inevitable. We too have slid into a deeper individualism and isolation from one another as brothers and from the poor of the world."

Recognizing, by our very presence in Brazil, "the urgent need to continue to speak and act against increasing poverty and the growing gap between the rich and poor of the world," we committed ourselves to invite others to a conviction that the principles of a "fraternal economy" might be embraced more systemically.

The other major area of "repair" that is needed in the *oikoumene,* as Francis' experience in San Damiano makes clear, is the Roman Church itself. As this theme runs throughout this book, it is not necessary to concentrate on it here. However, I find helpful a very honest approach to the complexities of "repairing" the ecclesiastical structure of the Roman Church in the work of Joseph Chinnici, O.F.M., the Franciscan church historian quoted above. In providing various definitions of "repair," he notes that "the word mutates depending on circumstances and people, political situations and ecclesiastical possibilities." Consequently our approach to the repair of the church will vary. Depending on our background we may consider repair according to the terms of an architect, a builder or a gardener. Our approach to the repair will depend on whether we see ourselves as its owners or servants. Our tools to repair may differ as well. In sum, when we consider our call to repair the Roman Church, especially in its hierarchical structures whose ruins we find all around us and our world, he urges a good dose of humility:

> All of this would seem to indicate that "repair" is a relational reality that operates circumstantially in the space between people-living-with-other people. And therein, for most of us, I think, lies the true rub: If only repair were based on an ideal, a model, a preconceived plan, and not a relationship; if only it involved things and not people; if only it remained static and did not engage moving targets; if only it could fixate its rules of behavior and was not so embedded in personal choices governed by personal and communal beliefs, talents, roles, responsibilities, virtues and vices, historical possibilities and political impossibilities. And when we are dealing with repair in the context of a holy patrimony, we best be very cautions, taking off our sandals lest we leave very unseemly footprints.[37]

4. Repairing the Oikología

Well before there was any concern about the "sins of the world" done at the level of our own lives or *oikías,* our middle-class lifestyle in our *oikonomías,* and the institutions in our *oikoumēne* that are adversely affecting climate change, Francis of Assisi realized the interconnectedness of persons, relations, and resources at all levels of creation. He considered both animate and inanimate creatures not as resources to be exploited but as "brothers" and "sisters" to whom he and his followers would be bound in a caring commonwealth. It is little wonder, then, that he is the patron saint of ecology.

We have already seen that "ecology" comes from *oikía* or *oikos*. As such, when we take it from its intrapersonal, communal, and institutional grounding and apply it to the interrelatedness of both living and nonliving creatures in the environment, it becomes "a study of organisms 'at home,' with everything that affects them there. In its broadest sense," Shantilai P. Bhagat writes in his *Creation in Crisis*, "it is the science of planetary housekeeping." He explains:

> For the environment is, so to speak, the house created on the earth by living things for living things. Included in this "at home" is the study of living beings, the place in which they live, and the interaction among and between the living and nonliving components of the place being studied. So ecology attempts to understand the complex web of interactions and interdependencies in a particular environment or ecosystem.[38]

Since the early 1990s, in my ministry of promoting socially responsible investing, I have been aware of the ecological ruination occurring all over the earth. While some of this may have a basis in natural, cyclic patterns, it is becoming increasingly clear that the "economism" in our culture's story, combined with the individualism in our personal stories is keeping us from doing what must be done to begin to repair this most important "house that we can see is falling into ruin."

My effort to do something to "repair the house" has led me to be part of the effort of my Midwest province of Capuchin Franciscans, along with other religious orders and denominations and various environmental groups, to challenge ExxonMobil (XOM), the largest corporation, as well as the largest energy company in the world. For many years it did all in its power to resist any pressure for "conversion" regarding the way it produces energy. This included funding groups that attacked our efforts, giving the impression that we are some kind of eco-terrorists intent on undermining the "free market."

In the course of this ministry I have found that efforts of a company like ExxonMobil to obfuscate the scientific conclusions relating to the human factors that contribute to global warming represented a high-stakes effort by the largest corporation in the *oikoumēne* that has had an effect on every other "house" in the world insofar as it has been able to impact government policy, specifically, to undermine efforts to develop alternatives to fossil fuels. I also find parallels of the kind of behavior exercised by Philip Morris, the largest U.S. tobacco company, as I tried to challenge its behavior and effect on society's health — until the release of its own internal documents showed that it was quite aware, at the very same time of its denials, of the health hazards associated with the continued sale of its products.

Whether it is the matter of the planet's or people's health, it is clearly not in the corporate interest of many significant businesses to promote a healthy *oikología;* to do so might affect their real "bottom line." The same can be said of the government itself when it becomes the servant of corporate interests. The result is that it does little or nothing to ensure that businesses "clean up their house" when they exploit the earth's resources but then walk away leaving the surrounding inhabitants sickly in both physical and financial ways.

In the face of the ruination of the lives of people and the planet, it is up to all stakeholders in the "house," not just some shareholders, like my group of Capuchin Franciscans or the others involved, to work to put in order the house of the *oikología* itself. Such "repair" of the house of the earth is the "business" of all of us. This begins by putting people and the planet ahead of production and profits in a way that makes us realize we are to be "at home" in the universe on equal terms with everyone, living in cooperation, not as lords and masters living in competition. In the wonderful words of Mislin and Latour:

> No thoughtful person can any longer doubt that the solution of our ecological crisis and control of the human environment in particular is possible only if man realizes that he is a concrete member of the biosphere, that is, of his living space. We must undergo a transformation in our learning process that will change our attitude from one of domination and usurpation to one of service. In his new partnership with nature, Francis of Assisi showed us how to overcome our proprietary, grasping mentality. What he accomplished was a breakthrough to a respectful, supporting, custodial participation in all of nature. Did not Francis conjure up the quintessence of primitive Christianity and show how unrealistic it is to attempt any solution of our problem without a religious foundation? What our time needs is a world-involved Franciscanism, in the original connotation of the word.[39]

FOUR

Finding a Father to Believe In

Listen to me, all of you, and understand. Until now I have called Pietro di Bernardone my father. But, because I have proposed to serve God, I return to him the money on account of which he was so upset, and also all the clothing which was his, wanting to say from now on: "Our Father who are in heaven," and not "My father, Pietro di Bernardone."

— Francis of Assisi, circa early 1206[1]

Francis' Early Years

While little is known about Francis' family background, we can safely say that it would hardly qualify for "Family of the Year." However, in a culture of "machismo" defined by violence, it would not be surprising if Francis of Assisi grew up in a home that reflected the dominant cultural patterns. Males "ruled the roost" at every level of the world, from local household to the commune and up to the emperor and pope. Consequently the household of Pietro and Joan ("Pica" ["Magpie"]) Bernardone probably was not that different from any other family. What was different about the Bernardones, however, was that they were definitely upwardly mobile.

Pietro Bernardone was a savvy merchant, an almost archetypal representative of the rapidly rising mercantile class. In the world of commerce, the Italians dominated the cloth trade. Although their grade of wool was inferior, they could profitably import French or Flemish or English woolen cloth and then rework and refinish it with superior techniques and superior dyes.[2] As one of the merchants capitalizing on making his money in the cloth industry, Pietro frequented the great trade fairs, such as Champagne in France.

Lester Little notes that these fairs were ancient in origin but had been revived in the twelfth century. By the time Francis was ten years old, "they had become organized into an annual pattern with six stages spread out from spring to early winter and with locations at Troyes, Provins, Lagny, and

Bar-sur-Aube. Jurisdiction over the fairs rested with the Count of Cham-pagne." He explains that merchants "from Italian and Provençal towns formed associations to facilitate travel to and from the fairs, to assure ade-quate protection of their lives, their goods, and their rights, and to be able to bargain effectively with the fair officials."[3] It is likely that Pietro was a member of one of these associations.

The art of the deal held such importance to him that he was in France on a business trip when his son was born. Even though men were not part of the birthing patterns of that day, most biographers interpret his absence at the birth of the baby as a sign that birthing was women's business; business was men's business.

Pica had given birth to a son. Being a good Catholic, she wanted him bap-tized as soon as possible. He was taken to Assisi's cathedral, San Rufino, to be baptized. Since much importance was attached to the name that would be given a baby, she had him named Giovanni di Pietro di Bernardone, in honor of John the Baptist, the precursor of Jesus of Nazareth. Upon his re-turn from France, Pietro wanted to give another name to his son that would reveal the honor he was receiving from his business. He insisted that the baby be called Francesco, an Italian version of "France" or "Little Francis." Although Assisi's records note that others had been given the name before, it was not a very common name, much less the name of a saint.

The culture that gave birth to Francis was defined by clear power arrange-ments and sexual roles — in the home as well as throughout the world as it was known. Women and children had no rights. Marriages were defined more by function than love. Beatings and verbal abuse were common. It should not be surprising if these dynamics defined life for Pica and her boys.

Among the two or three sons she bore her husband, Francis seemed to have a special, if not exclusive, place in her heart. He was affectionate and energetic, vivacious and endowed with "a remarkable memory,"[4] Thomas of Celano tells us. Pica and Pietro "reared him to arrogance in accordance with the vanity of the age. And by long imitating their worthless life and character he himself was made more vain and arrogant."[5] Despite these qualities, it never could be said that he ever was anything but generous, even before his "conversion."

For reasons of prestige as well as business, Pietro Bernardone could not countenance an illiterate and uneducated son. Francis needed to know the rudiments of reading, writing, and especially arithmetic, so he could transact business. Consequently Francis seems to have been placed in the grammar school at San Giorgio (St. George) — named for the mythic hero who chival-rously slayed a dragon that threatened a young maiden. There he was taught

Latin and the rudiments of reading and writing. This would help him pray the liturgy of the church, especially the Psalms.

It seems quite likely that, as soon as he was capable, Francis would be taken from both school and the protective nurturing of Pica to accompany Pietro on his business; after all, he was destined not to be a scholar or a momma's boy but a businessman. Book learning would not be as important as learning "the books." Entering the family business included trips to France. There Francis seems to have become enchanted with the French language and, especially, its songs about the chivalrous activities of the knights.

For the first half of his life, Francis seemed to be the delight of his father — as well as people throughout Assisi. Celano writes:

> He was an object of admiration to all, and he endeavored to surpass others in his flamboyant display of vain accomplishments: wit, curiosity, practical jokes and foolish talk, songs, and soft and flowing garments. Since he was very rich, he was not greedy but extravagant, not a hoarder of money but a squanderer of his property, a prudent dealer but a most unreliable steward. He was, nevertheless, a rather kindly person, adaptable and quite affable, even though it made him look foolish.[6]

Most likely Francis and his father were part of the group of Assisians in 1198 that stormed and razed the last symbol of feudalism in the city: the Rocco Maggiori. Then, when civil war broke out between the feudal lords and the townspeople (1199–1200), it also is most likely that merchants like Pietro and his son, Francesco, chaffing under the rule of the nobles, were very much involved. Buoyed by this success, Francis volunteered for Assisi's army when war finally broke out against Perugia, Assisi's perennial enemy, in 1202. At the battle of Collestrada Francis was taken prisoner, and Perugia ultimately prevailed. The resulting peace between Assisi and Perugia brought about a return of the nobility to Assisi, humiliating reparations paid by the business people, and a restoration of papal rule over the territory.

Meanwhile Francis languished in prison. The ransoming of prisoners of war was almost as big a business as the wars themselves. Probably because the Perugians knew Francis came from wealth, they demanded a high price for his head. For unknown reasons, some possibly reflecting his preoccupation with money more than family, Pietro stood by as Francis spent a year in prison. Only when word came that Francis had become very sick, did his father pay out ransom money.

Once home, Francis lingered for at least a year. Convinced that he was well enough to go back to warfare, in 1204 Francis decided to take up arms with the knight Walter of Brienne. We have already discussed what happened to him at Spoleto. This event led him to "withdraw" from the violence and return home. Once home, he continued hanging around with his former companions and taking part in their revelry (and, quite possibly, leading it!). However, this kind of dissipation was increasingly being accompanied by a newfound introspection that became more and more noticeable.

During this time he happened to go to Rome on a pilgrimage; this was a regular ritual among Assisians, even those whose faith was not strong. Once there he was so shocked at the meager offerings being made by the visitors to the church of St. Peter that he threw a handful of money through a grating in the altar. He left the church and encountered some beggars. He convinced one of them to exchange clothes with him. As the *Legend of the Three Companions* narrated: "Standing on the steps of the church with the other poor, he begged for alms in French, because he would speak French spontaneously, although he did not do so correctly."[7]

Was this scene spontaneous? Was it for real? Or was it a masquerade? Was it theatrics? Somehow, it does not compute. Francis' gesture hardly seems to have been that sincere or genuine because he soon asked the beggar to return his clothes. Regaled back in his regular finery, he returned to Assisi. But, while this "exchange" may have been somewhat questionable, without question, the experience contributed to the change already taking place in him.

Francis' Break with Pietro, His Father

As a result of the experience before the cross at San Damiano, Francis now became increasingly torn between the expectations of Pietro, his father, regarding his participation in the family business and Francis' sense of needing to be about the business of repairing San Damiano. Convincing himself that God's work was more important than domestic work, he decided to take some of the cloth from the family store and ride to Foligno, about ten miles away. There he sold both the cloth and the horse and returned to the church to present its priest with the money he had received from the sale.

Whether he was suspicious of the town playboy's sudden conversion or fearful of what would happen if Pietro Bernardone found out he had accepted Francis' largesse, the priest refused. Frustrated, Francis threw the money into the church. The priest, however, did allow Francis to stay with him at the church.

When Francis did not return home, a kind of search party was organized by Pietro. Knowing that they would ultimately come to San Damiano, Francis had previously found a nearby cave that he could use in such a case. *The Legend of the Three Companions* says he stayed for a whole month in the cave, with "only one person in his father's house" knowing of its existence. Who was this anonymous person whose trust Francis had elicited? Pica? A brother? A servant? It is not known. However, he used his cave-time to grow in prayer and discernment. The time in the cave produced a real change in Francis, so much so that, when he decided to leave it and face the consequences from his father, the latter reacted with rage when he emerged and returned to Assisi wearing the habit of a hermit. "Those who knew him earlier, seeing him now, reproached him harshly. Shouting that he was insane and out of his mind, they threw mud from the streets and stones at him," according to *The Legend*.

When Pietro discovered what was occurring, "glaring at him wild-eyed and savagely, he mercilessly took him in tow. Confining him to home and locking him up in a dark prison for several days, he strove, by words and blows, to turn his spirit [back] to the vanities of this world."[8]

Although it was not unusual for fathers to lock up their sons when they disobeyed and even to beat them, in the Bernardone case, Francis' "house arrest" represents a case of two ambitious and bull-headed men having unagreed-upon assumptions, unrealized expectations, and, increasingly, unresolved tensions. This found both of them unwilling to cede their convictions. On the contrary, for Francis, his father's abuse only served to harden his resolve, even if his actual "resolve" was far from resolved! What *was* clear for Francis was that his future would not be connected to this father's business nor Assisi's rising consumer culture, its class interests, and its military maneuverings. There was something greater and more compelling that had now attracted his imagination and sense of direction.

When Pietro was called from Assisi on urgent business, realizing that Francis would not be persuaded by her pleadings, Pica released Francis from his place of imprisonment and let him return to his former place of refuge in the cave near San Damiano. However, when Pietro returned and discovered what Pica had done, he beat her again and stormed to the palace of the commune to denounce his son before the civil authorities. He demanded restitution of the money that he said his son had robbed from him at Foligno.

When the civil authorities called Francis for a hearing, he stated that, since he now was a hermit, he no longer fell under their governance but that of the church. Consequently Pietro went before Guido, the bishop of Assisi, to make his accusation. Although Pietro, being a merchant, was no friend of

Guido's (whose economic interests were with the feudal lords), Guido summoned Francis and told him he had to return the money to his infuriated and scandalized father since he had, indeed, acquired it dishonestly. Neither the cloth nor the horse were his; thus the need to return the proceeds to his father. He urged him to "act courageously," realizing that divine providence would get for him whatever would be "necessary for the work of his church."[9]

At that moment *The Legend* describes the scene of the final confrontation between a father and a son who were equally convinced of the righteousness of their positions. It has become etched in the imagination and memories of devotees of Francis for centuries:

> Then the man of God got up, joyful and comforted by the bishop's words, and, as he brought the money to him, he said: "My Lord, I will gladly give back not only the money acquired from his things, but even all my clothes." And going into one of the bishop's rooms, he took off all his clothes, and, putting the money on top of them, came out naked before the bishop, his father, and all the bystanders, and said: "Listen to me, all of you, and understand. Until now I have called Pietro di Bernardone my father. But, because I have proposed to serve God, I return to him the money on account of which he was so upset, and also all the clothing which is his, wanting to say from now on: 'Our Father who are in heaven,' and not 'My father, Pietro di Bernardone.'"[10]

Thereupon began the next stage in Francis' mythic journey. Having renounced a significant symbol of that which was of "the world," he could continue on his path by embracing a world far bigger than that offered by his earthly father. In the "aesthetic Gospel gesture" of taking off his clothes and becoming naked, Ronald Rolheiser notes, Francis of Assisi "helped restructure the romantic imagination of Christianity and the world in general" in a way that would "inflame the romantic imagination of the church and the world."[11]

How Francis Understood God to Be His Heavenly Father

"O how glorious it is to have a holy and great Father in heaven!" Francis wrote in both his First and Second Letter to the Faithful.[12] Given the previous section, it is understandable that such a transference would have to be made!

That Francis made a complete physical break with his father is supported by the fact that we never hear a word about Pietro Bernardone again in his writings. The same is evident in the account of his life recorded by his first biographers. However, the fact that Francis made a complete ideological, as well as physical, break from his father is evident from his writings as well as his prayers. While he urged his followers to pray "day and night" the prayer Jesus taught, i.e., the "Our Father,"[13] Julio Micó has observed that "when he prayed alone, he rarely invoked God as Father." He opines what most psychologists would attest to: "his turbulent relationship with his own father, Pietro Bernardone, may have influenced his attitude to God the Father,"[14] especially when we consider his divestment of Pietro's paternity in front of Bishop Guido.

This disassociation of the attributes connected to God's fatherhood and those of any earthly father, such as Pietro Bernardone, is further supported by an analysis of Francis' use of the word "Father" in his writings. While he uses it over one hundred times, he refers to the notion of an earthly "father" or one with a blood-connection to a child only three times and, when he does so, it is in a pejorative sense based on the scriptures. These include the passages about leaving one's earthly father (and the patriarchal household) to follow Jesus (Luke 14:26 and Matt. 19:29), along with the admonition to "call no one on earth your father; for one is your Father, who is in heaven" (Matt. 23:9).[15] On the contrary, while he clearly alienated himself from any positive image of an "earthly" father as a model to be emulated, in one of his most quoted passages, he has no problem with offering the love of a mother for her son as a model for the kind of care the brothers should show to each other.[16] Indeed, in his Letter to Brother Leo Francis wrote that he was speaking to him "as a mother would."[17] Even more, in one place in his second biography of Francis Celano notes one brother referring to Francis as "mother."[18]

Furthermore, in his effort to be free of patriarchal dynamics in his community, it seems that Francis had no problem embracing a mother/son dynamic. He actually suggested that those who desired "to stay in hermitages in a religious way" divide their functions along the lines of mothers and sons rather than fathers and sons. If four brothers should be involved, he wrote in his Rule for Hermitages: "Let the two who are 'mothers' keep the life of Martha and the two 'sons' the life of Mary and let one have one enclosure in which each one may have his cell in which he may pray and sleep." As to how they should interact, he stated: "Let those brothers who are the 'mothers' strive to stay far from everyone and, because of obedience to their minister, protect their 'sons' from everyone so that no one can speak with them. And those 'sons' may not talk with anyone except with their 'mothers' and with the minister and his custodian when it pleases them to visit with the Lord's blessing." He concluded that the " 'sons,' however, may periodically assume the role of the 'mothers,' taking turns for a time as they have mutually decided."[19]

Such would seem to indicate that, as a model for human interaction, a familial model based on mother/son relationships would be quite appropriate for the brothers since it would be grounded in dynamics of care. Such would not be the case in those father/son dynamics that, at least in his experience, were grounded in control.

When considering the way he referred to God, however, God is never called "mother." On the other hand, his writings are replete with references to God as *Pater* ("Father"). Norbert Nguyên-Van-Khanh notes that, for Francis, "God's name is essentially that of Father"; however, the characteristics of this "Father" were very different from those of Pietro Bernardone. He explains: "He is Father because He is Creator. Francis saw an intimate connection between creation and the fatherhood of God. His vivid awareness that God the Creator is also Father led him to recognize a bond of solidarity that links not just human beings but all creatures to one another."[20] Nguyên-Van-Khanh also insists that this Creator God who is our Father was always understood by Francis to be Trinitarian and, therefore, the exemplar of the human family.

Thaddée Matura, one of the great Franciscan scholars, examined the use of the word *Pater* (or "Father") in the writings of St. Francis. He discovered that, next to the words *Dominus* ("Lord," 410 times) and *Deus* ("God," 258 times), *Pater*, or "Father," is used the third highest number of times: 104.[21] However, he notes that, when Francis does refer to God as "Father," it is with reservations:

> When God appears as Father in the writings of Francis — and this is very frequently — this fatherhood is rarely placed in direct relationship with human beings. God is Father because of the mystery of the Trinity, above all because of the Son and His relationship to Him. These are the relationships that Francis sets forth, meditates on, and admires. They are the unique and loftiest examples of what we can become by the grace of the Spirit who dwells in us.[22]

The Heavenly, Trinitarian Father Who Is "Our" Father

When Francis wrote in the Later Rule that, wherever the brothers would be and meet each other, they were to show "they are members of one family," he offered them — and the world — an alternative model for a way of relating that would create a new household (i.e., "family"). Not linked to any place, such as a monastery, their relationship of trust would characterize their household. All this would be in imitation of that divine household called the "Economic Trinity."

For Francis, God could not be "Father" without being Trinitarian. It is not surprising, then, that Trinitarian notions dominate Francis' use of the word "father," as well as references to Jesus' prayers, especially the "High Priestly Prayer" offered, according to John's Gospel, on the night before he died, where he prayed to God as "Father" many, many times. It is this notion of God as Father that would constitute Francis' fraternity as brothers, Clare's monasteries and a family of sisters, and the others who embraced the Gospel calling in their own professions, brothers and sisters with all.[23] In a wonderful summary of the Trinitarian underpinning that characterized Francis' approach to God as "Father," Micó writes:

> The Fatherhood of God, then, means that the Fraternity has been gathered together by the Holy Spirit to follow Christ in doing the will of the Father and that, among other things, it consists in making possible the network of fraternal relationships between equals in which love and solidarity are the normal and fundamental values of our life together. The community of the Trinity is the origin of and the model for Fraternity. Created as we are in the image of the Triune God, we brothers have been called to overcome our differences and reproduce between us the loving relationships within the Trinity.[24]

In the writings of Francis, we find references to God as "Father" most in the Earlier Rule (1221). There it is used twenty-five times. One third of these are in chapter 22, which is called Francis' "Admonition to the Brothers." There he urged the friars to ground their lives in the Holy Trinity: "always make a home a dwelling place there for Him Who is the Lord God Almighty, Father, Son and Holy Spirit."[25]

The second most frequent use of the word "Father" for God in the Earlier Rule comes in the Prayer and Thanksgiving Francis offers God in chapter 23. In this passage Francis urged the brothers to ground all their faith, their hope, and their love in the Triune God:

> Wherever we are,
> in every place, at every hour, at every time of the day, every day
>   and continually,
> let all of us truly and humbly believe,

hold in our heart and love, honor, adore, serve, praise and bless,
  glorify and exalt,
magnify and give thanks to the Most High and Supreme Eternal
  God Trinity and Unity,
Father, Son and Holy Spirit, Creator of all, Savior of all
Who believe and hope in Him, and love Him, Who, without
  beginning and end,
is unchangeable, invisible, indescribable, ineffable,
incomprehensible, unfathomable, blessed, praiseworthy,
  glorious, exalted,
sublime, most high, gentle, lovable, delightful,
and totally desirable above all else forever. Amen.[26]

The text speaks powerfully to our hearts about the abiding presence of
God in our lives. It speaks of living in the present moment with the Trinitarian Godhead in such a way that we become at peace with ourselves and
united with everyone and everything in creation because of the God who
abides in us and among us. The Franciscan exegete Thaddée Matura writes:
"No text better reveals the vision that Francis has of God in the mystery of
the Trinity. At the heart of this mystery we see clearly the kingship of the
Father, the principle and source from which all comes forth. An apparently
simple prayer brings us into the very depths of God."[27]

When Francis refers to God as "Father," it invariably has some kind of
connection to Trinitarian notions. The dominant images used by Francis in
referring to the relationship between the heavenly Father (*Pater*) and the Son
(*Filius*) revolve around adjectives of intimacy and awe rather than domination and fear. In other words, when using images related to God as "father,"
the notion of paternal care and relationality is used, not patriarchal control
and dominance over the other members of the Trinity. All authentic fatherhood, then, must be grounded on the "primordial experience of fatherhood"
that is celebrated between the persons of the Trinity. Thus, Francis' approach
to God as "Father," Margaret Carney writes, includes a "vision of a Trinitarian God — not centered on the Father/Patriarch as dominant figure —
but God understood as a 'Fountain-fullness' of pure Goodness poured out
in the act of Creation."[28]

The fact that Francis' notion of God as "Father" was grounded in his
Trinitarian understanding of God freed him from any kind of identification
of God based on the patriarchal dynamics that he experienced in his family
and the society around him. Indeed, the God who was "Father" for Francis

was more like the "patron" than the "patriarch." The distinction is critical for us today as we seek to move away from patriarchal dynamics that still undermine the integrity of our culture's story and the church's story. It also helps understand why, in the patriarchal system that had its apex with the *Pater Patriae,* or Caesar, in Rome, Jesus would teach his followers that their real "Father" was elsewhere, in heaven. This father would have another reign and another Gospel that would proclaim a new kind of peace different from Caesar's Pax Romana. As the language of grace that characterizes the whole New Testament is the language of patronage,[29] in the new evangelical social order envisioned by Francis, fathers would reflect the kind of heavenly patronage where all would be treated with respect rather than the earthly patriarchy characterized by abusive power.

The Heavenly Father Who Is to Be "Our" Father on Earth

When the brothers asked Francis, as Jesus' first disciples asked him, "to teach them how to pray," he echoed the words of Jesus as recorded in Matthew's Gospel: He said: "When you will pray, say, 'Our Father.'"[30]

Matura notes that an examination of Francis' writings shows that he never used the term "our Father" by itself. It is found only in connection with other attributes of God, especially God's transcendence — which has become immanent for us in Jesus Christ. Consequently, he notes: "A share in the relationship of the Son with the Father — this is the divine sonship offered to the believer — cannot be accepted except with the deepest reverence, with trembling. This is what Francis teaches us in his writings: 'O how glorious, and holy, and great it is to have a Father in heaven.'"[31]

Having a common Father in heaven made everyone calling that same God "our Father" brothers and sisters to each other, members of one family. Probably for this reason more than any other, Francis never allowed himself to be called "Father Francis." Indeed he wrote in the Earlier Rule: "*All of you are brothers. Do not call anyone on earth your father; you have but one Father in heaven.*"[32] Neither did he call himself "Francis"; it was always "Brother Francis." As brother, everyone and everything were his siblings under the one Trinitarian "Father in heaven."

As a child, like all Christian children of his day, Francis learned the words of the Our Father. Then, like most children, he probably projected onto the "Father in heaven" understandings of and dynamics around God as a "father" that were based on his personal experience of Pietro Bernardone.

However, as an adult, especially after the split he had with his earthly father, Francis spent much time reflecting on what it meant to call God "our Father."

First of all, he prayed the Our Father with the whole church at the Eucharist as well as at the various hours of the day when the Divine Office was prescribed for clerics to pray. However, in his Earlier Rule he noted that, in addition to the Our Father, they should realize their connectedness to each other in the "our" of the Our Father by adding the psalms "Have mercy on me, O God" (Ps. 51) "for the failings and negligence of the brothers" as well as "Out of the depths" (Ps. 130) "for the deceased brothers."[33] For those brothers unable to pray the Divine Office, he prescribed in both the Earlier and Later Rule that they should recite the Our Father.

Francis considered the Our Father to be the Prayer of All Prayers. He urged that it be prayed both by the Brothers as the beginning of their prayer[34] and throughout the day for everyone who would follow his way of life: *"Day and night* let us direct our praises and prayers to Him, saying: *Our Father, Who art in heaven...* for we should *pray always and not become weary."*[35] Just as Jesus taught the prayer to his followers, so Francis seems to have elaborated on its meaning for his followers. In the commentary on the Our Father attributed to him, each phrase receives an expanded interpretation that stresses the awesomeness of God and our need to show our devotedness to God in the way we invite all others into the praise of this God.[36]

In both his Letters to All the Faithful he invites his audience to develop a familial and intimate relationship with the members of the Trinity. In them he notes that happiness and blessedness will come to those who fulfill the Great Command and live religious lives:

> And the *Spirit of the Lord* will rest upon all those men and women who have done and persevered in these things and It will make a home and *dwelling place in them.* And they will be the children of the heavenly Father, Whose works they do. And they are spouses, brothers and mothers of our Lord Jesus Christ.
>
> We are spouses when the faithful soul is united by the Holy Spirit to our Lord Jesus Christ. We are brothers, moreover, when we do *the will of* His *Father* Who is in heaven, mothers when we carry Him in our heart and body through love and a pure and sincere conscience; and give Him birth through a holy activity, which must shine before others by example.[37]

The Holy Spirit who makes "a home and dwelling place" in women and men who allow this Spirit to rest upon them transforms them into a new creation free of hierarchy, patriarchy, or any other kind of discriminating dynamics. The result is the creation of a new community that is grounded in God and, thus, in Trinitarian relationships, and consciously connected to each other and, indeed, to all creation. Francis made this clear, as we read in Celano's "Second Life" of Francis. Even though it was written to promote a more clerical interpretation of Francis, the very fact that Celano would include the passage here speaks to its underlying power. Noting that Francis desired that the Order "should be for the poor and unlearned, not only for the rich and wise," he explained the real reason for this evangelical vision of Francis: " 'With God,' he said, there is *no respecting of persons,* and the Holy Spirit, the general minister of the religion [i.e., the Order] rests equally upon the poor and the simple." So convinced was he about the need for all in the Order to be equal under the one power of the heavenly Father, the Christ and their Spirit, Celano continues, that: "He really wanted to put these words in the *Rule,* but the papal seal already given to the rule precluded it."[38]

As noted in the previous chapter, in talking about the *oikología,* Francis came to an understanding of the connectedness, the relatedness, and the at-homeness that must exist throughout creation. Having decentered himself from needing anyone or anything to recognize his uniqueness, he was able to offer a unique approach to life on this earth that made all the earth's creatures his brothers and sisters under the God to whom he gave continual praise. This is most evident in the Canticle of Creation, which he penned quite spontaneously toward the end of his life. The *Assisi Compilation* notes that he sat down, concentrated awhile and then began to proclaim its verses and even composed a melody for the words.[39]

While he had extended his notion of the brotherhood beyond its male members to be able to communicate even to birds as "my brothers," almost from the beginning,[40] in writing the Canticle, in its original version, he considered himself in a familial relationship with all the basic elements of the earth. They were his sisters and brothers, members of one extended family under the Lord. This Lord is Seigneur of the household to whom praise and honor should be given by all.

In the Creed of the Church, Francis continually heard the proclamation that the God who is Father of all is also the Creator of all. Therefore all created things had to be part of God's family and, therefore, empowered by God to be his brothers and sisters. In awe at such a manifestation of God's love, he penned the Canticle of Creation. It became the earliest extant piece of literature in the Italian language.

At the front of the community of praise, of course, we find Francis, the servant of this Grand Patrón, who, like all good clients before the one to whom they are totally indebted, heaps praise upon praise to the ultimate and great benefactor under whose protection and governance all things are held together:

> Most High, all-powerful, good Lord,
>> Yours are *the praises, the glory,* and *the honor,* and all
>>> *blessing,*
> To You alone, Most High, do they belong,
>> and no human is worthy to mention Your name.
> Praised be You, my *Lord,* with all *Your creatures,*
>> especially Sir Brother Sun,
>> Who is the day and through whom You give us light.
> And he is beautiful and radiant with great splendor;
>> and bears a likeness of You, Most High One.
> *Praised* be You, My Lord, through Sister *Moon* and *the stars,*
>> in heaven You formed them clear and precious and beautiful.
> Praised be You, my Lord, through Brother Wind,
>> and through the air, cloudy and serene, and every kind of
>>> weather,
>> through whom You give sustenance to Your creatures.
> *Praised* be You, my Lord, through Sister Water,
>> who is very useful and humble and precious and chaste.
> *Praised* be You, my Lord, through Brother *Fire,*
>> through whom *You light the night,*
>> and he is beautiful and playful and robust and strong.
> *Praised* be You, my Lord, through our sister Mother *Earth,*
>> who sustains and governs us,
>> and who produces various *fruit* with colored flowers and *herbs.*[41]

Beginning by recognizing God as his patron, Francis notes that no human is worthy to even invoke God's name. From there, in the original verses of the Canticle, the basic elements of the earth are ordered in pairs with equal recognition balanced between the masculine and feminine: brother sun/sister moon, brother wind/sister water, brother fire/mother earth.

Other Images of God Used by Francis

Since the time of the Hebrews, we use concepts of God as one who is near or "immanent" as well as far away, "other," or transcendent. In Francis' writings both ways of considering God can be found. On the one hand, God's transcendence became immanent in Jesus through the Holy Spirit. On the other hand, especially conscious of his creatureliness, Francis never made God so immanent that God's transcendence went unacknowledged. The balance he was able to create between the two images of God in his way of praying to and relating to God is evident in his writings.

When we consider the images of God found in Francis' writings, many reflect notions of the knight serving a Lord, such as we find in the Canticle of Creation. Whether the word was used of the Father, the Son, or the Holy Spirit, it is a notion that acknowledged God's sovereignty over all creation as Creator and Lord of All. Julio Micó writes:

> In popular medieval piety, the images of the feudal lord and of the German king were projected on God the Creator. God is *Dominus,* the Lord of all things, who distributes them prodigally among men and women while still retaining His sovereignty over them. If we try to appropriate them for ourselves, we are denying God's lordship, and we create false expectations because in the end, "that which [we] thought [we] had shall be taken away from [us]." The right thing to do, then, is to respect God's ownership and thank Him for His generosity.[42]

Micó also notes that Francis' image of God as transcendent was influenced not only by the liturgy, the scriptures (especially the Psalms he learned as a child), and the prayers of his day, but also by the "Romanesque world," which was "dominated by the concept of majesty." While the word itself does not appear, majestic images are found throughout his writings, including "Lord," "Most High," "Eternal," "Omnipotent," "Supreme," "Almighty," and "Glorious."[43]

When Francis prayed to God, he often used such images. As a result, his prayer was more expressed in praise than petition and in gratitude more than repentance. Probably because his prayer was so contemplative he experienced God as the All-Powerful source of everything that invaded his soul and led him to the kind of compassion that revealed the authenticity of his prayer.

When we examine the words of God that Francis used in his writings, his speech and his prayers, we get the idea of a courtier approaching the throne of the ruler, bowing as far down as possible, unwilling to stand up straight without permission. And then, the only words worthy of the awesome patron were those of thanks and honor. A wonderful example of how many of these notions come together is found in his Second Letter to the Faithful:

Let *every creature in heaven, on earth, in the sea* and in the
    depths,
give praise, *glory, honor and blessing*
To Him Who suffered so much,
Who has given and will give in the future every good,
for He is our power and strength,
Who *alone is good,* Who alone is almighty,
Who alone is omnipotent, wonderful glorious
and who alone is holy, worthy of praise and blessing through
    endless ages.
Amen.[44]

Of all the images Francis used of God, the notion of the goodness of God
stands out. God alone is good; God is goodness personified; the highest
good, all good. God's goodness has become enfleshed in Jesus, who went
about doing good. Indeed, Octavian Schmucki has written, the notion of
God as "good" became central to his piety and a characteristic element of
his image of God.[45] Consequently, Francis urged the brothers in his Earlier
Rule: "Let us refer all good to the Lord, God Almighty and Most High,
acknowledge that every good is His, and thank Him 'from Whom all good
comes, for everything.' "[46]

FIVE

How Francis Made
Conversion Compelling

*The Lord gave me, Brother Francis, thus to begin doing penance in this
way: for when I was in sin, it seemed too bitter for me to see lepers.
And the Lord Himself led me among them and I showed mercy to
them. And when I left them, what had seemed bitter to me was turned
into sweetness of soul and body. And afterward I delayed a little and
left the world.*

— Francis of Assisi, Opening Words of His *Testament*[1]

The Context That Brought Francis to a Crisis
on His Mythic Journey

As noted in the introduction, the triad of Francis' experience of the violence
in and around him, his need to withdraw from this, and his experience of
the scriptures being fulfilled in him began with a crisis prompted by words
heard in a dream in 1205 that found him turning from visions of knighthood
with Walter of Brienne.

This time of "withdrawal" was quite extended for Francis. Despite
Thomas of Celano calling it the year of his "conversion," the whole period was more like two or three years. Beginning with the call to leave the
trappings of violence wrapped in glory to return to Assisi, there followed
a series of critical events that would have a profound effect on Francis' future and his sense of being called by God to offer a countercultural way of
living in the world. These included: (1) the experience of hearing the crucifix at San Damiano invite him to "repair my house" which was "falling
into ruin"; (2) his effort to rebuild this church, along with San Pietro della
Spina (which no longer exists) and the chapel of St. Mary of the Angels (the
"Portiuncula"); (3) the selling of his father's fine cloth and his horse with
the proceeds given to the poor; (4) his father's rage at what Francis had
done and his action in hauling Francis before the court and then the bishop

to seek restitution; (5) Francis' rejection of his father's patrimony and his election to live under the providence of his "Father in heaven"; and, finally, (6) the experience of meeting the leper, which prompted a dramatic turn in his life that would find the scriptures being fulfilled in him in a seminal, yet powerful way. It was this experience, he wrote in his *Testament*, that launched an entirely new way to "do penance" and "flee the world."

A New Way to Do Penance and to Flee the World

Traditionally people who entered monasteries did so as part of a structured dynamic that was characterized by two main terms: *fuga mundi* (flight from the world) and *exire de saeculo* (to leave the world), meaning the same thing. Sometimes this would be forced upon people, for example, as a way of atoning for some sin. The decision might be made by parents for their children. The resulting dynamic did not reflect a "withdrawal" from the conflicts and tensions of family or society, but a desire to be "removed" from them.

Fuga mundi or *exire de saeculo* involved leaving one's home to remain in a particular place with the same people of the same sex to work out one's salvation, apart from the wider "world" beyond. It involved *stabilitas loci* or "remaining in place" or "stability of life." If practiced individually, it would be called the heremetical (or "hermit") life. If done with others, it meant entering a monastery and staying there for the rest of one's life.

The decision to freely go into the desert or other remote places for hermits or to embrace the pattern of monastic living was characterized by the term *poenitentium* or "the life of penance." Far from the stereotypes reinforced in books like *The Da Vinci Code*, to embrace the "life of penance" was not just a denial or rejection of certain societal patterns; it included a *renovatia vitae* — a decision to live in this "world" in a markedly different way, a countercultural way of life radically alternative to the prevailing (and debilitating) societal patterns. Far from "leaving the world," it meant "withdrawal" from its violent (and, therefore, sinful) ways to become engaged in life rather than exploiting it. This way of conversion was called evangelical, or Gospel-living. Surrendering to this way of life involved a "no" to the establishment.[2]

By the time Francis of Assisi was born, a new understanding of the terms *fuga mundi, exire de saeculo,* and *poenitentium* had already evolved. Earlier reformers like Joachim of Fiore, Peter Valdes, and the "Poor Men of Lyons" had proclaimed penance in a way that raised concerns among the clergy about maintaining their hegemony over the people. Then, in 1140, the Cathari began preaching "penance" in such a way that they were listed as heretical, along with other groups like the Humiliati. Six years before Francis' birth, Peter Waldo began preaching in Lyons. In their efforts to bring about reform in the Roman Church, most of these preachers turned against the church's authority, especially when they experienced a hostile reception from the clergy.

Despite sanctions and threats, their preaching appealed to a people frustrated with the trappings and bureaucracy of existing religion. Their preaching of penance paralleled the breakdown of the feudal society, which was land based and agrarian (and, thus, promoted the notion of stability of place), and the rise of the mercantile or more mobile economy based on the movement of goods, which brought about increased urbanization. In this milieu, new forms of community began to appear. Prospero Rivi notes that these, in turn, influenced traditional notions once linked to monastic forms of life:

> The middle classes, increasingly aware of their own strength and rapidly organizing themselves into associative forms, showed a growing impatience, first of all with the fiscal laws and then with the legal and political encumbrances of the feudal powers. They demanded new arenas for Christian life in the Middle Ages — and the communitarian and evangelic project which inspired apostolic life, the penitential state in a certain sense appeared as a translation of the ideal of *fuga mundi* into new terms, as an essential element of conversion decreed in the Gospel.[3]

Around this time (i.e., the time of Francis' early years) the notions of *fuga mundi, exire de saeculo,* and *poenitentium* had already been adapted to apply equally to one's internal attitudes of "withdrawal" from "the world" that paralleled what had traditionally demanded an external "removal" from its negative influences. Until now this meant that such a life could be lived only as a hermit or monk or nun. Rivi writes that, with this "progressive interiorization of the concept of *fuga mundi* and of conversion, it was no longer simply identified with an exterior denial of social life in itself, but began more often to mean the struggle against sin in its various aspects."[4] The various aspects of sin from which one would turn would be personal, familial, and societal. As for those calling themselves *poenitentes* or "Penitents," this new phenomenon would show that "penance" would no longer be defined so much as a "removal from" as much as an embrace of a countercultural way of life grounded in the effort to live within the world with its tensions, conflicts, and violence, but in a way that would find its adherents in "withdrawal" from their controlling and all-pervasive dynamics. Rivi concludes: "Penitence was no longer a penalty, but had become a life choice that allowed the more ardent laity to follow Christian perfection without being forced to leave their work, their families, or society."[5] With this background, we now can probe more fully Francis' "conversion."

The Story of Francis' Embrace of the Leper

After giving up his fealty to his father, in 1207, Francis had a powerful experience in an encounter with a person suffering from Hansen's disease, commonly known then (and as we will henceforth call it) as leprosy. This would radically change his life.[6] In doing violence to himself via this encounter, he would embark on a way that would try to offer an alternative to the violence in and around him.

Throughout history lepers were considered among the most repulsive of all human beings; indeed they were considered inhuman and treated as such by society. Some of the most extensive passages in the Book of Leviticus cover the way lepers are to be treated, including how to cleanse a "leprous house" (Lev. 13:1–14:57).

Leprosy is attributed to a bacillus called *microbacterium leprae*. It was identified by G. W. A. Hansen in 1874, and leprosy has thus been called Hansen's disease. But for previous centuries, including the time of Jesus and Francis, the term "leprosy" covered a whole host of skin lesions. Two years before Francis' birth, the Third Lateran Council decreed that lepers should be segregated; they were forbidden to go to church or to share churches and cemeteries with those perceived to be healthy. Accompanying this decree was a ritual of separation from the community, modeled on the rite for the dead. In some places the priest would declare to the leper:

> I forbid you ever to enter the church or monastery, fair, mill, marketplace or company of persons . . . ever to leave your house without your leper's costume . . . to wash your hands or anything about you in the stream or fountain. I forbid you to enter a tavern . . . I forbid you, if you go on the road and you meet some person who speaks to you, to fail to put yourself downwind before you answer . . . I forbid you to go in a narrow lane so that if you should meet anyone he might catch the affliction from you . . . I forbid you ever to touch children or give them anything. I forbid you to eat or drink from any dishes but your own. I forbid you to eat or drink in company, unless with lepers.[7]

Since leprosy was believed to have come upon a person because of sin, the church felt no guilt in exposing such sinners and excoriating them. Indeed leprosy had long been identified with enmity to the church.[8] Since this decree came from the priest, it is clear that, despite professing to be committed to follow the pattern of Jesus' life, whose healings begin in Matthew's Gospel with the healing of a leper (Matt. 8:1–4), the church of Francis' day spent much more time finding ways to hurt lepers than to heal them, to be rid of them rather than to help them. As bad as this may have been, civil society was even more vindictive. Throughout Francis' life there was a virtual "barrage of legislation" determined to segregate lepers from the rest of society.[9] Fortini insists that such legislation, including that coming from communes like Assisi, was even more harsh than the church in dealing with these human beings. The statutes of the commune declared:

> The *podestà* must, a month after taking office, make a scrupulous search for lepers in the city and in the region. And if any leper, man or woman, be living in the city or in the *contado,* he is to be hunted out from these places, and from the *castelli* and from the *ville.* And the syndics of the cities and castellans of the castles shall take care to bring charges against the lepers.[10]

It is quite probable that in his first sixteen years, Francis more than once experienced what his fellow citizens would do with a leper who risked entering the city; such a person "was left to the mercy of the crowd, which hunted him down like a mangy dog." It was official law in the commune that "no leper may dare to enter the city or walk around in it, and if any one of them shall be found, everyone may strike him with impunity."[11]

One can rightly surmise from such accounts that Francis would be repulsed by the sight, sound, and smell of leprous people as much, if not more than any of his townspeople. Thomas of Celano recalls that the sight of lepers was so "bitter to him" that "when he saw their houses even two miles away, he would cover his nose with his hands."[12] He articulated this repulsion quite simply in his own words, when he recalled, at the end of his life: "the sight of lepers nauseated me beyond measure."

In effect, the leper was the embodiment of the least, the most abject, and most rejected "have nots" or *minores* among all the *minores* in society. The cultural dynamics of exclusion included their alienation not only from their family and the ordinary commerce of life; they were told by the church that their condition was the result of their sins or those they inherited from those sinners in their blood line before them; this was their consequence. They were scum and would be culturally recognized as such and treated as such. For years Francis had been inundated with such thinking and had made this ideology his own.

The actual religious experience of the kiss of the leper began with Francis' sense that there had to be something more to life than what he experienced around him. This sense led to his "withdrawal," which constituted two years of searching. It was accompanied by a sense that made Francis realize that, if he was going to draw close to God, he would have to turn away from whatever he had "loved and desired to possess" that might keep him from God. Encouraged by these words, as he was riding near Assisi, he saw a leper and, as they say, the rest is history. While Francis began the narration of his *Testament* by summarizing his experience, an elaboration of the event is described in the *Legend of the Three Companions:*

> One day he was riding his horse near Assisi, when he met a leper. And, even though he usually shuddered at lepers, he made himself dismount, and gave him a coin, kissing his hand as he did so. After he accepted a kiss of peace from him, Francis remounted and continued on his way. He then began to consider himself less and less, until, by God's grace, he came to complete victory over himself.[13]

Francis' solidarity with this individual person — who was part of the most oppressed group in society — may have begun when *he* gave the leper a coin. This was something many good Christians would do. However, this time, it went further: he kissed the leper's leprous hand. That kiss of Francis, the subject, empowered the object of his kiss, the leper, to do something unthinkable. It was precisely when the leper did not give Francis a kiss on the hand in return to Francis' kiss, but when he "gave him the kiss of peace," that Francis was brought to a totally new understanding, a new knowledge, a new realization of what was now truly, not just the right way to relate to the leper and all people, but the right way to live in a new way of connectedness to the most marginated in the world. The "kiss of peace" given him by the leper now meant that his surrender would embrace all those who were rejected by society. It would ground his gospel of peace.

The process of Francis' "surrender" and "catch" and his movement from the violence of a persecuting society to doing violence to himself is wonderfully summarized in the description of the event in military terms by Julian of Speyer, who wrote his biography of Francis between 1232 and 1235:

> When he was still wearing secular clothes, the Lord had visited him with his grace, when a certain leper happened to meet him. As usual, he was horrified by the sight, but doing violence to himself, he conquered

himself, and straightaway went up and kissed him. From then on, he fervently glowed with contempt of self, and began to wage constant war against himself until it was granted him from above to win perfect victory . . . [14]

In his own surrender of his previous way of looking at the leper — as well as the worldview that had supported his thinking, feeling, and acting — he had now found, in the embrace expressed in the leper's kiss of peace, a new way of looking at the world. This enabled Francis to see in the most abject person, not someone to be labeled a "minor," but the essence of one called "the Christ." That Francis would see this leper as "the Christ" and, consequently, find in all the most-rejected people he met icons of the Christ, seems clear in a statement he would make later of those who would continue to reflect the societal forms of rejection of such people that heretofore he himself had embodied: "Anyone who curses the poor insults Christ whose noble banner the poor carry, since Christ *made himself poor for us in this world.*"[15]

The kiss of peace from the leper, who became for Francis "the Christ," energized Francis to live in an entirely new way as he would go about in the world. By surrendering his former way of being in the world, including the very way his culture viewed "belonging" (and "alienation"), Francis discovered in the leper's kiss of peace, a challenge to proclaim a new kiss of peace throughout the world in a way that would bring about the reign of God. This would be accompanied by a totally new way of living in the world (i.e., the life of "penance" or conversion or transformation) that this entailed.

Nobody has explained the process of his resulting conversion better than Francis himself. This we find summarized in his words that began this chapter. Broken down, the pattern included the following elements: (1) his previous way of treating lepers reflected societal patterns; he was repulsed by this group of people to the point of avoiding them at all costs and being nauseated at their sight. (2) However, during the "withdrawal" from the violence around him that had begun in Apulia, he now felt "led by God" to go among these rejected ones. (3) This led him to make "company with them." (4) This identification or way of making "acquaintance with them" brought about an amazing transformation in him: "what had previously nauseated me became a source of spiritual and physical consolation for me."

This experience of Francis was seminal in terms of his future worldview. On the surface level, it immediately led him to go to begin nursing lepers; he did this off and on for the next year and still desired to do so in his last days. But at a deeper level, this experience was felt bodily in a way that became life-altering for Francis. At yet another dimension, it has become archetypal for all seekers insofar as its pattern mirrors the notion of "surrender and catch" that describes the process of authentic conversion for everyone. Its dynamics have been richly described, in contemporary images, in the writings of Kurt Wolff.

Francis' Embrace of the Leper:
The Archetypal Dynamic of "Surrender and Catch"

In the *Testament* Francis notes that it was precisely the engaging of that which before he perceived as "most bitter" that ended up converting his total perception of reality itself in a way that brought him "spiritual and physical consolation." The result was his embrace of what was called then, "the life of penance." However, because the notion today has such negative connotations, it would be better to realize that, since penance or conversion means a "turning from" and "a turning to," we would understand this experience negatively as Francis embracing a countercultural stance in society (his "turning from") and positively as a parallel embrace of an alternative way of living in his culture (his "turning to").

Centuries before the dynamic involved in Francis' embrace of the leper would be probed by philosophers, psychologists, and even sociologists, Francis of Assisi himself described the process. He outlined the kind of conversion that finds one no longer accepting the "givens" of one's world and, instead, finds one grounded in an absolute certainty that there is now another way. Embracing that way allows one to become a model for others. His process of personal change, conversion, or transformation became popularized in the dynamics of "surrender and catch" outlined by Kurt H. Wolff of Brandeis University as the heart of his sociology of knowledge.

"Surrender-and-catch is a protest against" whatever in our world and lives is violent, Wolff writes, as well as "an attempt at remembrance of what a human being can be." He sees this occurring in the ways we come to move from one set of beliefs to another. I find it applicable in moving from (i.e., "conversion from") the "isms" and their ideologies to the heart of those stories that speak to us in our culture and church.

While the sociology of knowledge analyzes people's observable practices, the notion of "surrender" reveals what may be intrinsic to what is external or observable. Indeed the sociology of knowledge needs this intrinsic element in order to "overcome the relativism it encounters in its practice by its remembrance, rediscovery, reinvention, the catch, of what is common to all human beings, what is universally human."[16] In fine, as the embrace between Francis and the leper shows, surrender is the way the subject and the object become one, enabling a radical change in one's life and stance in the world. The "radicalness" of surrender, Wolff explains, "is the state and the relation of cognitive love."[17] What he calls "catch" is the new reality that comes from true surrender: "it is a new conceiving, a new concept, a new being-in-the-world."[18]

The dynamics of "surrender" that bring about the "catch" outlined by Wolff uncannily match the phenomenon of Francis' religious conversion in a way that radically altered his worldview. The process began at Spoleto when Francis began a kind of "disarmament" or surrender and reached its apogee in the leper experience. Thus it is interesting that in describing the notion of surrender, Wolff himself is not unaware of its militaristic overtones. He writes:

> The term "surrender" itself, with its ironical military connotation, polemicizes against the official Western and potentially worldwide consciousness of the relation to the world, both nature and man's world and even man himself, which is not surrender but mastery, control, efficiency, handling, manipulating. Similarly, a synonym of "surrender," "total experience," which indicates the undifferentiated quality of the experience, polemicizes against totalitarianism, which is so closely and fatally related to that consciousness which "surrender" fights.[19]

What happened in Francis' leaving Spoleto was a deeper "leaving" that would reach its transformational peak in his experience with the leper. I find in Francis' narration of the event a retelling of how his actual surrender/catch experience occurred. However, using the words of Judith Feher, a colleague of Wolff, the experience was "outside the realm of words." Despite this indescribable dimension of the event, the words Francis chose to describe the experience of his conversion in his *Testament* provide us with an example in his own language that thus becomes "the only tool we possess to describe the experience of surrender."[20] Building on this "Franciscan" approach to surrender and catch we find how, in Francis' case, "the humanly unique and the humanly universal become *one* in surrender."[21] As Wolff writes, "though known by names that stress various aspects or components" of surrender and catch such as "conversion," "transformation," "metamorphosis," "enchantment," "inspiration," "mystical union," and "ecstasy," all represent the combination of both the emptying and fulfilling dimensions of a life lived authentically. This we call "spirituality."

According to Wolff, the experience of surrender itself is beyond human effort. It involves the "risk of being hurt," "suspension of received notions," "total involvement," "identification" in a way that results in the "pertinence of everything." From Wolff's explanation of these elements of surrender, it is clear Francis of Assisi can be considered its very embodiment. In his solitary experience of the embrace with the leper, as Francis describes it in his *Testament,* we have an outline of how we might go through a similar process in a way that will empower us to embrace a countercultural life of conversion in our own world. This process is what Wolff calls "surrendering to." While "surrender and catch" happen spontaneously, "surrendering to" is a process that can be embraced and developed. He notes:

> There is an important difference between "surrender" and "surrender-to." Surrender is something unpredictable, unachievable by an effort of the will (in that sense it resembles grace, which happens or does not [usually does not]). Surrender-to, instead, is something that can be willed, that one can want to bring about. Its characteristics are those of surrender, except that they are consciously aimed at.[22]

I find the difference between the spontaneous experience of "surrender and catch" and the cultivated process of "surrendering to" much like the distinction between contemplation and developing a contemplative approach or life. Indeed the two have many parallels. Primarily, the former comes unannounced; the latter is something that comes through concentration and practice. When we "surrender to" the characteristics of surrender are intentionally cultivated.

An examination of the five steps as they became realized in Francis' own "story" of his conversion has much to offer us in our own life stories as we try to "surrender to" the power of God's effort to bring us to transformation in the depth of our bodies and spirits. Indeed, as he considered his leper experience, such an approach to "surrender and catch" becomes a deeper way of experiencing salvation.[23] The process involves:

1. *"Risk of being hurt."* Being a child of his culture, with its civic and ecclesiastical expectations describing the treatment of lepers, Francis knew, in his very act of turning toward them, that he could be rejected by all those societal supports that once provided him meaning in his life. It also involved a realization that the search for his true identity might demand that he "leave" or "withdraw from" the "stories" that he had inherited from his parents and everyone else, especially as they were narrated in the ideologies of his culture and his church, including what they said about the way lepers should be treated. Such a risk was not so much connected with the act of

surrender itself, but the "catch" that came with his acting on that surrender by his embrace of the leper.

Being willing to risk being hurt is cultivated by prayer. Indeed, if prayer is authentic, it involves a conversion from one's self into the embrace of God. Wolff notes that "the most notable risk of prayer" being authentic is expressed in one's subsequent conversion itself.[24]

2. *"Suspension of received notions."* It follows, then, that surrender involves a willingness to experience some kind of desocialization and ideological critique. This involves what phenomenologists call "bracketing," or the willingness to suspend our prejudices and our day-to-day assumptions, once we become aware of them. It does not mean we reject everything we have learned; we actually affirm those things that can be affirmed because they have withstood the test associated with surrender.[25]

The need to suspend our received notions arises at that point when we realize that the pain of continuing in the same way, with its confusion and tension, demands another stance in the world. Wolff writes:

> Among the meanings of extreme situations is deep confusion, the unshakeable grip by something new, the feeling that everything is a riddle, that there is no sense to the world . . . But once one gets into a confusion in which the whole world is enigmatic or mysterious, the acceptance of things that previously were a matter of course is gone; the order of the world taken for granted before has vanished.[26]

In prayer, Wolff writes, we suspend our received notions via "recollection, the exclusion of everything else but the attempt to pray."[27] In so doing, we indicate our willingness to let go of whatever we bring to prayer that does not square with our experience of God.

3. *"Total experience or involvement."* In the surrender of the subject in the object, the object becomes the subject of one's affections. A "we" is created rather than an "I" alienated from a "thou." In this experience, "as in love itself," Wolff notes, "I am undifferentiatedly and indistinguishably involved in its occasion and in myself, my act or state, my object or partner." A kind of incarnation of the one in the other occurs. Referring to such a love, he exemplifies it in the embrace of Levin and Kitty in Tolstoy's *Anna Karenina*: "Then for the first he clearly understood . . . that he was not simply close to her, but that he could not tell where he ended and she began."[28]

Again, the goal of all mystical or contemplative prayer is just this kind of "total involvement." This kind of prayer nurtures the possibility of a mystical experience that invites personal, communal, and societal transformation via a prophetic life.

4. *"Identification."* In the experience of being embraced by the other, the leper, Francis was able to dissolve his ego in a way that found it reconstructed.[29] He died to this ego and found himself. In the process he became empowered in his body/person to move from his former ego-ism to a newly found autonomy that was not isolating but effective of solidarity with the most "leprous" or marginated in society. In himself he now discovered all creation, whether animate or inanimate. Wolff writes: "The lover, too, must lose himself to find himself, not to lose himself; otherwise he would be self-destructive."[30]

5. *"Pertinence of everything."* In his suspension of his uncritiqued worldview, with its story revealed in the ideology represented in its "isms," a new world order emerges. " 'Everything' is everything within the surrenderer's awareness — as for the lover it is everything about the beloved and the love," Wolff explains. "In the extreme concentration on the moment of surrender, 'everything' is important, but 'everything else' vanishes. In one process of contraction and expansion, the world becomes experienced in its infinity."[31]

It is clear from his experience of surrender/catch that Francis came to a new way of knowing that would now be defined by nondiscriminating love extending to the most rejected of humanity. In disarming himself in all the forms of "surrender" noted above, he fell "in love" in a way that captured the imagination of his world and continues to do so today. In the surrender of himself to another, he found himself welcoming all others in his very body. As a result of the way he moved from his head to his heart in the process of surrender/catch, Francis became the embodiment of the scriptural mandate found in the Great Command: love God with your whole heart and your neighbor as your *self*.

Francis' Embrace of the Leper: A Model of Focusing

In his *Varieties of Religious Experience,* William James told about his discovery that religion was actually more a matter of the "heart" than the "head." From his interviews with people, James discovered that religion is not primarily about ideas, concepts, or theological doctrines, despite what the proponents of various "religions" insist. In people's lives religion (or spirituality, as we would more likely call it today) represents the way that people have a *felt experience* with the divine; in fact he wrote: "I do believe that feeling is the deeper source of religion, and that philosophic and theological formulas are secondary products, like translations of a text into another text."[32] By the same token, he found that in most cases conversion is not prompted by intellectual arguments, but by an appeal to the heart or feeling.

For his part, Carl Jung came to realize that the process of human individuation and wholeness involves "waking up the divine within." Consequently for him, authentic religion could be found in those dynamics that brought about a sense of the divine/human connection — the biblical *shalom* or wholeness in an individual's life.

No doubt aware of these findings from James and Jung, Eugene Gendlin, a psychologist who taught at the University of Chicago until his retirement some years ago, also became intrigued by the question: "What makes people change?" More specifically, he wondered why some people he counseled made changes in their lives, even dramatic changes, while others never did. This led him to examine the transformation process, to probe what it was in those who changed that facilitated the process of "conversion."

The main finding of Gendlin came when he realized that those who made observable changes in their lives (among those who came to him for psychotherapy) were those who had spoken from their "hearts" or "feelings" rather than their "heads" or their "thinking." When people brought an affective approach to the change process rather than an intellectual effort, they were more often successful in getting "unstuck" and more able to bring about growth in their lives. Given this realization, Gendlin began to wonder whether an approach to therapy that would address the power of feeling in his clients' lives might help in bringing about desired changes. This led to the development of what he called "focusing," the process discussed earlier as developed by McMahon and Campbell.

With Gendlin's "focusing," as with Wolff's "surrender/catch," I find tools that help to explicate the solitary experience of Francis' conversion as recorded in his *Testament*. "First," Gendlin notes of the person who successfully experiences the process of focusing, "there is a kind of bodily awareness that profoundly influences our lives and that can help us reach personal goals. So little attention has been paid to this mode of awareness that I had no ready-made words to describe it, and I have had to coin my own term: 'felt sense.' " In Francis' own words, his bodily sense of thinking about lepers brought about a feeling of nausea "beyond measure." This feeling took root in him. However, at a certain point in his life he "stayed with his feeling" in a way that would no longer control him; he felt himself being led by a need to allow his feeling of repulsion for lepers to take him "into their company." In other words he surrendered his previously held feelings and embraced or welcomed the reality of that which had formerly repulsed him. In so doing, he became embraced by the reality itself.

What happened in him is described by Gendlin as the second dynamic that brings about change: "a felt sense will shift if you approach it in the right way. It will change even as you are making contact with it. When your felt sense of a situation changes, *you change* — and, therefore, so does your life."[33] Francis' former felt sense of repulsion changed not only to spiritual consolation but to consolation or peace in his body as well. In coming to be at peace bodily, Francis not only found his life itself changed; this change colored the way he would now live in the world.

Francis perfectly summarized the dynamic of change that took place within him: "When I had once become acquainted with them, what had previously nauseated me became a source of spiritual and physical consolation for me" ever after. So powerful was this experience of "surrender and catch" that he was actually changed in his body, a phenomenon described well by Wolff himself.[34]

Impelled by this religious experience, he embarked on a life of penance: "I did not wait long before leaving the world." No longer would this "leaving the world" be characterized along the model of hermits, monks, and nuns; in the embrace of the leper he found a way of conversion and transformation that had him surrender his previous worldview and the feelings that accompanied it to "catch" or "shift" to an entirely new way of looking at everything — from God to what before might have been considered the lowliest of creatures.

The Characteristics of Evangelical Conversion Embodied in Francis

In the opening line of his *Testament*, Francis characterizes the dynamics of his embrace of the leper as the beginning of his "Life of Penance." Later he would call this life "evangelical." The life of penance or change as articulated by phenomenologists like Wolff and psychologists like Gendlin has its echoes in spirituality. True religion for a Christian demands an embrace of the Gospel. In turn, authentic Gospel-living demands a new way of being in the world. This new countercultural way of being involves what has been traditionally called the "life of penance" or "conversion."

I have been fascinated by the notion of "conversion" for years. What began as my concern about social change eventually found me realizing the need to address my resistance to change in my own life. However, rather than being preoccupied with my own need for personal conversion, I was satisfied quoting from two documents that came from the 1971 Synod of Bishops in Rome. Ideally the church should be without spot or wrinkle and be able to call for conversion at all levels of the world. From this perspective the 1971 Synodal Document on "The Ministerial Priesthood" stated: "Impelled by the need to keep in view both the personal and social aspects of the announcement of the Gospel, so that in it an answer may be given to men's most fundamental questions, the Church not only preaches conversion to God to individuals, but also, almost as society's conscience, she speaks as best she can to society itself and performs a prophetic function in this regard, always taking pains to effect her own renewal."[35] But what about the conversion demanded of the church itself? The same Synod of Bishops addressed this question in its other document on "Justice in the World": "Anyone who purports to speak to others about justice must be seen by those others as just in their eyes. Hence we must undertake an examination of the church's own lifestyle, its possessions, and its mode of acting."[36]

That the institutional church needs conversion of its own house becomes clear to me from the irate letters I receive from both Catholics and non-Catholics in response to the shareholder resolutions we submit to various corporations in which they also hold stock. Oftentimes the "sins" of the church are highlighted and I am told to address these rather than harass the companies who "do more good for people than your preaching has ever done."

When I give workshops I often ask people: "How many of you think conversion is easy?" Rarely, if ever, does anyone raise a hand; instead I get groans and moans as though it is virtually impossible. With that I put my background in economics into action.

I ask if anyone has recently gone shopping and bought some item of clothing. When I get a volunteer we do some role-playing. I ask: "Was there something you were looking for?" Usually I get an affirmative answer, say a shirt. "So, in other words," I say, "you were seeking that shirt for some time?" Another affirmative reply. "So, when you found it, you must have been excited that it was just what you were looking for." A nod comes. "Was it good enough and at the right price that you were willing to part with your hard-earned money?" Oftentimes, the person will say something like, "I waited for a sale," generating laughs. "So, when the sale came," I say, "you bought the shirt." "Yes," the person says, usually with a smile. "It seems this has brought you happiness." "It sure has," will be the response.

At that I say: "You just went through conversion. And it brought you joy." Then I explain: "Our whole market economy, capitalism itself, is based on people like you and the rest of us going through conversions. Without conversion on our part the market will die. The reign of the market implodes without customers oriented to the process of seeking, finding, selling, and buying.

This leads to a discussion of what I consider the heart of the conversion to the reign of God that Jesus proclaimed in his parables. The process of seeking, finding, selling, and buying is found in two parables placed back-to-back in Matthew's Gospel. "The kingdom of heaven is like a treasure hidden in a field, which someone found and hid; then in his joy he goes and sells all that he has and buys that field. Again, the kingdom of heaven is like a merchant in search of fine pearls; on finding one pearl of great value, he went and sold all that he had and bought it" (Matt. 13:44–46).

The process of "surrender and catch" begins, Wolff writes, with seeking; such a search results in a "total experience" that transforms one's life.[37] Examining the dynamics of conversion more closely we see that many seek and do not find because they are looking in the wrong places or with the wrong set of eyes and a heart blinded by fears and anxieties, resentments and unforgiveness, or whatever. Some of these "find" or stumble upon a "find" without having done any seeking. However, there is no "selling" because what has been found does not measure up to what would have to be given up or because of fears related to the change that might be needed. This has brought me to the realization that the difference between Francis' conversion and our resistance to conversion is not in the unwillingness to "sell" but in the fact that we probably have not yet "found" a pearl of great price that is greater than our fears or other obstacles that keep us from the joy of conversion, such as the process of "falling in love."

Already in his initial conversion that took place after Spoleto, Celano writes, Francis "was filled with such great joy," he spoke to a "special friend about a *hidden treasure*" that he had discovered. "Even though he could not remain silent because of the greatness of the love inspired in him, he nevertheless spoke [to others] cautiously and in riddles...He said he did not want to go to Apulia, but promised to do great and noble deeds at home."[38]

The issue about evangelical conversion is the connection between finding, selling and buying. One buys what has been found, but one never sells anything unless what has been found is worthy of being bought. The issue, then is not in the "buying" as much as in the finding. And all finding begins with "seeking" or the desire for something or someone other than that possessed at this time.

For Francis, the "find" of his life, the pearl of great price, was not just what he called "the Gospel," but the Christ of the Gospel whom he had encountered. In the embrace of Christ, he was able to sell to the point where he could declare: "My God and my all!"[39]

The Contagious Character
of a Joy-Defined Conversion Experience

In the second chapter of the Gospel of Matthew, the first persons to encounter Jesus are the magi "from the East." They came *seeking* the newborn "king of the Jews." Upon *finding* "the place where the child was," Matthew writes: "they were overwhelmed with joy." Finding the child "with Mary his mother," they who experienced a religious conversion found no problem in going through an economic conversion. They *sold* or offered their "gifts of gold, frankincense, and myrrh." Having had the scriptures fulfilled in them, due to the impending violence resultant upon Herod's feeling duped, they "*anachorein*-ed" for their own country by another road. These were the first recipients of the Gospel, according to Matthew; the experience of Jesus brought about a conversion in their lives.

As Ilia Delio notes, Francis believed that when we embrace a truly evangelical way of life defined by penance it brings about a profound change in our relationship with God and others. She writes:

> Making room for the Lord's Spirit to dwell within us brings us into a consciousness of God as the source of overflowing goodness and our vocation as children of God. Sin brings about a twisted, distorted way of looking at reality that causes us to be easily deceived and prone to act according to what seems to be immediately good or beneficial. However, penance that leads to the indwelling of the Spirit leads to fundamental human relationships that embrace a well-rounded spiritual life...Penance, therefore, calls us to radicality, to new relationships that mirror Christ.[40]

Returning to the actual words of Francis wherein he describes his embrace of the leper as an experience that brought him deep delight, we find in this narration the unique reason that Francis would be willing to embrace the notion of conversion as his life's process. This involved the "payoff" called joy. While the power of this joy in his life, its witness and compelling power will be the subject of a later chapter, suffice it to say here that it was this joy-filled way of being countercultural that captured the imagination of the people in a way that led to their embrace of it as well.

Explaining why so many people were attracted to Francis' way, Prospero Rivi writes that the life of penitence proclaimed by the *viri poenitentiales* offered the people "the unique opportunity to find real peace, to build a fraternal world and allow them to reach the salvation that God offered." His way of preaching "penance," or "conversion," or "transformation" meant embracing a countercultural stance toward the world of that day. However, he notes that the actual attractiveness of the message of the Gospel was that it was promoted as "good" news, as something that was positive and joy-producing for whoever would embrace it. He notes that "penitence was for [Francis] intimately connected with the theme of gladness and joy" and this could explain "one of the reasons for the great response." In their way of "surrender" they would "catch" or embrace something so much better.

While the way that penance or countercultural living was proclaimed positively, with such joy, will be discussed in the final chapter, Rivi's words will give us a good summary of what we have written in this chapter about the contagiousness of this countercultural way of conversion:

> Recovering, with great spiritual finesse, the genuine evangelical sense of the penitential experience as a humble and joyful recognition of one's own condition of creaturehood before the Most High God who is revealed as Father in Christ Jesus, Francis and his friars were able to liberate it from that round of exteriority, sadness and negativity which penitence could assume in the midst of the people, even though one should bear in mind that for those living in medieval times the term "penitence" would certainly arouse more positive echoes than in our cultural context. They would be able to become fresh witnesses to penitence through joy, and would manage to be effective announcers of penitence as a road to true happiness. In effectively proclaiming penitence through joy, they could return to the Gospel its original and authentic character as a message of gladness. Here is the secret of the powerful grip that the life of penitence held on the Christians of the time, thanks to them. For Francis, true penitence and spiritual joy in reality constituted an inseparable duo.[41]

The way Francis could bring the two polarities together into "an inseparable duo" is best described in a saying that has been attributed to him.

> So great the good I have in sight
> that all my pain becomes delight.

SIX

Becoming the Christ

I am again in the pain of childbirth until Christ is formed [mor-
phooūsai] *in you.* — St. Paul's Letter to the Galatians (4:19)

The Centrality of Jesus Christ
and His Self-Emptying in Francis' Life

This chapter builds on notions contained in the previous chapter about "surrender and catch." When Francis considered Jesus Christ, he discovered a
God willing to surrender everything in love, and actually doing so in a way
that created in us the "catch" of being empowered with this divine love.
This was humility. This was the Christ revealed to him in the scriptures. It
became the core of what Francis considered "religion."[1] It became for him
the way of salvation.[2] Since Jesus Christ is the Word through whom everything in creation, including human beings, has been called to image, when
we go through the process of surrender and catch, we find ourselves "thrown
back" on what we really are and what we share with everyone else.[3]

This Jesus Christ was not just God-become-Human or divinity in humanity; he became for Francis the source, summit, and sacrament of God's
self-revelation. Since Jesus is the enfleshed word, and God's Word does what
it is (*dabar*), God's self-revelation and plan for the world are found in the
living and teaching of Jesus. For this reason Francis did not just "hear the
Gospel," as so many of us do; he heard "Christ in the Gospel" speak to him
and his disciples.[4]

Christ was not just divinity enfleshed; he was the Creator-become-
Creation. In fine, according to Giovanni Iammarrone, "Jesus Christ, the
God-man, is the summit of all creation. God has willed all other creatures
for the glory of Christ and ultimately, in and through Christ, for the glory
of the most Blessed Trinity. He, the first and absolute, is also the beginning
and the end, the center and culmination, the motive for the existence of all
creation. He is its glory and its hope."[5]

104

As the divinely human one, Jesus proclaimed in his outpost of the Roman Empire a way of life called "the Gospel." This set him apart from the prevailing imperial Gospel of the day as well as the limited and self-serving teachings of contemporary religious leaders.

"To live the Gospel," for Francis, meant to put into practice what Jesus taught so that the pattern of Jesus' life might be replicated in our own. When Jesus was approached by a Pharisee, who, trying to test him on his knowledge of the law and the prophets, asked:

> "Teacher, which commandment in the law is the greatest?" He said to him, " 'You shall love the Lord your God with all your heart, and with all your soul, and with all your mind.' This is the greatest and first commandment. And a second is like it: 'you shall love your neighbor as yourself.' On these two commandments hang all the law and the prophets." (Matt. 22:36–40; see Mark 12:28–34)

Since Jesus came to fulfill the law and the prophets (Matt. 3:15) and declared to his followers that their right way of living or righteousness had to exceed that of the scribes and Pharisees (Matt. 5:20), it follows that the same two key identifiers of Jesus should be reflected in the life and spirituality of each of his followers: to love God wholeheartedly and to concretize that love in ever widening circles of loving mercy, justice, and compassion.

In the Gospel, Francis found God's humility expressed in Jesus' self-giving love. He saw himself joined to Christ in such an intimate way (*coniungitur*) that his own life would replicate that humility in his own self-giving love. This could be realized because of the Spirit of Christ that had been shared with him.[6] As a result, like any lover, he could not stop thinking about or talking about the one he loved; he could not get his Beloved out of his mind. Celano tells us:

> The brothers who lived with him know that daily, constantly, talk of Jesus was always on his lips, *sweet and pleasant* conversations about Him, kind words full of love. *Out of the fullness of the heart his mouth spoke.* So the spring of radiant love that filled his heart within gushed forth. He was always with Jesus; Jesus in his heart, Jesus in his mouth, Jesus in his ears, Jesus in his eyes, Jesus in his hands, he bore Jesus always in his whole body. Often he sat down to dinner but on hearing or saying or even thinking "Jesus" he forgot bodily food, as we read about another saint: "Seeing, he did not see; hearing, he did not hear." Often as he walked along a road, thinking and singing of Jesus he would forget his destination and start inviting all the elements to praise Jesus.

With amazing love he bore *in his heart and always held onto Christ Jesus and Him crucified.* For this reason, he, above others, was stamped with Christ's brilliant seal as, in *rapture of spirit,* he contemplated in unspeakable and incomprehensible glory the One sitting "at the right hand of the Father," the Most High *Son of the Most High,* Who, with the Father, "in the unity of the Holy Spirit lives and reigns, conquers and commands, *God,* eternally glorified *throughout all the ages. Amen.*[7]

There have been two main ways of interpreting the reason why God would have chosen to be enfleshed in Jesus among us. One view considers Jesus to be the Word of God or divinity-enfleshed in order to redeem humanity and creation itself. The other considers the notion of divinity-enfleshed-in-humanity (and all creation by the enfleshment itself) as the means of God's self-revelation. As Giovanni Iammarrone writes, from this perspective: "God created the human race and the entire universe so that they might share in the fullness of his life and glory. Consequently, the primacy of Christ is the perfection of creation. He is the goal of all history and of the entire cosmos independently of his role as redeemer."[8]

Francis' knowing Jesus became his loving Jesus. To use the language of Kurt Wolff, his way of knowing became "cognitive love." This cognitive love becomes clear from even a cursory reading of the life and thought of St. Francis; he could not think of God's revelation in Jesus Christ in any way apart from God's love for us.

One cannot stress enough the experience Francis felt of God's freely offered love that was revealed in the humility of the Incarnation, crucifixion, and Eucharist. That the God of the universe would love in such a way that the very people who least deserved God's embrace would be "caught" into such a "surrender" totally confounded Francis.

As he examined the many signs of God's own "surrender and catch" revealed in Jesus Christ, Francis found it best exemplified in the words and deeds of Jesus found in the Gospels. However, among all the words and deeds he found in the Gospels, God's overwhelming generosity and grace fixated his imagination around three seminal events: the Incarnation, the crucifixion, and the Eucharist. Thomas of Celano writes that the "humility of the Incarnation" and "the charity of the passion" preoccupied him "to the extent that he wanted to think of hardly anything else."[9] Above all the Incarnation, the crucifixion, and their fulfillment in the Eucharist were human expressions of God's self-giving goodness. The "crib, the cross, and the altar" manifested the way Jesus Christ surrendered everything of equality with God as something to be exploited in a way that found him "catching" or embracing humanity in its weakest form, that of a slave. This very act highly exalted him in such a way that all would find a new way of life by imitating this same "surrender and catch" in their lives. What Wolff discovered about the very process of surrender and catch can be equally attributed to God's incarnate love for us: "I came to understand that moving from surrender to catch is moving from one world to another — here from the world of suspension itself to the world of everyday."[10]

God's own emptying or surrender has been outlined powerfully in the oft-quoted "kenotic" expression found in Paul's Letter to the Philippians. This passage is considered by all Christian writers to be the hallmark of the attitude needed for a life of authentic conversion or "surrender and catch": "Let the same mind be in you that was in Christ Jesus," Paul wrote:

> Who, though he was in the form of God,
> did not regard equality with God as something to be exploited,
> but emptied himself, taking the form of a slave, being born in
> human likeness.
> And being found in human form,
> he humbled himself and became obedient to the point of
> death —
> Even death on a cross.
> Therefore God also highly exalted him and gave him the name
> that is above every name,
> so that at the name of Jesus every knee should bend
> in heaven and on earth and under the earth,
> and every tongue should confess that
> Jesus Christ is Lord, to the glory of God the Father.
>
> (Phil. 2:5–11)

Many great schools of spirituality, whether Christian or not, involve such a notion of self-emptying at their core or heart. Buddhists seek the elimination of desire while Jesuits seek detachment. Those following the great mystics like John of the Cross and Teresa of Avila try to free themselves in prayer and asceticism so they will experience the *nada,* in which nothing will disturb them. Those whose lives have been changed because of Twelve-Step spirituality have found that "letting go" and "letting God" grounds their recovery (i.e., "conversion"). People committed to an eco-spirituality recognize the need to continually relinquish themselves and simplify their lives, their thinking, and their attachments in order to ensure the integrity of creation. Native American spirituality, grounded as it is in the earth, invites its adherents to continually work at their purification and to make no claims over anything. Still other spiritualities stress renunciation and abandonment.

For Francis, the *kenotic* imperative found him insisting on humility or nonappropriation (the surrender) combined with the self-giving embrace of Lady Poverty (the catch). This "surrender/catch" pattern is evident in his first Admonition, which he wrote for his followers. Octavian Schmucki writes: "The Pauline theology of the emptying of Christ according to Philippians 2:5–11, and the concept which is fundamental in John concerning Christ as the revelation of the Father, is merged with the promise of remaining with His own to the end of human history (see Matt. 28:20), by means of the mystical presence of the risen Christ."[11]

The Incarnation Revealing God's Self-Surrender in Jesus Christ

In the Incarnation Francis found the revelation par excellence of God's love for us. In the very act of becoming human, the God who became incarnate or enfleshed in Jesus showed humans, including the greatest of sinners, a way of life that would lead them to God. In the process of this divine revelation of God's way, truth, and life, everyone would be continually invited to enter the kenotic process themselves in a way that would bring them the freedom of the children of God.

Surrender for Wolff represents cognitive love or that love that comes to be known in our intellects as representing the core of all knowing.[12] Furthermore, if cognitive love represents the human way of true knowledge, its divine manifestation for humans, at least, can only be represented in that Cognitive Love revealed as the Word Enfleshed because of God's love for the world. In my understanding, as a Franciscan, this self-giving love is what is truly meant when the author of the Fourth Gospel declares: "For God so loved the world that he gave his only Son, so that everyone who believes in him may not perish but may have eternal life" (John 3:16).

Building on John's Gospel, Francis understood the Incarnation of Jesus as the Father's Word enfleshed through the power of the Spirit. Ilia Delio describes his thought well:

> It is because the persons in the Trinity are united in love that Francis understands the Incarnation within the context of the Trinity. For Francis, God's immanence is revealed to us in the person of Jesus Christ. In his second version of his Letter to the Faithful, Francis describes the kenosis of the Word, indicating that God comes to us in poverty and

humility. He writes: "The most high Father made known from heaven through His holy angel Gabriel this Word of the Father — so worthy, so holy and glorious — in the womb of the holy and glorious Virgin Mary, from whose womb He received the flesh of our humanity and frailty. Though He was rich, He wished, together with the most Blessed Virgin, His mother, to choose poverty in the world beyond all else."[13]

For Francis, God's love was first manifest in the Incarnation in a way that made all created matter holy; however, this love enfleshed in Mary's womb was made visible to the world in the public revelation of God's love that he found in the crèche. Francis' original idea of using real figures for the representation of Jesus' birth found in the Gospels was more than a way of meeting a childish whim. He himself said he wished "to enact the memory of that babe *who was born in Bethlehem:* to see as much as is possible with my own bodily eyes the discomfort of his infant needs, how he *lay in a* manger, and how, with an ox and an ass standing by, he rested on hay."[14] When the night came for the town of Greccio to experience the world's first "living crib," Francis stood "before the manger, filled with heartfelt sighs, contrite in his piety, and overcome with wondrous joy."[15]

The Incarnation represented for Francis what Wolff describes as the "total involvement" dimension of surrender. Through the Word Enfleshed everything in the world became charged with God's loving presence and power. Wolff writes: "In surrender as in love, differentiation between subject, act, and object disappears — an example of the suspension of even essential categories among our received notions."[16]

One of the most powerful "received notions" that gradually became suspended as his followers strove to be faithful to Francis was in the way Franciscan theologians came to a new understanding of the redemptive dimensions of the Incarnation itself. Possibly because of their understanding that God's love is greater than anything any human can do to obliterate it, thinkers like John Duns Scotus (1265–1308) at the University of Paris outlined a fresh way to understand why God became involved in human history in the person of Jesus Christ and his humble self-giving love. For Scotus God's love, not humanity's sin, was the "necessity" that demanded that God's redeeming presence appear in human form. They became convinced that, even if "Adam and Eve" never fell, God's all-inclusive love for everyone, including humans, would have driven God to "surrender" in a way that would find God revealed, incarnated among them in a way that would have been redemptive.

Few have made an intellectual link between the actual theology of Scotus with the words and witness of Francis himself, but the connection is clear. As Giovanni Iammarrone writes:

> Scholarly research has established the fact that the theology of Scotus must be looked upon for the most part as a theological reflection on the experience of St. Francis of Assisi as well as a reflection of the theological insights of the great Franciscan master who preceded Scotus himself. His reflection on Jesus Christ, especially on his centrality in the history of salvation, and on the reality of his human nature, is without doubt the area of his theology where we can trace the "scarlet thread" that stretches from Francis to Scotus, and through him connects with all succeeding Franciscan theological movements.[17]

The enfleshment of God's energy in Jesus Christ now makes everything holy: this encompasses Wolff's notion of the "pertinence of everything." In virtue of the Incarnation, God's Word enfleshed, all flesh, all matter, becomes godly. The Incarnation reveals God's energy at the heart of all reality.

In the notion of *identification,* the aim of surrender is realized. The enfleshment of God in the human form of the one called Jesus became, in itself, salvific, a sacrament of God's love itself. This act of freely offered love on behalf of those most in need shows the *total involvement* this represents; the absolute nature of that love that enables God not to lose God's self in the process, but to be found or most realized in it. Wolff writes of the one engaged in "cognitive love" words that can be equally applied to the cognitive love of the Word for the Word-er: "The lover, too, must lose himself to find himself, not to lose himself; otherwise he would be self-destructive."[18]

This process involves the "risk of being hurt" and, indeed, the very violence that surrounded the announcement of the presence of "the newborn king of the Jews."

The Incarnation Revealing "the Catch"

For centuries, including our own time today, a certain notion of redemption has dominated Christian thinking regarding "God's plan" for a fallen world. It begins with an unquestioning acceptance of the myth of an actual Fall by actual people, Adam and Eve. Their human act of disobedience to God (considered an "infinite offense") was so great that this demanded infinite reparation. Since only an Infinite being can do anything infinite, this necessitated divine intervention to save the fallen ones. In turn, this demanded an infinite sacrifice, namely, a bloody death. Only in this way could a fallen race be redeemed. In effect, Jesus had to come because of the sin of humans, if they were to be saved from their sin. He also had to suffer violence.

Besides the fact that most scholars have long rejected the historicity of any "Adam" or "Eve," the human logic that demands of God anything is preposterous. God is not required to do anything for anyone, much less humans. If God is required to do anything, being love itself, God is required only to love and to reveal that love in ever expanding revelations. This grounding of all salvation in love rather than in anything that involves violence as part of any divine necessity is best summarized in the school that arose from the original insights of St. Francis: the theory of the Absolute Primacy of Christ as proffered by Scotus.

Scotus taught, with St. Bonaventure (who succeeded Francis as the seventh Minister of the Order, thirty-one years after his death), that, from the beginning, everyone and everything in creation has been intended for Christ because Christ is the beloved Word of the Father through whom all creation has been made in the first place. However, Scotus went further than Bonaventure in insisting, from the notion of love itself, that, whether or not sin ever existed, Christ would have become enfleshed in creation. Both he and Bonaventure taught that Christ is first in God's intention to love because, in the Beloved One, all Love of the Lover is contained. Therefore, if the whole creation has been made in, for, and through this Word, it ultimately is made for Christ. Everything is patterned on the Word of God and, we might say, is a "little word" of God. Creation, as Ilia Delio writes, is therefore "not mere physical matter; rather, it expresses God's infinite love. God 'speaks' the depths of his heart in the rich diversity of creation. Because creation reveals the glory of God, in the same way that Jesus Christ reveals the Father, creation is sacred. It is a holy earth that speaks to us of the holy love of God."[19]

The cosmic implications of the surrender of the incarnated word in Jesus Christ and the "catch" that has transformed creation as a result has been expressed most eloquently in the paean attributed to Paul found more expansively in Ephesians 1:3–23 and again, in a more condensed version in Paul's Letter to the Colossians. It shows the cosmic implications of being consciously connected to the Christ who holds "primacy" over all that is:

He [the enfleshed word] is the image of the invisible God, the first-born of all creation; for in him all things in heaven and on earth were created, things visible and invisible, whether thrones or dominions or rulers or powers — all things have been created through him and for

him. He himself is before all things, and in him all things hold together. He is the head of the body, the church; he is the beginning, the
firstborn from the dead, so that he might come to have first place in
everything. For in him all the fullness of God was pleased to dwell,
and through him God was pleased to reconcile to himself all things,
whether on earth or in heaven, by making peace through the blood of
his cross (Col. 1:15–20).

The realization of the incarnated word enfleshed and encapsulated in the
members of Christ, called "the church," brings about the reconciliation of
all things in God. For Paul, as well as for Francis, this "peace" or new social
order of *shalom,* was realized or "made" through the blood of his cross as
well. This leads us to discover how Francis found in the crucifixion (more
than the resurrection), another example of "surrender and catch."

The Centrality of the Crucified One in Francis' Spirituality

Even after studying Francis for my whole adult life, I was never able to
appreciate why the cross and Christ Crucified constituted his central image of
Jesus. But then I became aware of Wolff's notion of surrender and catch. This
enabled me not only to understand and even appreciate it; even more, it led me
to believe that, in the surrender of Jesus on the cross, we find the *only human
way* we "catch" the resurrected Christ. The Crucified One encapsulated God's
humility, God's self-giving love. In the very surrender of his will — which,
humanly speaking, resisted the terror of the cross and the suffering and
death connected with it — Jesus became empowered as the "catch" who
brings about for us who believe the possibility of living in a resurrected way.
In the process of this surrender, Jesus became the Christ, the one anointed to
empower us in discipleship, the one giving us a share in his own Spirit that
we too might go through the same pattern in our own dying and rising.

In his surrender to everything, including the unjust traditions of his religious leaders and their system of meaning, Jesus was willing to go so far as
to embrace the cross they and the political leaders imposed on him as a sign
of his deviance and subversion to their way of thinking. Building on Wolff,
this is what Eleanor M. Godway calls the "epistemology of the cross"; this is
the salvation promised all who are willing to pass over from one worldview
to another. She writes: "We have to 'unlearn' what we have been colluding
with as we have been co-opted by privilege, and the outcome of this unlearning will allow us to handle the violence differently — that is why I make so

bold as to refer to an 'epistemology of the cross.' "[20] She notes in another place that her "reading" of the cross was "not in relation to an original Fall from grace, from which we are redeemed by Jesus' sacrifice," but in his surrender itself: "I think that the witness of Jesus — what makes him the Christ if you like — is that he surrendered — absolutely — and despaired — as we know; so he did not know the outcome. He is the clearest example of 'unlearning privilege,' and to accept the Gospel is [for us] to learn to do likewise."[21] The author of life willingly gave his life on the cross.

Along with his dream in Spoleto that promised Francis that he would be able to "catch" an entirely new way of becoming a knight, the next most life-altering experience in these initial years of his conversion came at the Chapel of San Damiano when he heard the words from the cross: "Francis, don't you see that my house is being destroyed? Go, then, and rebuild it for me." The Christ who challenged him spoke from a crucified body.

Upon responding that he would gladly do so, the *Legend of the Three Companions* notes that the marks of the Crucified Christ were impressed in the depths of his being: "From that hour, therefore, his heart was wounded and it melted when remembering the Lord's passion. While he lived, he always carried the wounds of the Lord Jesus in his heart."[22] That the imprint of this interior identification in himself with the Crucified Christ that originated at San Damiano would find its visible expression in his body itself in the form of the stigmata will be discussed later.[23] Suffice it to say that, in the image of the crucified Christ, Francis somehow placed himself in solidarity with the Mother of Jesus, and with all those living members of his body who were being crucified through persecution, marginalization, and poverty all around him.

Not only did the cross at San Damiano's lead him to greater solidarity with the victims of injustice in the world; it made another kind of indelible mark in Francis' life. While it is true that he never seemed to place much stress on the resurrection in Christ's life and even composed an Office of the Passion, one can wonder if it was not because, as a student of John's Gospel, he found the resurrection contained in the death of Jesus on the cross and the release of the Spirit in the pouring out of the blood and water when the soldier pierced the side of Jesus (John 19:34). Indeed the glorified Christ is the one whose voice he heard from the cross at San Damiano. Therefore we can ask if it also could be that Francis intuited from other images that surrounded the Crucified One on that cross of San Damiano's that he might be part of the church that would take Jesus' Mother to create a new kind of "house"? Could it be that he believed it would be by fidelity to Christ

Crucified that the "house" called the church could be repaired of its sins and thus be kept from falling into ruin?

This line of thought seems to guide the perspective of the Franciscan Thaddée Matura when he finds key images of house ("palace," "tabernacle," and "home") used by Francis of Mary with regard to the church itself. He concludes: "If the attribution to the church of such ties to God and his mystery appear exorbitant, let us not forget that elsewhere, with great serenity, Francis identifies this same link comparing believers to spouses, brothers, and mothers of Christ (2LtF, 51–53). And a simple believer is certainly less than the entire church in its mystery."[24]

After Francis' experience of the cross at San Damiano, the next critical moment came in the way he surrendered his previously ordered life, which included avoidance of lepers. In his *Testament*, immediately after noting "how God inspired" him to go among the lepers in a way that resulted in the "surrender/catch" dynamic that took him more deeply into the "catch" of his conversion, he then writes: "And the Lord gave me such faith in churches that I would pray with simplicity in this way and say: 'We adore You, Lord Jesus Christ, in all Your churches throughout the whole world and we bless You because by Your holy cross You have redeemed the world."[25]

Finally, upon receiving the hermit's habit from Bishop Guido when he renounced his patrimony in favor of his heavenly Father's patronage, Francis indicated his desire to put on more than a habit. By chalking the back of the habit with a "Tau," he was indicating to himself and anyone who might see it that he was taking up his cross and committing himself to the evangelical following of Jesus.[26] Later, after hearing a sermon preached by Pope Innocent III at the Fourth Lateran Council on November 11, 1215, on the power of the Tau cross (based on Ezek. 9:4), Francis took the message personally and used it to mark his communal effort to "repair" the ecclesiastical house called "the church."[27] However, rather than just following the original revelation about the Tau being placed on the foreheads of those who groaned "over all the abominations" that were being "committed" in Israel (i.e., the institutional church), Francis also embraced the Tau as a continual reminder to himself, his followers, and the world that to be his follower meant embracing the effort to bring about a restoration of the ruins rather than only groaning about their destruction.

If Jesus was the revelation of God, then, in his humanity he revealed to the world the divinity of the one who was originally revealed to Moses as the "I am" (Yahweh). Indeed, it was just his self-referencing as "I am" in John's Gospel that elicited from the leaders of the Jews such anger and, ultimately, the decision to kill him.

Of all the "I am" statements of Jesus in John's Gospel, none were used more frequently in Francis' writings than the one where Jesus declared himself to be the Good Shepherd. Here Francis found the Shepherd's *goodness* another image of the surrender of divinity on behalf of humanity. The cognitive knowing of the Good Shepherd was revealed in the love that motivated him to be willing to freely lay down his life because of that love (John 10:14–18). Indeed, he was convinced of the truth of Jesus' words later in John that there could be no greater love than to lay down one's life for one's friends (John 15:13). In turn, as a reciprocal sign of this friendship, the one so befriended would feel impelled to embrace the ways of the friend: "You are my friends if you do what I command you" (John 15:14). For Francis, as we will see in the next chapter, this involved embracing the Gospel; it also served as a reminder that his followers should be willing to lay down their lives for each other and the world, as did the saints of the church, not just wax eloquently about their sacrifice. He wrote in his Sixth Admonition:

> Let all of us, brothers, consider the Good Shepherd Who bore the sufferings of the cross to sheep.
>
> The Lord's sheep followed Him in tribulation and persecution, in shame and hunger, in weakness and temptation, and in other ways; and for these things they received eternal life from the Lord.
>
> Therefore, it is a great shame for us, the servants of God, that the saints have accomplished great things and we want only to receive glory and honor by recounting them.[28]

The Crucified Christ represented and symbolized for Francis the ultimate surrender of God into human hands in a way that "caught" up humanity into divinity. Not only did the image of the Good Shepherd reflect for Francis the love between the Father and the Son; because the Son was willing to lay down his life for his friends, a new reality was brought about, linking earth with heaven. In surrendering his life for us and all creation, Jesus invited us to turn to him and be empowered in a way that would find us united with the Father in heaven and working to create restored relationships of communion among all people and the planet without reliance on traditional categories of "majores and minores," "father and children," "master and slaves." This notion is made clear in an extended passage found in his Earlier Rule that he wrote for his followers:

> Let us have recourse to Him as *to the Shepherd and Guardian of our souls,* Who says, "I am the Good Shepherd Who feeds my sheep and I lay down My life for my sheep."

All of you are brothers. Do not call anyone on earth your father;
you have but one Father in heaven. Do not call yourselves teachers;
you have but one Teacher in heaven.[29]

Since it was from the cross that Francis heard the words, "Repair my
house," the cross continually challenged Francis to build up the "house"
of human beings and all creation wherever they might be in need. "When
he was tempted to turn his back on the world completely and spend all his
time in solitary contemplation, it was the vision of the cross that restrained
him," Leonhard Lehmann reminds us. He continues:

The same cross that led Francis out of the world led him back into
it. It was a question of leaving a certain kind of world, and of finding a new approach to it. This could come about only through an
existential return, that is, through penance. It meant transcending all
previous earthly standards and finding a new route through the world.
Since God himself continually gives Himself to the world through Jesus
Christ, our response cannot consist in turning from the world but in
a critical facing up to its reality. Our model is Jesus, Who possessed
nothing in this world, had no place whereon to lay His head, and yet
gave Himself totally for us. Francis followed His example.[30]

When he returned from his effort to convert the sultan in Egypt and
found many leaders of the Order trying to move it in ways that appeared
quite diametrically opposed to his vision, the *Assisi Compilation* notes that
he "was tormented inside and out, in body and spirit." It seems his response
was neither fight nor flight but a kind of depression or torment. From my
understanding of spirituality that would have meant that he had to endure
both a "dark night" of his senses ("tormented in body") as well as a "dark
night" of his soul ("tormented in soul"). It adds: "He was troubled by this
temptation day and night for more than two years." Consequently, given this
crisis that penetrated the depths of his being as he experienced his dream
being violently ripped away, he entered into his Great Temptation: the triad
of conflict and withdrawal that ultimately resulted in an empowerment in
the Word that freed him by grounding him again in faith. The *Assisi Compilation* tells us that he "withdrew from the close company of the brothers."
In this state of withdrawal, one day "he happened to hear in spirit that
saying of the holy Gospel: '*If you have faith like a mustard seed, and you
tell* that *mountain to move* from its place *and move* to another place, it will
happen." Then he heard " 'That mountain is your temptation.' 'In that case,
Lord,' said blessed Francis, 'be it done to me as you have said.' " With that

response to God's Word, his depression was removed; he became free of the conflict that had torn him apart.[31]

What, more specifically, constituted this "Great Temptation"? Francis had become disillusioned with the way his dream was being realized in the direction of the Order (including the fact itself that it had become an Order or structure more than a fraternity of equals). At first this led him to renounce the exercise of all power over his brothers, asking for a cardinal of the Roman Church to be a "protector" of the Order to keep it from conflicts and divisions. When this did not change the mind-set of many, he distanced himself from the brothers. However his way of "withdrawal" seemed far from healthy or holy; yet, because this form of his depression did not turn to despair, it seems it still could serve as the context for a transformation. This crucifixion was turned to resurrection.

Grado Giovanni Merlo writes of this period: "Before the stigmata, which the oldest sources say took place in September 1224, Brother Francis experienced a long period of resentful solitude. He was painfully dissatisfied at how the consequences of his and his brothers' religious experience were being expressed in the choices and life of the Order." However, upon receiving the stigmata, Merlo concludes: "He is no longer resentful, no longer tormented, but at peace, yet even more determined to insist on the fundamental and essential points of his Christian experience."[32] This is what he discovered by surrendering to everything that came to him as his "cross," including his own will: the catch of being grounded in God alone.

Taking Up the Cross Imposed by the World

In Matthew's Gospel, at three different times Jesus told "his disciples that he must go to Jerusalem and undergo great suffering at the hands of the leaders and chief priests and scribes, and be killed, and on the third day be raised" (Matt. 16:21; see 17:22–23; 20:18–19). However, after the first "prediction," Matthew narrates:

> Jesus told his disciples, "If any want to become my followers, let them deny themselves and take up their cross and follow me. For those who want to save their life will lose it [note the kenotic stress], and those who lose their life for my sake will find it. For what will it profit them if they gain the whole world but forfeit their life? Or what will they give in return for their life?" (Matt. 16:24–26).

In 1208, when Francis, Bernard, and Peter went to the Church of St. Nicholas to divine what God might have in mind for their trio, they opened the scriptures three times. The third time they prayed and then opened the Gospels they fell upon this passage. Hearing that they must deny themselves according to the kenosis of Jesus, Francis declared: "Brothers, this is our life and rule and that of all those who will want to join our company. Go, therefore, and fulfill what you have heard."[33]

The words "Take up your cross" have become a familiar expression, even in our secular world, to indicate the sufferings we and all other creatures must undergo on our respective journeys. However, many times people go the opposite way: they will embrace a cross, but it will be a cross free of anyone who may be crucified. When we remove the crucified one from the cross, we can effectively free ourselves from our responsibility in that crucifixion — whether it is of Jesus himself or his members being crucified today. Thus, we read: "If we are able to view the cross of Jesus without removing the scandal of the crucifixion, we are more likely to face without rationalization or denial the scandal of the world's suffering."[34]

Despite the consolation that can come when people realize that the crosses they must bear can be linked to that of Jesus, in many ways taking up such a cross can also have its downside insofar as the notion delinks it from its real context and, thus, from its actual meaning then and for now as well. In many ways "take up your cross" is much like another passage from Matthew's Gospel that has been separated from its context: "You always have the poor with you" (Matt. 26:11). Just as the story about the woman who poured costly ointment on Jesus was the "good deed" that he said must be remembered (Matt. 26:10, 13), only to be forgotten in face of the passage about the poor always being with us, so "taking up your cross" also has been separated from its historical context.

Just as Jesus' taking the cross was the consequence of choices he made that put him at odds with those in his religion who remained locked into its ideological story and those in the Roman world who viewed him as a threat to the Pax Romana, so the cross they inflicted on him is the cross that we too must take up when our story stands against the church's story and the culture's story, insofar as they stand opposed to "the story" of the Gospel proclaimed by Jesus Christ. "In the Gospel context," Barbara Reid writes: " 'cross' has a very specific meaning: it refers to the suffering that comes as a consequence of proclaiming and living the Gospel."[35] The cross was the consequence for the effort to bring about justice in an unjust empire. "Bearing the cross" meant to accept something humbly that had been unjustly imposed.

The phrase "take up your cross" has lost the power of its original meaning due to the increasing spiritualization and personalization of the Gospel. However, John Howard Yoder argued years ago, if we realize that the cross was "the standard punishment for insurrection or for the refusal to confess Caesar's lordship," it is easy to see why the "cross" became so depoliticized, especially after the Constantinianization of the Gospels. He noted: " 'Take up your cross' may have been a standard phrase of Zealot recruiting (the Zealots were deemed insurrectionists by Caesar). The disciple's cross is not a metaphor for self-mortification or even generally for innocent suffering: 'If you follow me, your fate will be like mine, the fate of a revolutionary. You cannot follow me without facing that fate.' "[36]

One need not watch such movies as *Gladiator* or *Ben Hur* to realize the truth of Yoder's contention. However, when people have become accustomed to wear the cross as jewelry and a good part of the jewelry market involves crosses of all kinds, it is a little hard to be reminded that the cross was once a standard form of violence used by the state to intimidate those at the periphery and those who might otherwise try to challenge the "gospel" of the empire in any way.

The Eucharist as Sign and Summit of the "Surrender and Catch" of Jesus Christ

Francis was no theologian. This was true, especially in his understanding of the Eucharist. Yet, in an amazing passage in his Letter to the Entire Order, he wrote: "I implore all of you brothers to show all possible reverence and honor to the most holy Body and Blood of our Lord Jesus Christ [referring to the passage from Colossians 1:20 noted above which summarizes the theology of the Primacy of Christ] in Whom that which is in heaven and on earth has been brought to peace and reconciled to almighty God."[37]

Just as his devotion to the Incarnation and crucifixion revolved around the humbling or "emptying" that was articulated in Paul's Letter to the Philippians, so when Francis wrote his First Admonition to his followers, he linked this very self-emptying of the enfleshed Word in Jesus with what happened every time the Eucharist is celebrated: "Behold, each day he humbles Himself as when He came *from the royal throne* into the Virgin's womb; each day He Himself comes to us, appearing humbly; each day He comes down *from the bosom of the Father* upon the altar in the hands of a priest."[38]

The extent of Francis' theological training can be found in his grammar school education at San Giorgio's, where he spent some time. Consequently his notion of the Eucharist was not very developed and, possibly because the Mass represented something a priest "did" and the people "observed," Francis developed his thoughts regarding the Eucharist as a way of total surrender and catch (i.e., salvation) more around the notion of the "real presence" in the consecrated bread and wine that was reserved in the churches. This notion, called "transubstantiation," was authorized by a decree of the Fourth Lateran Council (1215), which tradition has Francis attending. With this stress Francis reflected the Eucharistic piety of the medieval and even modern times, which Jean Carroll McGowan describes as being "oriented to a *cultus* of the real presence of Jesus Christ in the Blessed Sacrament."[39]

In at least seven of the ten letters Francis wrote, he speaks about the body and blood of Christ, even though he never mentions the word "Eucharist." At least five of his letters have as their primary concern proper participation in and devotion to the Eucharist: the First and Second Letters to the Custodians, A Letter to the Entire Order, and A Letter to the Clergy (earlier and later editions wherein he used the word "we" when he spoke about the term "clergymen").[40]

He wrote in his *Testament* that "in this world, I see nothing corporally of the most high Son of God except His most holy Body and Blood."[41] He wrote in his Letter to All Clerics in a way that brought together both the Incarnation and the crucifixion: "For we have and see nothing bodily of the Most High in this world except His Body and Blood, His names and words through which we have been made and redeemed *from death to life.*"[42]

As noted above, Francis began his "Admonitions" with a summary of the self-emptying love, or humility, that was involved when the Word was enfleshed in a way that made the Jesus of history the Christ of our faith. The love of the incarnated Word revealed in the historical Jesus, in his mind, reaches its apogee in that "mystery of our faith" called the Eucharist. After declaring: "Behold, each day he humbles Himself as when he came *from the royal throne* into the into the Virgin' womb," he continues:

> Each day He comes down *from the bosom of the Father* upon the altar in the hands of a priest.
>
> As he revealed Himself to the holy apostles in true flesh, so he reveals Himself to us now in sacred bread. And as they saw only His flesh by an insight of their flesh, yet believed that He was God as they contemplated Him with their spiritual eyes, let us, as we see bread and wine with our bodily eyes, see and firmly believe that they are his most holy body and Blood living and true. And in this way the Lord is always with His faithful, as He Himself says: *Behold, I am with you until the end of the age.*[43]

In the Eucharist, the surrender of Christ seemed concretized in a way that brought the Incarnation and crucifixion together; it served as an invitation for all who would be in its presence to go through the process of surrender and catch themselves because: "It is the Spirit of the Lord, therefore, That lives in Its faithful, that receives the Body and Blood of the Lord."[44]

The realization of this unfathomable love of God, with its cosmic implications, should evoke in all Franciscans a sense of deep wonder, gratitude, and a commitment to surrender themselves in imitation of that which they celebrate. Thus he wrote to the brothers gathered in General Chapter:

> Let everyone be struck with fear, let the whole world tremble, and let the heavens exult when Christ, the Son of the living God, is present on the altar in the hands of a priest! O wonderful loftiness and stupendous dignity! O sublime humility! O humble sublimity! The Lord of the universe, God and the Son of God, so humbles Himself that for salvation He hides Himself under an ordinary piece of bread! Brothers, look at the humility of God, and *pour out your hearts before Him!* Humble yourselves that you may be exalted by Him! Hold back nothing of yourselves for yourselves, that He Who gives Himself totally to you may receive you totally.[45]

Truly, when we participate fully in the Eucharist we enter into the humbling of our God in a way that finds us truly exalted: partakers in the very body and blood that finds us in communion with God, with each other, and with all creation itself.

The Eucharist Celebrated in the Church and Celebrating the Church

For Francis, the Eucharist was the Body of Christ, but the Body of Christ was the Church. All three: the Eucharist, the Body of Christ, and the Church were part of an essential triad. To be fully involved in the Eucharist, he had to find the fullness of his identity in the Body of Christ called the Church. Furthermore this "Church" was not just a mystical communion but also the actual Church of Rome. He had been born into this church and, despite its failings, it was the context in which he felt God had called him to lead a Gospel way of life.

It is critical to realize that, at the time of Francis, Christianity had no divisions between Protestant and Catholics. The only split within Christendom itself had come in 1054 between the Orthodox and the Uniates. Furthermore, no Orthodox Christians lived in, near, or anywhere in the environs of Assisi. The only "unbelievers" ("infidels") were heretics and the adherents of Islam. In other words, if heresy meant unbelief, the only "game in town" had to be the Roman Church. In no way could Francis even imagine being separated from it. However, within the way it told its story, he offered another way of living: the Gospel story, which he enshrined in his Rule.

Once Francis was able to get Rome to accept his way of life as "the Gospel" incarnated in his Rule, he made sure that he would seek to put greater stress on repairing any of its faults or those of its ministers rather than pointing out their way of ruination. Rather than challenging the authority of the bishops, he nonviolently accepted their decision when they determined any friar should not preach in their diocese; it was a matter of jurisdiction, not evangelization. Yet, in a way it was a matter of evangelization, or, more precisely, the realization that the Gospel could not be preached there, which would necessitate the brothers taking their gospel of peace elsewhere. Thus, on the one hand, he incorporated a one-line admonition in his Later Rule that was not found in his Earlier Rule — a point that had to be included, probably because there had been incidents when friars insisted on challenging or circumventing bishops who would not allow them to preach in their dioceses: "The brothers may not preach in the diocese of any bishop when he has opposed their doing so."[46] Yet, on the other hand, in his *Testament* he makes it clear that he interpreted a bishop's rejection of the evangelical message of the brothers from the perspective of Jesus' admonition to his followers to "shake off the dust from your feet as you leave that house or town" (Matt. 10:14): "Wherever they have not been received, *let them flee into another* country and do penance with the blessing of God."[47]

When it came to priests publicly recognized as sinners,[48] Francis chose not to berate them as had often been the custom of other preachers. While not sweeping their sinfulness under the rug (and even writing the clergy a private letter [wherein he referred to himself as part of the clergy] inviting them to conversion),[49] he urged his followers to have an attitude of faith and respect toward them. Indeed, according to Thaddée Matura: The words that he employs to describe this attitude are "venerate" (ER, 19.3; 2LtF, 2.33), "reverence" (2LtF, 2:33), "honor" (Test 8), "love" (Test 8), and "fear" (Test 8).[50]

While deferring to the clergy because of their unique role in bringing into the world the sacramental presence of the Christ, Francis never ceased to treat them as he did everyone else: as his equals. Thus he called them by the same names he called others, including inanimate creatures: "brothers" and even "lords" (albeit with "all others" as well!). He had no problem in acknowledging their unique role in his life: through them he was able to participate in the Eucharist. Without them, he could not find this manifestation of the Real Presence of Jesus Christ in his life. Indeed he wrote that it was divine inspiration that had led him to view priests in this way, even when they may be public sinners:

> The Lord gave me, and gives me still, such faith in priests who live according to the rite of the holy Roman Church because of their orders that, were they to persecute me, I would still want to have recourse to them. And if I had as much *wisdom as Solomon* and found impoverished priests of this world, I would not preach in their parishes against their will. And I desire to respect, love, and honor them and all others as my lords. And I do not want to consider any sin in them because I discern the Son of God in them and they are my lords. And I act in this way because, in this world, I see nothing corporally of the most high Son of God except His most holy Body and Blood, which they receive and they alone administer to others.[51]

The kind of respect he had for priests of the "holy Roman Church" came precisely because they were of the institutional church itself. While some might think of this as evidencing a noncritical stance toward their public sins and aberrations, it also might be considered a nonviolent way of shaming them into change. Respect for them in the midst of societal disrespect might do more to bring about conversion than merely echoing the disdain hurled at erring priests.

Within his own Gospel-grounded way of life, priests who sinned would not get off so easily. If they did something publicly and seriously wrong, they were to be treated no differently than any other brothers. The Gospel demanded as much; the fraternity's notion of equality expected as much to be institutionalized:

> If any brother, at the instigation of the enemy, sins mortally in regard to those sins concerning which it has been decreed among the brothers to have recourse only to the provincial ministers, let him have recourse as quickly as possible and without delay. If these ministers are priests, with a heart full of mercy let them impose on him a penance; but, if the ministers are not priests, let them have it imposed by others who are priests of the order, as in the sight of God appears to them more expedient. They must be careful not to be angry or disturbed at the sin of another, for anger and disturbance impede charity in themselves and in others.[52]

I have often considered that, when he was faced with resistant bishops and impenitent priests, Francis offered a nonviolent way of "withdrawal" that might serve us well. Basically he would not return rejection for rejection and get angry (and thereby sin) when they might sin. In this way, he imitated Jesus when he invited his followers not to retaliate with an eye for an eye, evil for evil, or violence with violence. While he did not invite his followers to fight, neither did he urge them to flight. Instead he offered an alternative, nonviolent way of "withdrawal" that was *disarming*.[53] In this way charity would not only not be impeded; instead, this way of surrender just might invite such bishops and priests to conversion themselves!

SEVEN

The Gospel as Francis' Life-Project

No one showed me what I had to do, but the Most High Himself revealed to me that I should live according to the pattern of the Holy Gospel.[1]   —St. Francis of Assisi, *Testament*, 14

Francis' Understanding and Embrace of the Gospel as His Way of Life

Francis did not invent the idea of "living the Gospel" or a way of life called "evangelical," even though his popularity certainly helped the rise of this movement among lay Christians in the Middle Ages.

An examination of the writings of Francis of Assisi, especially in his Earlier Rule of 1221, reveals a marked familiarity with the Gospels. Indeed it reveals his approach to the Rule revolved around various New Testament texts used as proof-texts to support the way of life he then spelled out in further detail.

Francis did not come to such an awareness of the scriptures overnight. In a society where most of the laity, including many among the *majores*, were unable to read or write, Francis learned many of his favorite passages from memory. His early knowledge of the scriptures arose from attendance at Mass, where he heard them read, as well as in grammar school where he learned the psalms, found in what is known as the Psalter. "Because of the use of the Psalter as the principal text," used in grammar school for the students to learn, Octavian Schmucki writes, "it is easier to explain the exceptional knowledge which Francis had of the psalms which appear with revealing frequency in his writings, above all in the mosaic of prayers put together from memory in the Office of the Passion" which he created.[2]

The first specific notation of Francis being influenced by anything connected directly with the Gospel came around 1208, well into his initial conversion experience. As the *Legend of the Three Companions* describes it, Francis was participating in a Mass. The Gospel reading told how "Christ tells the disciples who were sent out to preach, instructing them to carry no *gold* or *silver, a wallet* or *a purse, bread, walking stick,* or *shoes,* or *two tunics."* When Francis heard the priest explain the meaning of the passage "he was filled with indescribable joy. 'This,' he said, 'is what I want do with all my strength.' "[3]

Francis was well into his way of surrender that began at Spoleto and evolved more clearly with the words from the cross at San Damiano and his embrace of the leper. This passage was the "catch." It capsulated the journey that had begun at Spoleto. The son of the merchant became a salesman of a different kind. This is wonderfully captured in a paragraph from Julian of Speyer:

> Francis then removed himself from the tumult of business and made himself a *salesman* of the Gospel. He sought *good pearls,* as it were, until *he came upon one precious one, and while he was coming to see what was more pleasing to God, he meditatively entered the workshop of various virtues. And when he went away to meditate on the lord's field, he found there* and hid the Lord's *hidden treasure,* and, *having sold everything,* he proposed to buy it along with the *field.*[4]

Given the fact that Francis had such a good mind, if not being very literate, he committed "to memory everything he had heard; he joyfully fulfilled them." This meant doing literally what the passage talked about: divesting himself of his second garment, going shoeless without a staff or haversack. He changed from his hermit's habit to "a very cheap and plain tunic," which ultimately became the habit of the friars. "Applying all the care of his heart to observe the words of new grace as much as possible, he began, inspired by God, to be a messenger of evangelical perfection and," the *Legend* continues, "to preach penance in public. His words were neither hollow nor ridiculous, but filled with the power of the Holy Spirit, penetrating the marrow of the heart, so that listeners were turned to great amazement."[5]

Two years after this we read about Francis' next significant encounter with the Gospel. Bernard of Quintavalle, a wealthy Assisian, came to him indicating interest in his way of living. He had observed Francis working on the churches and what a difficult life he was living, but with how much joy he did so. He approached Francis, "disclosed his plan to him, and arranged to have him come that evening to his home."[6]

One can only imagine the conversation the two shared. Whatever transpired between the two, the result was that Bernard decided to join Francis. He sold all his goods and gave the proceeds to the poor in such a way that Celano writes: "His conversion to God stood out as a model for those being converted in the way he sold his possessions and distributed them to the poor. The holy man Francis *rejoiced with very great joy* over the arrival and conversion of such a man, because the Lord seemed to be caring for him, giving him a needed companion and a *faithful friend.*"[7]

The next day Francis, Bernard and another, Peter of Cantanio, went to the church of St. Nicholas so they might "take up the Gospel Book, and seek the counsel of Christ" about what might be the direction God had in mind for them. The "Gospel Book" they consulted was most likely the Lectionary used for Mass.

After intense prayer, they followed the popular practice (repeatedly criticized by the hierarchy) of opening the scriptures to determine what God's will might be. It seems a priest helped them in this process because, *The Anonymous of Perugia* tells us, "none of them knew how to read very well."[8] Accordingly, Celano writes, the first passage declared: *"If you wish to be perfect, go and sell all you own, and give it to the poor."*[9] After more prayer, they opened the Gospels "a second time and found: *'Take nothing for your journey.'* "[10] For their third try they found the text: "If anyone would follow me, let him deny himself."[11]

Upon hearing these passages, Francis came to the simple but powerful realization that these Gospel passages were to constitute "our life and rule and that of all who will want to join our company."[12] Embracing these words literally, the brothers put on the habit that has now come to identify Franciscans throughout the world. Thus began the corporate witness of his evangelical life and that of his followers. Simply put, it was *vivere secundum formam sancti Evangelii* ("to live according to the pattern of the Holy Gospel")[13] or, even more simply, *sequela Christi* (following Christ).

When the brotherhood had grown to eight, following the pattern of Jesus in the Gospels, Francis created four groups of two brothers each. He then commissioned them to proclaim the Gospel in echoes of the same words used by Jesus when he sent out his first disciples:

> "Go, my dear brothers," he said to them, *"two by two* through different parts of the world, *announcing peace* to the people and *penance for the remission of sins.* Be *patient in trials,* confident that the Lord will fulfill His plan and promise. Respond humbly to those who question you. *Bless those who persecute you.* Give thanks to those who harm you and bring false charges against you, for because of these things an *eternal kingdom is prepared for us."*[14]

Soon, when the number of his followers had reached eleven, Francis concluded that it would be advisable to seek official approval for his way of life. This demanded Roman approval for the vision he would present. As he later recalled what happened next, Francis wrote in his *Testament* that, "after the Lord gave me some brothers, no one showed me what I had to do, but the Most High Himself revealed to me that I should live according to the pattern of the Holy Gospel." He then had them "written down simply and in a few words."[15]

What Francis wrote down is no longer extant. However, it is believed that the rule was mainly various passages from the Gospels and some other scripture passages. Guided by these teachings, Francis and his followers were willing to make such their "Rule."

Rome's Acceptance of Francis' Way of Life

On the way to Rome Francis suggested that they choose a leader who would determine details about the journey. Bernard was the one.[16] However, once Francis and his crew got to Rome it became very clear who was in charge of the fraternity. At the same time the ecclesiastical powers-that-be there were not quite as ready to accept as "gospel" their way of life. Upon their arrival there it happened that they met Bishop Guido of Assisi. He received them warmly but was apprehensive that they might be thinking of leaving his diocese where he found them doing so much good. So, when he heard the reason for their coming and the Gospel-plan for themselves that they envisioned, he promised them his advice and help.

Guido was a friend of the cardinal whose church was Santa Sabina — John of St. Paul. He was a well-respected Benedictine. When Bishop Guido interceded with him on behalf of Francis and his companions, Cardinal John of St. Paul sent for them. They spent several days with him. During that time he was impressed with their words and example. The *Legend of the Three Companions* notes that he "saw that their works corresponded to what he had heard." Aware of their desire to "live according to the manner of the Gospel," he offered to plead their cause at the papal court.

At the Curia he said to Pope Innocent III: "I found a most perfect man, who wishes to live according to the form of the holy Gospel, and to observe evangelical perfection in all things. I believe that the Lord wills, through him, to reform the faith of the holy Church throughout the world."[17] This idea amazed the pope to such a degree that he asked the cardinal to bring Francis to the court.

Once he was received by the pope and explained to him his vision of living the Gospel in a literal manner, the pope took the long view of the request. While he believed Francis and his followers possessed the necessary zeal to live such a life in the way he proposed, he thought it would become too burdensome for those who would succeed them. He asked Francis to go back and pray about it and, if he came to know it to be God's will, he would accede to his request.

A few nights before Francis returned, convinced of God's support for his proposed Gospel way of life, Innocent III had a powerful dream. According to the *Legend of the Three Companions,* the dream involved St. John Lateran, the "mother church" of Christendom. In his vision the church of St. John Lateran seemed ready to collapse. However, it was being held up on the shoulders of a man wearing a habit. He was small and of shabby appearance. When he awoke, recalling the previous visit of Francis, "he began to say to himself: 'This is indeed that holy and religious man through whom the church of God will be sustained and supported.' " The *Legend* concludes that, upon Francis' return visit to Innocent III, "he embraced him and approved the rule he had written. He also gave him and his brothers permission to preach penance everywhere, with the stipulation that the brothers who preach obtain permission from blessed Francis. Afterward he approved this in a consistory."[18]

I often think that we underestimate the fuller meaning of what transpired between the pope and Francis of Assisi. In a church that had embraced in its institutional expression and mode of operating a style of life based more on imperial ways than evangelical ones, Francis did not come pointing out how this had led to its impending ruination rather than its repair, as envisioned in his dream by Innocent III himself. That was how he had come to envision the church: as in ruins. However, for Francis, despite his avowed loyalty and willingness to submit to the pope, there was one thing that he could not in conscience do, even for the pope: change his way of thinking about what it would mean for him as a Catholic to "live the Gospel" in the Catholic Church. In no way could he be convinced by anyone, cleric or lay, that his vision had not come directly from God. This "evangelical" way of life, which he enshrined in his Rule, made it clear that:

1. In a world and church defined by clericalism, Francis' Gospel way of life invited its adherents to find a way of obedience whereby nobody would lord it over others. Indeed, all would ultimately be equal.

2. In a world and church that structured women and men into unequal relationships, Francis' Gospel way of life invited its adherents to see all as brothers and sisters under a common Father in heaven.

3. In a world and church that believed the universe revolved around the earth, Francis' Gospel way of life proclaimed to "all creation" that

all humans must decenter themselves in a way that finds them making common cause between people and the planet.

4. In a world and church that fought over competing property claims, Francis' Gospel way of life invited its adherents to "sell" whatever might be in the way of proclaiming good news to the poor.

5. In a world and church that understood that the "apostolic" life must be lived apart from society, Francis' Gospel way of life invited its adherents to realize this Gospel must be global and can never be separated from the cry of those marginalized by the world and the church.

6. In a world and church that limited prayer for the people to the liturgical prayer of the church and official prayer to the priests and canons, the monks and the nuns, Francis' Gospel way of life honored these forms but also insisted on a way of prayer available to all which sought never to distinguish the power of the Spirit in whatever would be done.

7. In a world and church that understood obedience to be structured from the top down, Francis' Gospel way of life grounded all obedience in the fraternity first in a way that made all superiors accountable to the fraternity and all members of the fraternity responsible not only to them but to their consciences as well.

8. In a world and church that could not even imagine the promotion of religion apart from the promotion of armaments, Francis' Gospel proclamation of peace to every *oikía, oikonomía, oikoumēne* in the whole *oikología* witnessed to a radical alternative.

It was Francis' conviction about this alternative vision of living the Gospel that intrigued the pope. Francis and his followers were convinced that God had revealed to their original three members that the church could be reconstituted, repaired, and rebuilt only by a return to the Gospel. Yet, to accomplish this in "the church," he needed to submit this evangelical life as enshrined in the Rule to get the canonical authority to agree that this way of life was indeed "the Gospel way of life." I am convinced that it is this notion of "submission" of his divinely inspired vision of the Gospel that received the authorization from the official church that brought about the delicate dance that is articulated for his friars in the last chapter of the Final Rule. While he demanded that we be "always submissive and subject at the feet of the same Holy Church and steadfast in the Catholic Faith," this submissiveness and subjection itself would always be defined by the observance of that "poverty and humility" that he found in "the Holy Gospel of our Lord Jesus Christ" which the brothers "have firmly promised."[19]

Francis was viscerally opposed to challenging anything in the institutional church that might not reflect the "Gospel" and that might be part of the reason for it falling into ruin. Rather, as he seems to have intuited (more than any conscious seeking of an alternative ecclesiastical model), Francis would ask the institution, via its representatives, to agree that his way of life was not just "catholic" but "evangelical." The implication of this intuition for those concerned today about church "reform" seems clear: (1) we will be more effective (and pleasant as well!) when we offer creative alternatives to being "catholic" that are evangelically grounded rather than attacking the institutional church for any perceived unevangelical ways, and (2) when we are grounded in this Gospel theologically as well as in our personal consciences, we will have a more reliable basis to dissent from those teachings that appear to undermine the Gospel's vision of a justice of right relationships grounded in the Trinitarian reign of God.[20]

How Francis Grounded the Fraternity in the Gospel of the Reign of God

Julian of Speyer notes that, as they were returning from Rome, "these zealots of a new justice" had a discussion "whether in the future they should live in solitary places or among [the] people."[21] He notes that Francis made it clear that their zeal would take them to their neighbors. Upon their return from Assisi the fraternity spread out from there and began proclaiming the Gospel of penance (countercultural/alternative living) and peace throughout Italy. However, because it increased so rapidly there was a real need for them to leave their various ministries and come together to plan their future.

Around 1212 Francis received on loan the church of St. Mary of the Portiuncula (Little Portion) from the Benedictines on Mount Subasio near Assisi. After repairing San Damiano (quite rapidly) and San Pietro della Spina, Francis had started on the Portiuncula because it had been deserted and had no caretaker. Not wanting to possess any property, Francis had agreed to lease the church from the Benedictines for a basket of fish each year. To this day the payment is still made.

With the Portiuncula as the new "home" of the expanding fraternity, the brothers convened there for a Chapter twice a year, at Pentecost and on the feast of St. Michael, late in September. There, using Bible quotes in a way that urged his followers to remain faithful to the Gospel Rule of Life they had embraced, Francis "zealously used to admonish the brothers to observe the holy Gospel and the *Rule* which they had firmly promised."[22] "Anyone who can expound Gospel texts in such an admirable and penetrating manner," Schmucki once wrote: "must not only have been already steeped in it intellectually but also have experienced it intellectually."[23] Celano summarizes it best, I believe, when he wrote how the Gospel Story became Francis' Story: "*He filled the* whole *world* with the Gospel of Christ; . . . edifying his listeners by his example as much as by his words, as he made of his whole body a tongue."[24]

The Gospel of the Trinitarian Reign of God Proclaimed by Jesus

Celano tells us that Francis often visited "four or five *towns and villages,* proclaiming to everyone the *good news of the kingdom of God.*"[25] His form of evangelization turned hardened hearts into welcoming homes for God's reign. In his evangelization, he was merely following the model of Jesus. This model constitutes the "old" and the "new" evangelization. As for the latter, the words of then-Cardinal Joseph Ratzinger are clear: the "new evangelization," revolves essentially "in the words Christ himself used when starting to evangelize: 'The time is fulfilled, and the kingdom of God is at hand; repent, and believe in the Gospel' (Mark 1:15). The Church must ask herself if she does not talk too much about herself and relegate talking about God to the shadows of her proclamation." "The message of the Church is not a collection of dogmas and prescriptions, but simply talk of God who in Christ turns to us."[26]

While it is clear that evangelization demands a return to the proclamation of the Gospel as articulated by Jesus, it is clear that his Gospel was a proclamation of the "Kingdom" (really the "kin-dom,") or the "Reign" (really the "rule") of God.

At the time of Jesus, the notion of "kingdom" had definite political overtones. In the context of his world, it would have been political suicide for Jesus to announce the coming of a new "empire," given the hegemony of the Romans in his Mediterranean world. For him to inaugurate his ministry declaring: "Repent, for another empire is at hand" (see Matt. 4:17) would have ended his evangelization before it began. "Kingdom" was a phrase he could use in a way that had greater subtlety, although the word for kingdom (*basileia*) can also be translated as empire. Even if he did preach "the kingdom," this image combined with the fact that he went about preaching the good news (*euangelion*) of this kingdom in the midst of the empire was not that subtle. According to Wes Howard-Brook the image of *euangelion* was quite unique in the New Testament insofar as it had been used only once in all of the Septuagint (2 Sam. 4:10).[27] This evidences the fact that the image of "good news" did not come from Israel's tradition but was "one *expropriated from the Roman Empire.*"

Although "good news" once covered a wide range, gradually, when people in the empire heard someone announce an *euangelion* it often was linked to the news of the empire's conquest of a new territory, the birth of a new emperor, or the proclamation of a *dogmata* or decree of an existing emperor. In this imperial context of "good news" for another *euangelion* to be proclaimed had within itself a very subversive message. For Jesus to be going "throughout Galilee" and "all the cities and villages" "proclaiming the good news of the kingdom" as Matthew portrays him doing (4:23; 9:35), especially in a way that resulted in his fame rather than Caesar's being spread, was tantamount to treason. Furthermore, when it became clear that Jesus' kingdom would stand in resistance to the dynamics of the kingdom defined by empire, those members of the household who were discipled to him could expect trouble.

As envisioned by Matthew's Jesus, the kingdom of God was not a special place nor was it geographically located. Rather it was a place in one's heart in which God reigned. Such a vision of life, then and now, the African Jesuit Mattam Joseph has written, involves "the transformation of the present earth, human beings and their relationships. It is the radical reorientation of our life; a radically new vision of reality. It is a negation of the present as final."[28]

For Matthew, God's reign is a holistic concept covering a wide range of dimensions. It involves salvific-historical perspectives as well as political-economic implications. The salvific-historical dimension refers to God's reign as transcendent and eschatological — something not yet here. In Jesus and his church, that reign has now broken into history even though it will be fully realized only at the last harvest (13:24–30, 36–43). However, now on earth, in the present, God's reign has political-economic consequences. Matthew places in the mouth of John (3:2) and Jesus (4:17) the proclamation that God's reign is "at hand" (*eggizein* [3:2; 10:7]).

The idea of having God's "reign come about" (*erchomai e basileia sou*) "on earth as it is in heaven" dominates Matthew's Gospel. This will be accomplished by the one proclaimed "Son of David" by the people in a way that threatened the religious leaders (21:9–16) and "King of the Jews" by the "soldiers of the governor" (27:37, 27). Thus Matthew makes it clear that Jesus' kingship surpasses any authority in the existing empire or the religion of the Judeans.

Proclaiming the inbreaking of God's reign on earth became the heart of Jesus' message as well as the heart of the evangelizing efforts of the early community. That economic, political, and religious implications were contained in this proclamation cannot be denied for the notion itself was inseparable from the impact these had on people's lives as they lived in the midst of imperial culture and its ideology.

Since we have seen that the reality as well as notion of "God" surpasses all categories of space and time and that "heaven" cannot be limited to any place, the notion of God's reign as life everlasting, eternal relationship, or highest household seems the best a contemporary person can use to understand the meaning of the phrase for *basileia*. God's "kingdom" is heaven; it is God's rule, God's domain, God's commonwealth, God's polity, God's realm, God's empire, principality and territory. It is also God's reign. As such it involves God's dominion, God's governance, God's jurisdiction; it entails everything that constitutes God's sphere of influence. In effect, God's "kingdom" is not just God's reign; it is God's reality, God's energy, God's being and rule, God's essence and existence; it is God's actuality; it is God. Since God's actuality has been revealed to us as a community and commonwealth, it can best be understood by us as a household, as an *oikía* or *oikonomía*: a community of persons relating to each other in a way that empowers each member to have full access to all the resources available to the other members. This is what is called the "economic trinity."

The dynamics of the economic trinity constituted the fraternal economy of the evangelical community envisioned by Francis. His was to be a community of equals wherein all the persons involved would relate to each other in such a way that they could confidently make known to each other their needs. This would be his unique way of living the Gospel. Francis sought to create this fraternal economy or social ordering as a nonviolent alternative to the destructive, patriarchal and hierarchical dynamics around him that were sustained by resorting to a "God wills it" ideology. In contrast, his fraternity would be based on the dynamics of the Trinitarian God; its way of relating would be a Fraternal Economy based on the model of the "Economic Trinity." It follows then, as Micó declares: "The community of the Trinity is the origin of and the model for the Fraternity."[29]

Since we also have stated that the *oikonomía* within which Matthew developed his Gospel was that wherein the house was the primary metaphor, we will remain with this image in this chapter. Since households revolved around relationships among people in them and connected to them (i.e., "kin") and the resources shared within them, from here on (unless the word is in a direct quote) I'll simply refer to God's "kingdom" as God's kin(g)dom or reign, always assuming this involves an *oikonomía* or household wherein the relationships bring about a new familial order of kin-dom.

Matthew's Jesus makes it clear that the immanence of God's reign — signified in a special way by Jesus' various healings — places the household of those who believe in him (12:29) against the house of Satan's reign. Furthermore, the expulsion of the demons by *exousía*, by the Spirit of God, represents the evident proclamation that "the kingdom of God has come upon you" (12:28). Here the kingdom (*basileia*), the city (*polis*), and the house (*oikía*) are viewed in the same context (12:25). Thus, when Matthew's Jesus told his disciples to base their operations for preaching God's inbreaking kindom from the household (*oikía*) in every town (*politeía*) they enter (10:11–12), the social stratification of that society is being addressed. The house is the base of the town, the town is the core of the kindom; the kindoms constitute a totally new Kindom (*basileia*) of equal relationships under God.

When we Christians pray to God as our "Father," we do so knowing and agreeing among ourselves that our God is a Trinitarian community of persons. Each one is essential in constituting the original family of equals. As the revised *Catechism of the Catholic Church* states so well: "The *Holy Trinity* is consubstantial and indivisible. When we pray to the Father, we adore and glorify him together with the Son and the Holy Spirit."[30] It is in the name of this God revealed as Father, Son and Holy Spirit that we ourselves are constituted as members of the Christian family (28:19). When we pray to this God, we do so acknowledging God's triune composition or nature.

The Trinitarian understanding of God grounds religious experience and, therefore, truly humanitarian and communitarian life on earth as it is in heaven. In God's revelation to us in Jesus and in the Spirit they share with us in baptism (28:19) we find the model of all human community: three persons who relate to each other in such a way that everything available to the one is there for the other.

In the Trinity each person images the other precisely because each person has total access to the other's resources. This is the essence of that community of God we call the economic (household) trinity. Through the Christ, God-with-us (1:23) in human form, we are called to participate in this perfection of God by having access to the resources we need for living as fully as possible. The essence of every human being, made in God's image, is to be-in-relationship in a way that models the way resources are shared in the reign of our God. All reality involves each person living as an individual and in interpersonal relations that create communities that respond to the members' needs. All this takes place within societal infrastructures that honor the integrity of all creation. The divine *oikonomía* must be imaged in the human *oikonomía*. A description of this mirroring might look like the chart below:

The Economic Trinity	The Discipline of Economics
1. Every PERSON	1. The ALLOCATION (= ordering, relating)
2. Is in RELATIONSHIP to the Other so the Other	2. of scarce RESOURCES
3. Has equal access to all available RESOURCES	3. among (competing) PERSONS to meet needs

Economic Trinity's Vision for Human Economy

1. God made each PERSON, male and female, in the divine image,
2. God entered into RELATIONSHIP with each in the blessing,
3. So that all RESOURCES would be shared to help increase, etc.

If God creates all persons in the divine image, they will be blessed to the degree they can increase, multiply, fill the earth, and have a collaborative relationship with all others in creation itself. From Genesis 1:26–28 we discover the fundamental requirements for all people if they are to be in a community that reflects the reign of the Trinitarian God: (1) all persons made in the divine image must have that dignity realized in freedom; (2) all resources must be shared equitably in ways that meet the basic needs of all involved; and (3) all ways of relating among the different persons with regard to the resources available must promote the fullest solidarity, mutuality, and participation possible.

As in heaven, so on earth, all persons exist for each other. The resources of this earth exist for everyone. When all persons share with the greatest amount of equity in resource-allocation, justice defines those relationships. To use one's power to deny others access to resources needed for the greater good is to make oneself a god alien to the God revealed in Jesus' Prayer. When power is thus abused at any level of this world — individual, interpersonal, or infrastructural — that use of power undermines the divine power and, to that degree, is untrinitarian and sinful.

The Gospel of Jesus Proclaimed by the Early Church

In the previous section I declared that Jesus' proclamation of the Gospel revolved around his effort to bring about God's reign on earth as it was/is in heaven. For this he was delivered by his religious leaders, who saw his preaching as a threat to their "story," and to the representatives of Rome, who were told he was a threat to its "story" as well. With his death, his followers thought everything had collapsed. With the devastating impact of Jesus' death, his followers' experience of his aliveness-with-them within a very few days became the basis for another kind of "gospel." With their experience of Christ's risen presence, the Gospel proclaimed by Jesus was amplified by a new sense of "good news" that they felt compelled to proclaim.

The overwhelming "good news" in this experience, along with the collective experience of his Spirit-among-them shared by his disciples, soon eclipsed the original "good news of God's reign," which demanded a change of heart. Now the change of heart for a convert had much less to do with challenges to and alternatives for the culture's story and the religion's story. Later the community began preaching this "good news" that now revolved around the Jesus-Event itself and how Jesus had risen from an empire-imposed and religion-inspired death to offer eternal life to those who would believe in him. Now he, not Caesar, would be worthy of faith and people's worship. The proclamation of this "good news," which understood Jesus to be the Christ in whom the scriptures were fulfilled, began on the very day of Pentecost. On that day Peter declared not only to his peers but to all the people of Jerusalem that the last days prophesied by prophets like Joel had now been fulfilled in a way that had brought about a new creation of a cosmic community of equals all made so by the outpouring of the Holy Spirit:

> In the last days it will be, God declares,
> that I will pour out my Spirit upon all flesh,
> and your sons and your daughters shall prophesy,
> and your young men shall see visions, and your old men shall
>   dream dreams.
> Even upon my slaves, both men and women,
> in those days I will pour out my Spirit and they shall prophesy.
> And I will show portents in the heaven above and signs on the
>   earth below,
> blood, and fire, and smoky mist.
> The sun shall be turned to darkness and the moon to blood,
> Before the coming of the Lord's great and glorious day.
> Then everyone who calls on the name of the Lord shall be saved.
>   (Acts 2:17–21)

As we read in the Acts of the Apostles (more properly called the Acts of the Evolving Church) and know from the way the scriptures were used in the

Tradition to turn from the original community of equals, both women and men, slave and free, empowered by the Spirit, to return to previously rejected clerical forms of domination and abuse, the "good news" was domesticated as it began to revolve around more personalized, individualized acceptance of the Risen One into one's life. Rather than all the parts of Joel's prophesy that preceded the last sentence, only the last sentence would be remembered as the "good news" by those proclaiming themselves to be evangelicals and "born again": "Then everyone who calls on the name of the Lord shall be saved" (Acts 2:21).

The Church's Proclamation of the Gospel at the Time of Francis

After more than a thousand years of a gradual ossification of the original vision, in the late twelfth and thirteenth centuries there was a great desire to return to the "Gospel" by following Jesus Christ without entering a monastery. An early group espousing this view was the Cathari (The "Pure Ones"). They believed two primary forces controlled the universe: good and evil. As a consequence, they rejected the physical world, including the abandonment of material possessions and abstinence both from sex and from the food of any animal that had a parent.[31] Because of their anti-Roman stance, they gained many adherents until they were outlawed in 1163. They later morphed into other equally heretical groups such as the Albigensians and "Bulgars."

During the first part of Francis' life, until about 1220, the Humiliati ("Humble Ones") thrived in three forms of life that included women and men: canons, monastics, and lay. Their Rule combined various elements of the Benedictine and Augustinian rules. Its members as well as the Order itself (approved by Innocent III in 1201) were not to own any land; its members were not to do manual labor. Instead they were deputed to conduct lay preaching.

About ten years before Francis of Assisi was born, Peter Waldes of Lyon, like Francis' father a rich trader in cloth from southern France, divested himself of his wealth. He gave some of it to his wife and some for the care of his daughters; he gave the rest to the poor and began preaching to them. Rather than doing manual labor he and his followers took up a life of begging for alms and preaching the Gospel. He had the Bible translated into French and used it to challenge wealthy merchants and the corrupt clergy. In 1179 his way of life was approved by Rome. His followers, the

"Waldensians," called themselves "The Poor Men of Lyons." When Francis was three years old, Pope Lucius III declared the Waldensians to be heretics because they would not submit to papal authority.

The Liège diocese in the Low Countries not only birthed the group founded by St. Norbert of Xanten (1080–1134) called the Premonstratensians after Premontré, where they were founded in 1120; it also was the birthplace of the Beguine movement of women committed to a radical living of the Gospel. The earliest Beguine was Mary of Oignies (1177–1213), a woman of exemplary charity and mystical piety. Not only was she a contemporary of Francis of Assisi; she shared his core values. A chief goal of the Beguines was to be able to know God in perfect love. Pope Honorius III approved their way of life, which encompassed a full range of social classes. According to Lester Little, their movement flourished in the northern commercial and industrial cities in the latter half of the twelfth century. He articulated four distinct phases of the women who joined the Beguines. In general, they lived in communities but sustained themselves by outside work or wealthy benefactors.[32] The height of the Beguine movement produced two of the greatest mystics of the Middle Ages: Hadewijch of Antwerp (ca. early to mid-thirteenth century) and Mechthild of Magdeburg (1212–1281/1301).

At the time of Francis, preaching in the local parish churches "attended" by the people was anything but inspiring. Even more so the preaching-in-practice evidenced by the lifestyle of many priests, local bishops, and the Roman Curia of Innocent III bespoke a way of life that seemed far removed from the way of discipleship outlined by Jesus in the Gospels.

This institutionalization of the Gospel in the trappings of and abuse of power by ecclesiastical clerics had evoked a strong counterreaction in the preaching of the "gospel" of many reform movements of the age, especially the Waldensians and the Humiliati. So great was their frustration with the trappings of power and its concomitant abuse that they proclaimed Rome to be the "great whore" prophesied in the Book of Revelation.

Quite aware of what had happened when such groups were condemned by the official church as heretical, Francis made a move that was at once both wholeheartedly sincere and strategically brilliant. He would have his "Gospel way of life" approved by the very authority whose mode of operating seemed by other reformers to be most antithetical to the Gospel. He would recognize the authority of the institutional church in a way that would have its highest officials recognize his way of living the Gospel to be divinely inspired.

Repairing the Church for the Christ of the Gospels

In his *Life of St. Francis,* Thomas of Celano viewed Francis as one called to restore the church from its entrapment by the culture. He considered Francis not only to be *"in faith and truth a minister of the Gospel,"*[33] but as the new evangelist who "preached the way of the Son of God and the teaching of truth in his deeds." He adds that, as a result: "In him and through him an unexpected joy and a holy newness came into the world."[34]

In the last years of the pontificate of Pope John Paul II, the slogan "the new evangelization" became almost a mantra in certain sectors of the Catholic Church. While many believed it meant finding a way to become more orthodox as a Catholic, such a notion was rejected while Cardinal Joseph Ratzinger was prefect of the Congregation for the Doctrine of the Faith. He noted that, since all evangelization involves the proclamation of God's reign, "the church ought to ask herself whether she does not talk too much about herself, thereby casting a shadow over the proclamation of God."[35]

John Haughey, a Jesuit theologian at Loyola University in Chicago, has reflected on the problem of translating theology into faith. Haughey writes: "Faith statements made in a classroom are pure gold for a teacher of theology, because they legitimize conversations that go beyond theology to the convictions in the hearts of the students." This conviction led him to realize that, while non-Catholic Christians, especially Lutheran and evangelical students "are not shy about making personal faith statements" in his classes, "Catholic students, on the other hand, are very slow to make faith statements or statements about a personal relationship with Christ, even though Pope John Paul II... insisted that a personal, even intimate relationships with Christ should be the aim of our programs of catechesis in the church." This insight became the basis of an article he published in *America* in 2004. He opined that Catholics are slow to profess their faith because they have been given a faith in "Church-ianity" more than "Christ-ianity."[36]

From my experience in preaching in many parts of the developed world, Haughey's insight is critical. A key reason we are experiencing a crisis in faith among so many Catholics is not that they don't believe in Jesus Christ or the Triune God; it's just that they find issues identified with the institutional church eclipsing both Jesus Christ and the Trinity. When this happens the "church" becomes a "what" rather than a "who." The consequences are telling, as the chart on the next page details.

The confusion in the Catholic Church over its ultimate identity as a "what" or as a "who" is expressed in deep polarities that have found some absolutely convinced of their position when, in fact, allowing for the

"Church" Is Seen as a "What"	*"Church" Is Seen as a "Who"*
An organization	An organism
With an established structure	Where all parts are essential to the whole
Of those with power and those without	With a shared mission for good of whole
That sets apart the clergy as over others	That sees the common good as goal
Which makes "others" observers	Which makes all members basically equal
In the effort to maintain the organization	Participants in the common mission
Which is the responsibility of the clergy	Because of their unique "charisms"
The "people" see "church" as outside themselves	The "people" find themselves to be "the church"
"Truth" is seen as an objective body of facts that the members must believe	"Truth" is grounded in the living Person of Christ, to whom members adhere and listen
"What does the church say" means what is the "official" teaching (of the clergy)	"What does the church say" means what do the people and leaders believe
Stress is on the intellectual adherence to the body of truths	Stress is on the personal integration of meaning
Faith is expressed by adherence to a body of "truths" defined by those in power	Faith is found in a personal relationship to Jesus Christ
Fidelity is seen as adherence to the "truths"	Fidelity is seen as adherence to Jesus Christ, Head of the Body
Stress is on preserving a "Catholic Culture"	Stress is on proclaiming the Good News
"Churchianity" and Christendom	"Christianity" and Discipleship
Cohesion comes through obedience	Cohesion comes through shared vision
Body is "over/against" wider society	Body is to be a leaven in wider society

ultimate grounding in the Church as a "who," it can never be without a "what," a structure founded in authentic teaching about the scriptures and Tradition (or "the Story" and the "Church's Story"). This invites us to find ourselves on a continuum of belief rather than polarized by our beliefs. Francis found this balance in his embrace of the Gospel within the Roman Church. The Church today is hungering for that genius.

EIGHT

The Contagious Character
That Created a Classless Community

*Wherever the brothers may be and meet one another, let them show
that they are members of the same family. Let each one confidently
make known his need to the other, for if a mother loves and cares
for her son according to the flesh, how much more diligently must
someone love and care for his brother according to the Spirit!*
— St. Francis, Later Rule, 6.7–8[1]

The Structured Classism of Unequal Relationships

The Assisi of Francis' time experienced the beginnings of the movement
from one "ism" to another: from feudalism with its proud nobles alienated
from their serfs, to materialism with its avaricious merchants seeking to
ensure their newfound power as greedily as the nobles they had replaced.
Even though he may not have been of the nobility itself, Arnoldo Fortini
writes, the bishop of Assisi, by shrewdly steering a course between popes
and emperors had been able to acquire such an enormous amount of land,
that he apparently owned half the property of the commune when Francis
was growing up.[2]

Whether feudalism or the episcopacy, Celano's notion of the "fatal disease"[3] that infected the secular world of Francis of Assisi was grounded
in the sins of pride and avarice. While these deadly sins also infected the
churchmen of his day, these churchmen were able to sustain their position
in the world through another deadly sin: clericalism. As a canopy keeping
all these sins covered over and justified, without the possibility of the sun of
conversion, reigned classism itself: the structured and systemic separation of
peoples into unequal power relationships. All these class differences, violent
in themselves, could be sustained only by war.

Fortini also notes of the young man who dreamed of knightly honor:
"Perhaps the young merchant son of Pietro Bernardone grieved over nothing

more bitterly than his sin of pride, which the biographers defined as his 'greed for glory.' " Since all forms of class are sustained by power, which, in turn, is nurtured and revealed in pride, it is not surprising when Fortini also notes that pride became the organizing principle "on which all factions will find they can agree. It will be the basis of a pact in 1210, in which all [previously conflicted parties] will swear to act together for the grandeur of the commune and the power of all the citizens, *pro honore et salute et augmento Comunis Assisi.*"[4]

The pact of 1210 may have been signed in the hopes of stopping wars, as had happened with the old agreement of 1203. However, when the same attitudes remain, something written on paper will not have the power to change them. Consequently, because Assisi's historical classism merely experienced a cosmetic change, the underlying stance of needing arms to protect the structured difference remained. Fortini notes:

> The two social classes remained armed, one against the other. The *maiores* are against the *minores,* the nobles against the people, the *milites* against the *pedites.* The feudal lords, who have been vanquished in the country and been forced to come into the city, do not renounce combat. The dualism remains, the formulae appears empty abstractions, the ancient quarrel, determined by pride and wealth, becomes ever sharper.[5]

Francis' Choice of a Classless Society under God the Father in Heaven

Since the phenomenon of Francis of Assisi has come to represent an archetype of the way one who has been assimilated into a culturally conditioned and religiously sanctioned form of violence is able to make a clear break from it with the modeling of a nonviolent alternative, Arnoldo Fortini makes it clear that anyone studying the way Francis was able to accomplish this countercultural alternative would be right to conclude its origin as a reaction to the classism that infected his world. While the rising merchant class may have supplanted the nobility during the early years of Francis, both were characterized by an arrogance grounded in class differences. As Fortini succinctly explains: "The Franciscan movement came into being as a reaction to that class war and to the conditions prevailing in Assisi at the time of Francis's youth."[6]

Given the endemic social division of his society, Francis never directly confronted its beneficiaries (who were also its perpetrators); instead he consciously opted for its victims: the *paupers* and the *minores*. In the process, he modeled a new way to live in the world that would be putting the Gospel into practice in a way that would make the "Gospel story" more compelling than the social dynamics found in the "church's story" or his "culture's story" (as though church and culture at that time had stories that were different!). In this sense Leonhard Lehmann is correct when he writes:

> This much is clear: social reform or political theories did not play a decisive role in his departure from the world. The inspiration came directly from the Gospel, or, in Francis's words, from the Lord Himself. This fact of course does not exclude the possibility that the social conditions he witnessed in Assisi made him especially receptive to the Gospel call. They provided the negative backdrop against which the positive image of an alternate social order stood out in bold relief, one in which a Gospel-based brotherhood could take shape.[7]

Stanislaus da Campagnola writes, in his "Francis of Assisi and the Social Problems of His Time": "He desired to lift up all classes of people who in whatever way and for whatever reason were suffering from social inferiority. His social ideal and aspiration was not a pauper society, but a leveling and a maximum of equality, marked by the same notion of fraternity which had inspired his religious movement." He notes that Francis' alternative rested in the creation of "a fraternal social model based on the concept of family, in which social differences would not be dictated by riches, power or knowledge."[8] Instead, his family model would be a community of equals under the one Father in heaven. This would find his fraternity serving as an evangelical model of "a classless society, based on a kind of uniformity which would tend to wipe out all differences and inequalities, by overcoming them on a lower, humbler level," da Campagnola writes. Then he concludes that these fraternal dynamics:

> would include not only differences between *majores* and *minores*, lettered and unlettered, clergy and laity, but also every real exercise of power by one person over another. Such a society would be ruled by a hierarchy not of status, but one purely functional or related to service (ministers, guardians, custodians). Its members were to "live in peace with everyone; and toward all without exception they should conduct themselves as lesser ones" and subjects, while awaiting from God "their reward."[9]

It is critical to realize that Francis' vision of his community was a community of equal brothers wherein there would be absolutely no structured hierarchies that separated one group from another, including himself. Indeed, as the original group of twelve made their way to Rome to present their "Gospel" rule of life, Francis—the founder of the group—refused to be its leader. Instead, we have already seen the brothers chose Bernard to be the "vicar" for the fledgling fraternity.[10]

All who followed his Gospel interpretation of life in its various forms were to live as brothers and sisters, equal children of their common Father in heaven. In a further explication of the role of the "Father" in his Trinitarian-type of community — which Francis wanted to model as *evangelical* for the whole world to see — Micó concludes: "The Fatherhood of God, then, means that the Fraternity has been gathered together by the Holy Spirit to follow Christ in doing the will of the Father and that, among other things, it consists in making possible the network of fraternal relationships between equals in which love and solidarity are the normal and fundamental values of our life together (1LtF 1:13)."[11]

While various names identified the newly emerging group of Assisians that stood in stark contrast to the cultural patterns around them ("the brothers of penance," "the delegation of peace"), when it came time to give them a name Francis' choice of a name, as in biblical times, was meant to declare the beginning of certain reality about to be revealed in their way of living. In the flowery way of hagiography prevalent at that time, Celano writes: "He himself originally planted the Order of Lesser Brothers and on the occasion of its founding gave it this name. For when it was written in the Rule, 'Let them be lesser...,' at the uttering of this statement, at the same moment he said, 'I want this fraternity to be called the Order of Lesser Brothers.' "[12]

In contrast to the prevailing feudal power relationships that structured the way of life of the Benedictines, whose Rule even detailed how the monks were to sit in choir in order of rank or seniority,[13] Francis wrote in the Earlier Rule of 1221: "Let no one be called "prior," but let everyone in general be called a lesser brother. Let one wash the feet of the other."[14] This kind of care the brothers were to show each other is evident in the fact that his writings use the word "brother" more than any other: a total of 242 times. That they were to have a unique kind of familiarity is evidenced in an additional fact that, oftentimes, the word is accompanied by adjectives of care such as "my brothers," "my beloved brothers," "my dearest brothers."

In many ways, it seems, Francis was most concerned about abolishing any unequal power relationships, in the name of the Gospel, that existed as much in the ecclesiastical world he had now entered as in the civil world he had left — if not in the world itself, at least in his fraternity. Despite having only the title of "brother" in his fraternity, Francis continually showed respect to the very ones whose way of life he chose not to follow, such as acknowledging their proper titles to those holding ecclesiastical office. While Francis greeted the cardinal of Ostia as "Signore," or Lord, he responded to the cardinal's offer to make the brothers bishops in the Church with an alternative vision of how relationships should be structured in an evangelical way: "My brothers are called 'lesser' so that they will not presume to *become 'greater.'* They have been called this to teach them to stay down to earth, and to *follow the footprints of Christ's* humility, which in the end will exalt them above others in the sight of the Saints."[15]

Lest it be thought that Francis' approach was limited only to reacting against the classism around him, it became clear in his Rule — which he saw as a concretization of the Gospel pattern of life proclaimed by Jesus himself — that he felt called by God to structure an observably different form of life based on equality. As Julio Micó notes: "Francis adopted the fraternal structure for his group because he saw it as a demand of the Gospel. But as well as that, the socio-religious atmosphere of his times influenced him to follow that path and no other." He continues: "His participation in the emergence of Assisi as a free commune of equal citizens had familiarized him with 'horizontal' relationships in contrast with those of the feudal system, which were hierarchical and 'vertical.'"[16]

Micó notes that the new relations Francis found in Assisi were based on a different way of understanding power itself and how God was associated with power. "The whole feudal system was based on the false premise that God had organized society in a hierarchical form, and to change or disrupt that organization would be to go against His will." In realizing that power need not be hierarchical and patriarchal Francis realized that what the Trinitarian God of equal relationships desired was a world that would reflect its Maker; creation would mirror the Triune Creative Power at its heart. Therefore, Micó concludes: "what God really willed was the welfare of all and not just that of a privileged few at the expense of everyone else."[17]

Creating an Evangelical Fraternity
of Equal Power Relations

It is quite clear that Francis had no initial intention of founding a formal religious community. However, when Bernard of Quintavalle and Peter of Cantanio indicated their desire to join in his way of conversion, it seems that he looked around at the pious fraternities that were already in existence in Assisi and the Umbrian valley as a model. These twelfth- and thirteenth-century groups of equality stood side-by-side the hierarchal forms that predominated, just as it was at the time when the Gospel writers tried to describe the incipient Jesus' movement.

What I argued in my *House of Disciples: Church, Economics and Justice in Matthew* and what I hold today is that the First Gospel portrayed Jesus as the one who created a community or "house" within yet alternative to the social arrangements of the imperial structures and religion of his day. This, I argued, could be found in the pivotal passage that serves as the anchor dividing the five main "books" of the Gospel itself. It also proved to be one of the favorite passages used by Francis in his own writings:[18]

> While he was still speaking to the crowds, his mother and his brothers were standing outside [the house], wanting to speak to him. Someone told him, "Look, your mother and your brothers are standing outside, wanting to speak to you." But to the one who had told him this, Jesus replied, "Who is my mother, and who are my brothers?" And pointing to his disciples, he said, "here are my mother and my brothers! For whoever does the will of my Father in heaven is my brother and sister and mother." (Matt. 12:46–50)

As noted before, in the Hebrew scriptures (*bet*) and at the time of the writing of the Gospels, where there was no word for family, the "house" (*oikía/oikos*) served as the basic unit of all social relationships and their organization. The ordering (*nomos*) of the "house" (*oikos, oikía*) constellated around the *persons* involved, the style of their relationships and the way they would (or would not) have access to the resources available. This *oikonomía* (*oikos* + *nomos*) served as the basic economic underpinning of the *polis* or society. The household gods in a hierarchy extending all the way to the imperial household sustained it.

Within the dominant, patriarchal system of households there could also be found parallel, collegial, or more-or-less egalitarian households in loose associations, such as burial societies.[19] Even a cursory reading of Matthew's Gospel supports the thought that, as evidenced in the text of 12:46–50 that serves as the Gospel's pivot, the author was trying to portray Jesus as transferring the notion of "house" from that of the traditional forms around him, including his own family model, to a new group of disciples, freely choosing to associate with him, in a way that would constitute a new community of equals under his heavenly Father. This is clear from the calling of the first four apostles themselves:

As he walked by the Sea of Galilee, he saw two brothers, Simon, who is called Peter, and Andrew his brother, casting a net into the sea — for they were fisherman. And he said to them, "Follow me, and I will make you fish for people." Immediately they left their nets and followed him. As he went from there, he saw two other brothers, James son of Zebedee and his brother John, in the boat with their father Zebedee, mending their nets, and he called them. Immediately they [sons] left [reordering the relationships of their *oikía* consisting of] the boat [resources] and their father [persons], and followed him [into a new *oikía* with its economic and ecclesial implications]. (Matt. 4:18–22)

In other words, from one kind of household and its *oikonomía,* with its religious underpinnings, Jesus invited some of its members to create a new *oikonomía* as well as a new house-based *ekklesía.* Understanding the context in which it was written helps such a reading of not only the Matthean texts noted above, but also of the words from the cross of San Damiano about "repairing the house," which was based on John 19:25–26. In bringing these two texts together, what Francis seems to have created in his alternative community is a new vision of what the whole church could be if it would become truly "evangelical." In the words of the Franciscan historian Joseph Chinnici (who also links the passages from Matthew and John): "What is created here is the fundamental reality of a Church marked by maternal, fraternal and sororal relationships. The image is meant to be a counterweight to other styles of leadership and governance."[20] Showing how Francis wrote in his Earlier Letter to the Faithful about becoming members of this kind of a family under "the Father in heaven," Chinnici concludes, with Fortini, that Francis' vision of a classless society was truly "penitential" in the sense of it being a way of life that truly countered the prevailing culture of classism at that time:

This sense of relational connection — the creation under God of a new kinship group not based on race, property, money, social status and power but on the free consent of anyone who chooses to do penance — permeates the entire vision of Francis and Clare for themselves, their Church and their society. The project of universal kinship stands in stark contrast to the economic and political consortia that dominated Assisi.[21]

The repeated New Testament use of the term *oikos* (112 times) and *oikía* (94 times) indicates the Gospels' and epistles' contextualization within their environment. Historically, "household" and its related terms described the foundation and context of the Christian movement. Religiously, the movement originated in and owed its growth to the conversion of entire households or of certain individuals within households; generally cultic activities like the Eucharist took place in the house. Economically, the household constituted the context for the sharing of resources among co-believers as well as the wandering charismatics. Socially, the household provided a practical basis and theological model for Christian organization as well as its preaching. These various dimensions of "house" help support my contention made years ago that "house" serves as an assumed primary metaphor in the New Testament, especially Matthew.[22]

Not only was it an assumed primary metaphor helping to understand the new kind of social relationships envisioned by Jesus; it helps to understand why the specific form of *oikía* Jesus chose to create would not be that of the hierarchical types around him, all the way to the imperial household itself; rather it would be a more egalitarian group committed to pursuing a new way of living and relating. It would represent a new kinship.

When Francis heard from the cross, "repair my house," I believe an argument can be made, if not from other supporting sources, but from the very dynamics that unfolded, that the way he chose to live in the hierarchical church of unequal power relationships defined by classism and clericalism would be by creating another kind of *oikía,* one that would opt for an across-the-board *minority* status as well as one in whom all priests would be equal to the brothers in authority relationships. It was de-clericalized.

As a young man Francis seemed to belong to a " 'club' or group of young men who used to meet for banquets and other types of entertainment (1C 2; L3S 7), proof that he was attracted to this kind of association, so popular at the time," Micó notes. Thus it would not be surprising, he concludes: "When Francis was converted, his reading of the Gospel was strongly influenced by the social conditioning of his surroundings."[23]

Notwithstanding the support from such ecclesiastical figures as Pope Innocent III, Cardinal John of St. Paul, and Bishop Guido of Assisi, at first, the initial reaction to the new Franciscan movement on the part of many in the clergy was hostile and violent. A good reason can be found in the fact that such clerics — from the local priest to the bishop — were the custodians and teachers of the Gospel. When another group came "proclaiming the Gospel" accompanied by nonhierarchical social relations of equality, it threatened their "evangelical" life. Even though they were not authorized to expound on great theological themes but limited to "ferverinos" by the papal authorization of their way of life, the way they preached by their lives the words that they proclaimed represented a phenomenon that won over many of their subjects. Consequently, Micó explains at some length (and with a universalization that invites greater nuance):

> The official Church reaction to the new Fraternities was always a negative one. Besides denying them any existence in law by not including them in the *Corpus Juris* ("the body of law"), the local authorities acknowledged their presence only to denounce and condemn them for their supposed abuses. The hierarchy's attitude was fundamentally due to their profound mistrust of the Fraternities, which, they believed, were a threat to the whole social and ecclesiastical structure of the time. The Fraternities represented a new concept of power, based on mutual agreement, which made feudal obedience meaningless and obsolete, and which, consequently, could lead to social and economic destabilization. In a hierarchical, "vertical" society, in which every person was bound to superiors and inferiors but with no account being taken of relationships between equals, an oath or promise to help and support one's associates would presuppose and necessitate a solid social organization that would challenge the whole feudal system.[24]

An Authentically and Evangelically "Franciscan" Fraternity

Four key qualities would mark the new "household" of the Franciscan Fraternity. These would separate their way of relating from the institutions, including the religious structures, around them. Three would refer to their internal dynamics and one would characterize how they "went about in the world." The first three involved their form of governance, their day-to-day way of relating, and, especially, the kind of trusting relationships they would have, which, in turn, would impact the governance. The fourth defined how they would go about in the world and be interpreted as authentic or not.

First, regarding the basis for their evangelical brotherhood, Francis made sure it would be characterized as a community of equals within which and from which all governance would be grounded. Francis envisioned his form of authority and obedience, within a very clerical system in the Roman Church, to be "evangelical" to the degree that the brothers would be equal in power. Thus he wrote in the Early Rule:

> Let all the brothers not have power or control...especially among themselves; for, as the Lord says in the Gospel: *The rulers of the Gentiles lord it over them and the great ones make their authority over them felt; it shall not be so among the brothers. Let whoever wishes to*

be the greater among them be their minister and servant. Let whoever is the greater among them become the least.[25]

The ministers (superiors) of the brothers were to be elected among the brothers. All brothers of any rank, as long as they were in their final commitment in the brotherhood, would be eligible; it would make no difference if a brother were ordained a priest in the church or not. Such forms of clericalism, which reserved power to one group over another, represented that kind of classism that Francis rejected as unevangelical.

From this core form of equality actual governance and accountability would take place. As he wrote in the Later Rule, the brothers were entrusted with electing from their own those to whom they would obey "in everything they have promised the Lord to observe" as long as it would not be "against their soul or our Rule." In turn, "the brothers who are the ministers and servants of the others [were to] visit and admonish their brothers and humbly and charitably correct them, not commanding them anything that is against their soul and our rule."[26]

Far from being elected the highest superior and then acting autonomously, Francis made sure that structures would be in place to remove such a person if it were perceived that the brother was not acting in the best interests of the brotherhood. Thus, at the highest level of the Order reserved for the general minister of the Order, who gave obedience to the pope, if it ever would be concluded among "the body of the provincial ministers and custodians that the aforesaid general minister is not qualified for the service and general welfare of the brothers," they would "be bound to elect another as custodian in the name of the Lord."[27]

The second key characteristic of the new community would be recognized in the way the brothers would create their communities among themselves. Rather than being defined by a building or monastery to which they were attached, the attachment of the brothers would be precisely in the fact that they were brothers. Their houses would not be "somewhere" or "some place" but "wherever" and "every place." Consequently their personal relationships would define their community, rather than any place. Francis summarized this vision in the Later Rule in words that have become indelibly marked in the psyches of his followers ever since as the goal they share in common: "Wherever the brothers may be and meet one another, let them show that they are members of the same family. Let each one confidently make known his need to the other, for if a mother loves and cares for her son according to the flesh, how much more diligently must someone love and care for his brother according to the Spirit."[28] Such an ideal seemed to have been genuinely embraced, if we are to believe one of the earliest accounts of Francis and the early brotherhood, *The Anonymous of Perugia:* "They loved one another from the heart and each one served and took care of the other, as a mother serves and cares for her son. The fire of love burned so intensely in them, that they would have willingly sacrificed their lives not only for the name of our Lord Jesus Christ, but also for one another."[29]

Well before modern physics revealed the interrelationship of all previously held forms of materiality, Francis intuited that the heart of everyone, everywhere, and at all times should be determined by the quality of their relationships. These, in turn, should be based on mutuality in meeting each other's needs.

What were these needs that should be expected to be met if the brotherhood were truly living evangelically? Francis did not say. However, as we have broadened our understanding of "need" to be not limited to physical and corporal needs such as health, education, and welfare but to be expanded to the deeper psychological needs such as acceptance, freedom, and respect as well as such spiritual needs as understanding, mercy, and forgiveness, all these "needs" must be met in contemporary forms if the brothers are to experience authentic fraternity within the competing claims of the hierarchical church and capitalist society in which they are called to live out their vocation. Indeed, by the very choice of the word "fraternity" Francis would be called "feminist" today because, as Mary Elizabeth Imler writes: "Interestingly, Francis never uses the word 'community.' He always uses the word *fraternitas.* What a fascinating word this is: it's a feminine one used to describe a male relationship. It describes a nurturing, caring experience in a male relationship. It's more intimate than being friends. It's what we're called to bring forth as brothers and sisters in Christ."[30]

While Francis may not have defined the "needs" that had to be met in his *fraternitas* wherever the brothers might find each other, within this context of meeting needs he did make it clear that there were three categories of brothers with special needs that demanded the concern of the friars as a whole: the sick, those with shortcomings, and those discovered to be "sinners."[31]

In the same passage where Francis talked about the mandate to have the brothers relate to each other in ways that would meet their needs, he gives special mention to those who might fall sick: "the other brothers must serve him as they would wish to be served themselves."[32] In Francis' mind, it was so important that the brothers serve the sick, that, if the necessity arose, even though money was to be refused, a possible mitigation could be made by the highest superiors if the needs of the sick so demanded it. In this case money could be used to take care of them; it just could not be received. It was a technicality that indicated Francis' willingness to bend when it came to those who were sick. With this understanding Francis wrote in the Later Rule:

> I strictly command all my brothers not to receive coins or money in any form, either personally or through intermediaries. Nevertheless, the ministers and custodians alone may take special care through their spiritual friends to provide for the needs of the sick and the clothing of the others according to places, seasons and cold climates, as they judge necessary, saving always that, as stated above, they do not receive coins or money.[33]

The second group of brothers inviting the whole community to be responsive included those who had evident shortcomings. These shortcomings were not those defined as such by the social categories of society, such as the fact that one had been poor or marginated before entering the Order. No, the shortcomings were of the type of disabilities that kept them from showing mutual care and concern for one another, always trying to overcome those obstacles that might otherwise divide them. Thus, in a beautiful admonition developed around the subjunctive words: "Let them," Francis wrote in the Earlier Rule:

> Let all the brothers be careful not to slander or engage in disputes; let them strive, instead, to keep silence whether God gives them the grace. Let them not quarrel among themselves or with others but strive to respond humbly, saying: *I am a useless servant*. Let them not become angry because *whoever is angry with his brother is liable to judgment; whoever says to his brother "fool" shall be answerable to the Council; whoever says "fool" will be liable to fiery Gehenna.*
>
> Let them love one another, as the Lord says: *This is my commandment: love one another as I have loved you.* Let them express the love they have for one another by their deeds, as the Apostle says: *Let us not love in word or speech, but in deed and truth.*
>
> *Let them revile no one.* Let them not grumble or detract from others, for it is written: *Gossips* and *detractors* are *detestable* to God. Let them be *modest by showing graciousness toward everyone.* Let them not judge or condemn. As the Lord says, let them not consider the least sins of others; instead, let them reflect more upon their own sins *in the bitterness of their soul.* Let them struggle *to enter through the narrow*

gate, for the Lord says: *The gate is narrow and the road that leads to life constricted; those who find it are few.*[34]

The third group of brothers demanding special care was those recognized as sinners by the brotherhood in certain matters. If any brother would seriously sin "in regard to those sins concerning which it has been decreed among the brothers to have recourse only to the provincial ministers," the erring brothers were to go to those ministers "as quickly as possible and without delay," knowing, from what we have said before, that they would be treated with kindness. Indeed, the Later Rule demanded as much from those ministers. They were to invite them to penance "with a heart full of mercy." Furthermore, the ministers were to "be careful not to be angry or disturbed at the sin of another" because, Francis reasoned such anger would undermine the integrity of the communal bonds: anger and disturbance impede charity in themselves and in others.[35]

The uniquely "Franciscan" character regarding the way of relating among the brothers that would find them meeting (and, thereby, fulfilling) each other's needs revolved around *trust:* "Wherever" a brother would meet another, he was to "confidently make known his need to the other." This is what confidence means in this context: a style of relating among the brothers that would find them sharing their needs with each other in a way that was based on trust that those needs would be met, making each brother assume responsibility for the other. This is the third unique quality of an evangelical fraternity as envisioned by Francis.

Years before the word "psychology" would characterize the study of persons or "sociology" would be recognized as the study of communal dynamics, Francis realized that all healthy relationships, especially those geared to the development of intimacy, must be grounded on trust. This trust would be developed within a fraternity whose members showed care for each other in such a way that they could "confidently make known their needs." Confidence, any counselor will tell us, is the characteristic of a community of care. Trust must be the earmark of its members' relationships. Without trust and trustworthiness in a relationship there will only be individualism. Trust is the bridge that must be built between the two poles of individualism and obedience if we are to find new ways of communal commitment. Without trust among persons in a relationship, commitment will be compromised and faith in the community itself will erode. Trust is the glue of every committed relationship. If the brothers would not find ways to "confidently make known to each other their needs" the community itself would not survive.

As I "see" the Fraternity-Become-the Order, it seems to me that the only way we will be able to "repair" this *house* which has become overly defined by our individualism is by dreaming and developing Francis' original insights about the way we are to relate to each other in a model generative and expressive of trust. Indeed, given the institutionalization of the original charism, it will only be by creating such "envelopes of care" or "holding environments," to use the images of Donald Winnicott,[36] that we will be able to evidence the kind of freely given trust that will define us embracing this as our "new obedience" rather than institutionalized forms that often deny our God-given freedom and individuality.

Assuming that such characteristics would define their lives with each other in fraternity, Francis also exhorted the brothers to go about the world in a way that would be nonviolent and peace-filled at all times. When they would go about, he wrote, they should not ride horseback — a symbol connected to those who were the *majores*. Rather, he wrote: "I counsel, admonish, and exhort my brothers in the Lord Jesus Christ not to quarrel or argue or judge others when they go about in the world; but let them be meek, peaceful, modest, gentle, and humble, speaking courteously to everyone, as is becoming."[37]

I am increasingly convinced that, grounded in the trusting relationships that ensured the meeting of the friars' physical and psychological needs as well as their religious and spiritual needs, the contagious character of the early Franciscan community revolved around the way they were perceived by "the world" precisely in the manner described by Francis above. In addition to these characteristics, we have seen (and will discuss further in chapter 11), their joy would also contribute to the contagious quality of their way of life that would be so invitational to so many people of every kind of sex, class, and grouping. Because of these characteristics, the growth of the movement was phenomenal.

Within a decade of its founding, the original group of twelve friars who journeyed to Rome for approval of their evangelical way of life had grown to five thousand when the Chapter of 1219 took place. At this Chapter Cardinal Hugolino, at the instigation of those provincial leaders who never really embraced Francis' vision of the evangelical life linked to poverty, penance, and peace, tried to persuade him to revert to one of the traditional Rules from Augustine, Bernard, or Benedict. Taking the cardinal by the hand he led him into the Chapter "and spoke to the brothers in this way: 'My brothers! My brothers! God has called me by the way of simplicity and showed me the way of simplicity. I do not want you to mention to me any *Rule*, whether of St. Augustine, or of St. Bernard, or of St. Benedict. And the Lord told me what He wanted . . . "[38] This egalitarian dream would be dashed at a subsequent Chapter after Francis died. The Chapter of Narbonne (1260) legislated in its Constitution for the Order the clericalization that has come to define its structure to the present time. Without special permission lay brothers would no longer be allowed to hold office.

Earlier, in 1212, when he was thirty and she was eighteen, Clare Offreduccio, the daughter of a noble family of Assisi, ran away from home. Connecting with Francis at the Portiuncula, he cut off her hair as a sign of her commitment to Christ. From there she went on to found a parallel group of women who also would not be defined by male categories but by that divine inspiration that would find them embracing their own form of the evangelical life, even if it meant they would remain in monasteries. Their first permanent home would be San Damiano, in expanded quarters prepared for them by their Franciscan brothers. Her group as well would expand, even in her lifetime, well beyond the Alps.

The third group to be founded as "Franciscan" were the seculars themselves. As seems evident in Francis' two "Letters to the Faithful," as well as in his Earlier Rule, where he mentions the different types of people apart from the friars and Clares who embraced his Gospel way of life, such people discovered they did not need to become celibates as were the Little Brothers and the Poor Ladies; they could live the Gospel by remaining not only in their homes but in their own unique professions. Their entrance into the *Ordo Poenitentium* would be marked by their very different way of living in the world in such a joyful way that their very embrace of the penitential life would be contagious.

In an extended passage (and with the flowery language characteristic of that time) Celano notes how, within a very short time, the way of life of the brothers became contagious: soon all sorts of people were finding the evangelical way of life fit for their way of living:

> Francis, Christ's bravest soldier, went around the cities and
>   villages,
> proclaiming the kingdom of God
> and preaching peace and penance for the remission of sins,
> not in the persuasive words of human wisdom but in the
>   learning and power of the Spirit . . .
>
> Men ran, women also ran, clerics hurried, and religious rushed
>   to see and hear
> the holy one of God, who seemed to everyone a person of
>   another age.

People of all ages and both sexes hurried to behold the wonders
which the Lord worked anew in the world through his servant...
Thus, in a short time, the appearance of the entire region was
changed and,
Once rid of its earlier ugliness, it revealed a happier expression
everywhere...
Many people, well-born and lowly, cleric and lay, driven by
divine inspiration,
began to come to St. Francis,
for they desired to serve under his constant training and
leadership...
He is without question an outstanding craftsman [of the Gospel],
for through his spreading message,
The Church of Christ is being renewed in both sexes
according to his form, rule, and teaching,
and there is victory for the triple army of those being saved.
Furthermore, to all he gave a norm of life
and to those of every rank he sincerely pointed out the way
of salvation.[39]

A Creation Community Constituting All as Brothers and Sisters

For Francis, real fraternity had to extend beyond the borders defined by the brotherhood. As Celano notes: "He used to call all creatures by the name of 'brother' and 'sister' and in a wonderful way, unknown to others, he could discern the *secrets of the heart* of creatures like someone who has already passed *into the freedom of the glory of the children of God*." Thus, he writes: "Fields and vineyards, rocks and woods, and all *the beauties of the field*, flowing springs and blooming gardens, earth and fire, air and wind: all these he urged to love of God and to willing service."[40]

According to Micó, the reason why Francis was able to treat everyone and everything quite equally as brothers and sisters came from his realization that we all have a common origin — the loving care of God:

It even broke human barriers; it extended to more than persons.
Things, as well as people, come from the hands and heart of God and,
therefore, are related to people. God, One in Three, is the Creator of all
things, spiritual and material, but especially of men and women, who
are made in His image and likeness (RegNB XXIII). Francis knew that

everything comes from God and is kept in existence by His creative love or providence, as we call it. Those who came to the Fraternity to share his life were brothers whom the Lord had given him (Test 14). All Christians and everyone on earth were his brothers and sisters whom he had to serve (2EpFid 1:2), while all other creatures were also a gift, and they, too, were his brothers and sisters (CantSol).[41]

Francis' cosmic consciousness led him to dethrone himself as the center of creation. He moved from being a self-possessed individual around whom the world revolved and whose world owed him a living to seeing himself as just one creature in the midst of all creation, under one heavenly source that had been revealed in Jesus Christ. Such a cosmic consciousness made him connected to the Christ and all creation in a way that not only made him "universal"; it led him to feel a part of everyone in a way that everyone could claim him as their own.

Furthermore, there also was a certain quality that he brought to his cosmic-connectedness and his Christic-consciousness: the quality of compassion. He could not be at peace if he knew anyone or anything suffered need or had been victimized in any way. Thus Celano would write: "The holy man overflowed with the spirit of charity, bearing within himself a deep sense of concern not only toward other humans in need but also toward mute, brute animals: reptiles, birds, and all other creatures whether sensate or not."[42] Francis' compassion made him feel the pain of Christ Crucified as well as the anguish of another who felt humiliated. It led him to identify with both in a way that would further the work of redemption itself.

Francis' Kind of Fraternity
as an Antidote to the "American Way"

In 2005 both the *Wall Street Journal* and the *New York Times* featured a series of articles on the issue of "class" in the United States of America. The fact is significant that both papers, one perceived to be conservative and the other liberal, saw it as "news" that the division between rich and poor was real and serious enough that they should run a series about the problem. That they saw this as "news" was news in itself.

The title for the *Wall Street Journal* series on the growing class divide among U.S. citizens was: "Challenges to the American Dream." In that series, as well as in subsequent features, headlines declared the division loudly and clearly: "As Rich-Poor Gap Widens in the U.S., Class Mobility Stalls"[43] and "Wage Winners and Losers: Most Paychecks Fell in 2004."[44]

The *New York Times* series, "Class Matters,"[45] had eleven different articles. The clear message was that class affects our jobs, our income, our homes, and our health. It influences whom we marry, where we live (including which zip code will say more about who we are), and what we buy. In effect, class defines us in ways that we never believed nor could have imagined. Of the powerful articles included in the series, the most devastating for me, was the ninth. The main headline declared: "Richest Are Leaving Even the Rich Far Behind." The sub-headline declared why this had occurred: "Tax Laws Help to Widen Gap at Very Top." The article showed in graphs that the "share of the nation's income earned by the taxpayers in the top 0.1 percent has more than doubled since the 1970s, and in the year 2000 exceeded 10 percent, a level last seen in the 1920s."[46] This led Paul Krugman, a *Times* columnist, to write:

> As The Times's series on class in America reminds us the middle class society no longer exists...The wealthy have done very well indeed. Since 1973 the average income of the top 1 percent of Americans has doubled, and the income of the top 0.1 percent has tripled...Above all, the partisans engage in name-calling. To suggest that sustaining programs like Social Security, which protects working Americans from economic risk, should have priority over tax cuts for the rich is to practice "class warfare." To show concern over the growing inequality is to engage in the "politics of envy."[47]

Meanwhile the *Wall Street Journal*'s series made it clear, as did that in the *Times,* that it is no longer a simple case of the "rich are getting richer and the poor are getting poorer" in the United States. Indeed, while there is no doubt that the rich are getting richer, the poor are becoming less poor. Furthermore the rich are getting richer, not so much at the expense of the poor, but at the expense of the middle class that is rapidly decreasing into the ranks of the poor. Meanwhile, because of the previously discussed myth that perpetuates the "narrative of the lie" controlling their psyches, the middle class refuses to accept its fate. Its ever decreasing numbers still believe they are doing well, even as the other two groups, relatively speaking, are doing better and they are falling into the ranks of the poor faster than the ranks of the rich are rising. According to the *Journal:*

> Many Americans believe their country remains a land of unbounded opportunity. That perception explains why Americans, much more

than Europeans, have tolerated the widening inequality in recent years. It is OK to have ever-greater differences between rich and poor, they seem to believe, as long as their children have a good chance of grasping the brass ring.

Why are so many being duped? The *Journal*'s series made it abundantly clear: there's a myth that is being exploited by those who would benefit from it not being challenged. Key among these are the politicians (who, in turn, the *Journal* did not say, have campaigns largely financed by the corporations most bound to lose if laws are changed to benefit the average American rather than themselves): "This continuing belief shapes American politics and economic policy. Technology, globalization, and unfettered markets tend to erode wages at the bottom and lift wages at the top. But Americans have elected politicians who oppose using the muscle of government to restrain the forces of widening inequality."[48]

The politicians who are elected not only oppose governmental efforts to restrain the forces of widening equality, they actually do the opposite. Indeed, an analysis of congressional votes and other data shows that, for the past century, political polarization and economic inequality have moved hand in hand. The political polarization was able to reach its apogee in the terrible aftermath of September 11, 2001. Exploiting the fear of terrorism and faith in "Americanism," economic policies were created that favored a narrow elite of the people. In the effort to keep average people from realizing that this was being done at their expense, as Paul Krugman wrote in a column called "Class War Politics," the party that benefited from these social arrangements successfully accused "the other party of being unpatriotic and godless."[49]

A concrete example of this leapt from the pages of the *Wall Street Journal* shortly after it and the *New York Times* featured their respective series on "class." On page 2, two articles spelled out clearly the problem. At the top, one headline read: "Recovery Bypasses Many Americans: Despite Economic Growth, Median Household Income and Wages Fell Last Year."[50] Below, in a smaller column (almost showing an embarrassment at what it would discuss), another article noted: "Study Finds CEO Pay Has Soared since 2001." Of particular interest to me was the statement from the findings of the Institute for Policy Studies it highlighted: "In 2004, chief executive officers made 431 times as much as the average worker. This is up from a 301–1 ratio in 2001."[51] In 1982 the ratio was 42–1. Around the rest of the industrialized world, the ratio is closer to 25–1. This reinforces in a negative way the American mind-set of it being the greatest: indeed it has the greatest disparity between the top executives and the workers who create the wealth than any other nation.

There is a particularly clear face revealing the reality of the true underclass in the United States. Despite its absence from the psyche of the nation, this face became revealed corporately for the world to see during Hurricane Katrina and its aftermath in New Orleans in 2005. As we read our morning papers, watched the evening news, and surfed the Internet in between, it became increasingly clear that the face of poverty and the underclass in the United States is black. As one columnist stated: "If September 11 showed the power of a nation united in response to a devastating attack, Hurricane Katrina exposed the fault lines of a region — and a nation — rent by profound social divisions."[52] However, despite seeing this face of poverty so starkly and the racial class divide it revealed, another statistic indicated another ideological divide between blacks and whites regarding the aftermath of Katrina. By three to one, African Americans believed that federal aid took so long to arrive in New Orleans in part because the city was poor and black. By an equally large margin, whites disagreed.[53]

What we find in the United States is replicated globally. For instance, the 2005 UN Report on Human Development (09.10.05) noted that "every hour poverty kills 1,200 children" and that "the rich and poor divergence increases": "The 500 wealthiest men earn all together more than the 416 million poorest people in the world."

While researchers have in recent years described limits to class mobility in the United States and decried the growing wage gap among Americans, things are much worse south of the border[54] and in other developing nations, especially those in Africa, the underside of the global economy. Its poverty is endemic due to many factors, including the residue of former colonialism and present corrupt regimes, deforestation and drought, superstition and secrecy.

This stark scene was well visualized in a political cartoon I saw as I was writing this book. In the place of George Washington on a U.S. dollar bill a face of a starving black child, bowl in hand, looks out with deeply sunk eyes. Above the dollar bill is the caption: "Half the World's People Live on Less than $2 a day..." Below the bill it says: "...And We Wonder Why the World Has Problems?"[55]

NINE

Nonpossessiveness

Lord, if we had any possessions, we would need arms to protect them because they cause many disputes and lawsuits. And possessions usually impede the love of God and neighbor. Therefore we do not want to possess anything in this world.[1]

—St. Francis of Assisi, quoted in
The Anonymous of Perugia, 3.17

How Francis Recognized
the Violence Inherent in Conflicts over Property

From his earliest years, Francis had seen one group after another fighting with each other. Invariably, he discovered, these conflicts revolved around different expectations and assumptions, opposing claims and counterclaims associated with one thing: property. Hence there were wars between Islam and Christianity over the Holy Land; Holy Roman emperors and popes competing for territory; cities battling with each other over land; pitched battles between the entrenched noble class and the rising merchant class over property. Even the battles Francis had with his father ultimately took place because of Francis' failure to measure up to his father's expectations about the way the family business should be run — about making money.

Arnold Fortini, the mayor of Assisi-turned-biographer of Francis, writes that these same dynamics were in play in the conflicts occurring in and around Assisi at the time of Francis where war was "the very life of the commune":

Thus the principal explanation for the conflict of peoples was their opposing material desires. "The political economy governed all the battles. Its calculations measured the anger, dispersed the furors, ruled over those unfathomable psychic currents that unleashed multitudes of Italians, one against another. These struggles were all subordinated to the income and expenditures, the debit and the credit, the capital and the speculations, of the merchants who chose the consuls."[2]

Fortini also notes that, when previously warring groups found reason to come together, the reason was invariably because the resolution of their conflicts would promote economic gain for both:

> It is clear that in the struggle between the two social classes of Assisi the pact of 1203 is nothing, after all, but an agreement to join together for the conquest of material gain, to the detriment of other classes and other people. "And thus we say that all the citizens of Assisi must help each other maintain all their goods and their things and their rights and their way of life and possessions that they have and that they shall acquire . . . " It does not, as is often taught, deal with an ideological movement. It is purely economic. "And whoever, noble or other person, of our city is entitled to collect revenues or whatever else from another city or *castello* or from any man outside our jurisdiction, all the people of the city are bound to help him come into possession of it."

The battles waged by religions like Islam and Christianity, and within Christendom between Holy Roman Emperor and pope and even among townspeople and their priests seemed to everyone to be incessant. Conflicts over property were a way of life. Even in Assisi, Francis watched one of the parish priests seemingly more preoccupied with keeping his property than serving the people. Fortini writes of him:

> The priest of San Giacomo, Domino Egidio, who held the investiture all during Francis's lifetime, was continually before the consuls, be-cause of quarrels with greedy neighbors who gathered and took away his olives or to draft documents of acknowledgement and donation or to complain of robbers whom he cursed and chased with shouts and stones. The huge orchard that the church owned within the ancient wall, rich with fruit and plants, was not enough for him. He laid claim to the walls of houses that had been destroyed, to abandoned lands, to slopes on the borders.[3]

All these wars, conflicts and disputes, in Francis' eyes, came about for one reason and one reason alone: the desire for money and property. Thus his almost obsessive insistence on not having property. If his brothers were to proclaim the gospel of peace, they could not have the main obstacle to peace among people interfering with that proclamation: consequently the brothers were not to have property in any form lest they have to take up arms to protect it.

The same underlying recognition that violence was often linked to conflicting claims related to property led Francis to write in the Earlier Rule: "Wherever the brothers may be, either in hermitages or other places, let them be careful not to make any place their own or contend with anyone for it."[4] Contentiousness involves conflicting claims around issues of power, property, and prestige. The development of his countercultural way of dealing with these issues would be the concrete way Francis would "withdraw" from the world of violence around him and, with his followers, offer the world another vision of how to live as equals, as minors, in society. Because "Francis and his brothers were keenly aware of the vicious cycles of violence which permeated medieval society," Michael Cusato writes, "this refusal to resort to violence in defense of their places also implied the rejection of *all* forms of violence."[5]

Francis' Response to the Tendency to Be Possessive: Nonappropriation

If everything around him spoke of people's effort to appropriate more and more property and possessions, Francis' countercultural response would result in him legislating an alternative economic model, a fraternal economy. It would be based on fraternal trust among the brothers and a covenant between the brothers and their benefactors that would keep all from being conflicted in any way. While some of the dynamics of this *oikonomía,* along with its implications for almsgiving in a way that would restructure the *oikoumēne* for the integrity of the *oikología* were developed in chapter 3, this chapter will concentrate on three key points that were to characterize the friars' evangelical way of life as one "without property."

Chapter 4 of the Later Rule mandated that the brothers were "not to receive coins or money in any form, either personally or through intermediaries." Chapter 5 of the same showed that the ordinary way the brothers were to make their living would be by the "grace of working," for which they could "receive whatever is necessary for the bodily support of themselves and their brothers, excepting coin or money." Finally, in chapter 6 of the Rule he laid down clearly what this way of nonappropriation would entail and how the brothers should then go about in the world. "Let the brothers not make anything their own, neither house, nor place, nor anything at all."[6]

Francis' Alternative to Possessiveness: Nonacceptance of Coin or Money

At one time, when society revolved around what was known as a "gift economy," money was either hoarded or buried with the dead; it had no meaning in itself. Then, with the rise of the "money economy," things changed, especially attitudes toward money. Once money became the key medium of exchange, it worked its way into every type of human activity and transaction. Lester K. Little writes that, while the "keystone of feudal government was the personal agreement between lord and vassal to exchange protection for advice and military support," by the "early twelfth century, this personal agreement began to be replaced by a money payment."[7]

From Carolingian times through the time Francis was born the only type of coin in existence was the silver penny. As in biblical times, it was called a *denarius* or a penny. A pound consisted of 240 pennies, although there was no coin called a pound; the word represented how much 240 denarii weighed. At the turn of the century Venice minted the first silver coin that was larger than a penny, the *grossus denarius*.[8] To use a play on words, Francis would soon discover it truly was more "gross" than a denarius.

For centuries in the feudal society, it was not surprising that pride would be considered the chief capital sin; because pride flowed from power and its abuse, this would be understandable. Avarice was considered a subset of pride. However, with the rise of money as a means of exchange in the eleventh century, according to Lester Little, reformers like "Peter Damian heralded a significant change when stating unequivocally: 'Avarice is the root of all evil.' Peter advised the archbishop of his native city of Ravenna in 1043 that avarice was the most serious problem in the church at that time."[9]

In the twelfth century, the one in which Francis was born, Marbod of Rennes wrote a poem, "De nummo" (Of the Coin), in which he showed that money had become power itself; now greed and avarice trumped pride and power. Its power had captured everyone:

> Monk and senate, prince and prelate,
> Layman, cleric, mistress, man,
> Give them what you like, they'll sell it,
> Get good money if they can.
> Money! He's the whole world's master,
> His the voice that makes men run:
> Speak! Be quiet! Slower! Faster!
> Money orders — and it's done.[10]

At the time of Francis in Italy money came in two forms of coins: *pecunia grossa*, "strong money," because it contained silver, was the "coin of the ruling classes"; the other was *pecunia piccolae*, "weak money," not only because it had been debased of value in itself but because of the lesser worth the money of the poor had compared to the money of the rich. Michael Cusato notes that, as a result, "the poor, in other words, were at the mercy and the whims and wiles of the powerful. Money was a pernicious instrument of the exploitation of the weak in society."[11]

Francis had witnessed what such an approach to money had done in his own family. In his father's drive to make more and more money, Francis found someone becoming increasingly alienated from the values he had begun to cultivate, especially in his concern to use money for the needs of the poor and the repair of dilapidated churches. The final break with his father came when Pietro Bernardone went to "small claims court" before the bishop demanding the return of the monies gained by the sale of his cloth and horse. This certainly had to contribute to Francis' almost abhorrence of "coin or money" in any form. He saw what it had done to his father; he would have none of it. Neither would he even allow his brothers the merest possibility of coming into contact with it. In his mind, money corrupted. To the degree the friars' economic activity mirrored the underlying pattern of the market, it would destroy the original dream. Now, eight hundred years after the dream began, its followers have become highly versed in negotiating salaries and working with investment counselors to ensure the proper returns to keep solvent. Too often, money itself has now come to define our Franciscan identity much more clearly than the dream itself.

Francis and the Grace of Working

A second way Francis offered an alternative economic model was by prescribing something for all the brothers that the Benedictines had restricted only to the lay members of the community: work. Far from being seen by Francis as something demanded because of original sin, he viewed work as a grace that linked all humans to their Creator, who was originally revealed in the work of creation itself. Thus he wrote: "Those brothers to whom the Lord has given the grace of working may work faithfully and devotedly so that, while avoiding idleness, the enemy of the soul, they do not extinguish the Spirit of holy prayer and devotion to which all temporal things must contribute."[12] In his evangelically grounded community, work would be the great equalizer; it would be classless and its remuneration would be the same for all: "whatever is necessary for the bodily support of themselves and their brothers."

As he sculpted his policy toward labor, "the grace of working" involved a *why* (to avoid idleness), a *who* (inclusive of all the brothers to such a degree that those [presumably the clerics] who did not know how to work had to learn), as well as a *how*. On the one hand the "how" demanded that they work faithfully and devotedly; on the other hand, the "how" stated that it be done in such a way that those who worked would never "extinguish the Spirit of holy prayer and devotion to which all temporal things must contribute." It is this latter dimension that offered the friars of his day as well as people of our day a truly countercultural approach to work. It grounds all work in a meditative stance of mindfulness that puts everything in its proper relatedness.

In his wonderful book *The Left Hand of God,* based on many interviews with people throughout the United States, Michael Lerner discovered that more and more people talked about the way work has become purely utilitarian and workers have become equally utilitarian. Consequently they talked about the way work had been cheapened as had workers themselves. Where once it seems work was considered a way of life if not an actual calling based on "a higher mission or purpose, work became vulgar or debased."[13] Furthermore, what Lerner and his associates discovered, was that work no longer was a "grace"; it actually had led "to a general psychological depression permeating the workforce that was better described in spiritual than in psychological terms." In other words, the way work is done today is not energizing the spirit of prayer and devotion; it is actually deenergizing. He concluded:

> This spiritual depression is characterized by a sense of loneliness or alienation, a feeling that we are not really being recognized or dealt with in an authentic way, a feeling that our deepest life energies are being depleted or at best have been put to sleep temporarily, a loss of awareness of the beauty and holiness that surrounds us, a sense that our world is filled with meaningless activity and is lacking in love and joy, a sense that, rather than expressing our inner being, we and others are going through mechanical motions that have been imposed upon us by an outside force.[14]

For Francis work was not a necessity occasioned by any outside force or even by original sin; rather it identified the worker as an *imago Dei.* As such it involved an outpouring of divine grace in the one who so works. Bringing the attitude of nonappropriation or true poverty into the way they approached their work, the brothers were not even to claim compensation for what they did; rather than embracing an attitude of entitlement, they were to humbly accept whatever would be given them, as long as it was not money.

Returning to the way the friars were to work mindfully or in a way that would not extinguish the spirit of prayer and devotion to which all things must be subservient, such an approach itself would also ground all work in grace. The "mindful" way the brothers were to work was graced insofar as the way the work was done would be grounded in a sense of prayer and devotedness. As Leonhard Lehmann describes it so well:

> Together with its evident solidarity with the poor, work for the friars took on the quality of divine worship, as expressed in the words: "in the spirit of [holy prayer] and devotion." Honest work does not erect a barrier between the laborer and God. *Ora et labora* ("pray and work") was the watchword for the Benedictines, but Francis seemed to have associated prayer and work even more closely. In any case, the priority of contemplation must be respected, whether the friars are working with their hands or mind. "Sanctification of the world through work," expresses their ideal succinctly. "Work for the Franciscan took on a sacral character, and therefore always had a cosmic dimension."[15]

In his *Testament* Francis embraced the approach to work found in the scriptures. Paul notes this from a meeting he had with the representatives of the church of Ephesus: "I coveted no one's silver or gold or clothing. You know for yourselves that I worked with my own hands to support myself and my companions. In all this I have given you an example that by such work we must support the weak, remembering the words of the Lord Jesus, for he himself said, 'It is more blessed to give than to receive'" (Acts 20:33–35). Bound by this way of "making a living," Francis offered his own example of being a worker as a model for the way the brothers should earn their living — not like clerics but like the laypeople whose lives were defined by work:

> And *I worked with* my *hands,* and I still desire to work; and I earnestly desire all brothers to give themselves to honest work. Let those who do not know how to work learn, not from desire to receive wages, but for example and to avoid idleness. And when we are not paid for our work, let us have recourse to the table of the Lord, begging alms from door to door. The Lord revealed a greeting to me that we should say: *"May the Lord give you peace."*[16]

In Francis' understanding, an economy based on evangelical principles begins with work; however, if what is necessary for the well-being of the friars would not be forthcoming, the friars should experience no embarrassment if they have to beg. Indeed, in the Matthean version of the Gospel text that originally inspired Francis wherein Jesus tells his followers that they should "take nothing for their journey" as they go to proclaim the "good news" of the reign of God and its gospel of peace, we read two nuances that put another "spin" on why Francis might have found begging to be a natural consequence of the failure to get adequate recompense for work. First of all, they were not to charge for their preaching: "You received without payment; give without payment" (Matt. 10:8b). Second, however (which is more to the point of Francis' vision of an evangelical economy), the followers of Jesus (and of Francis) were to "take no gold, or silver, or copper in our belts, no bag for your journey, or two tunics, or sandals, or a staff" precisely because "laborers deserve their food" (Matt. 10:9–10). In other words, as they entered the various *oikías* with their gospel of peace, the fact that those in the house would be receiving them would assure them their basic needs would be met. This economic ordering of resources would bring about an evangelical *oikonomía* that grounded in a mutual sharing the resources that might be needed. Grounded in such an economic order, the gospel of peace would find a worthy reception. And, if the laborers were not paid directly, asking alms from door-to-door, along with the gospel of peace, would be justified insofar as it would be another way of paying for the work of preaching the Gospel being done by the brothers.

Francis' Response to Materialism: Nonappropriation

After insisting the brothers not receive coin or money in any form, either as gifts or as payment for working, and then discussing the "grace of working" itself, Francis developed the rest of chapter 6 in the Later Rule around two other themes: one negative and one positive. First, they were not to "make anything their own, neither house, nor place, nor anything at all"; this has come to be called "nonappropriation." Second, from this countercultural stance of conversion, they were to create another economic model based on the meeting of each other's needs rather than their wants.

By requiring his followers to embrace a life of nonappropriation of anything upon entering the new community, Francis created an alternative society. No longer would property claims create the divisions between the haves and the have-nots, the *majores* and the *minores*. To become a Friar

Minor demanded the relinquishment of all the wealth that might even hint that one might be a *major;* instead they were told to give what they had to the poor. This would be Francis' way of almsgiving.

By such almsgiving, the newly recruited would contribute to a new order of justice. This may be precisely why Julian of Speyer would note that, before his conversion, Francis may have been "very rich in passing wealth, but poor *in the works of* justice."[17] It also may explain why Celano would define Bernard of Quintavalle's way of disposing his wealth as alms to the poor as a "conversion to God [that] stood out as a model for those being converted in the way he sold his possessions and distributed them to the poor."[18] At the same time, if having done what they could with their resources to create the new order of justice, by joining the new community, if none of the members possessed anything, then there would be economic equality and if there would be economic equality they could be equal brothers.

First of all, the friars were not to appropriate "anything" to themselves. While Francis articulated in this text itself material things such as a "house" and a "place," as well as "anything at all," it is clear from his personal life and his writing that the "nothing" appropriated had to go far beyond material things that were property related.

If economists consider property to be just one form of wealth, Francis was talking not just about property. By living *sine proprio,* their poverty would be a countercultural rejection of wealth in all its forms. Their poverty would affect the way they related to each other and all others with regard to their time, treasure, and talents. While this might include property and other kinds of possessions, it would also include other dimensions of wealth such as power over anyone, especially offices of power. It would also include honors and titles, symbols of prestige, and, above all, the human tendency to pride. When people make their will their "own" in a way that exalts themselves without recognizing the source of their good, they replicate the dynamics of original sin.[19]

In Admonition after Admonition Francis urged his followers to develop a style of life and relating among each other that would be based on non-appropriation of "anything": not just property and possession but power and prestige as well. Ilia Delio, the Franciscan scholar, has summarized succinctly the triad of nonappropriation that became encompassed in Francis' vision of himself and the brothers being *sine proprio:*

Three areas where he speaks of living *sine proprio* are: (1) our inner selves and what we possess for ourselves; (2) our relationships with

others and what we possess in relation to others; and (3) our relationship to God and what we possess in relation to God. In all three areas
Francis asked of his followers to "hold back nothing of yourselves for
yourselves, so that he who gives himself totally to you may receive you
totally."[20]

Second, with all the friars free of property and its allurements, they would
be able to more easily and readily bring about a new economic order based
on *meeting each other's needs* rather than the market economy based on
meeting one's own wants. While I have written about this way of relating
in chapter 8, I would like to highlight the uniqueness of this Franciscan way
of creating a viable economy of other-interest that differentiates it from the
prevailing economic model based on self-interest.

A Fraternal Economy Based on the Brothers' Needs

While the economic patterns of Assisi at Francis' time did not characterize
our full-blown capitalism, the mind-set of the people (as evidenced in his
own father) was becoming ever clearer to Francis: self-interest around property and material goods must trump relationships that had once grounded
trust among disparate peoples. While Adam Smith would not write his opus
on political economy for another five hundred years, the seeds of our present
expression of capitalism were already being sown: "It is not from the benev-
olence of the butcher, the brewer, or the baker, that we expect our dinner,
but from their regard to their own interest. We address ourselves, not to
their humanity but to their self-love, and never talk to them of our own
necessities but of their advantages."[21]

Francis would have none of this; he refused to accept as inevitable any
way of life that would be based on individualism and self-interest. Rather his
economic mind-set would reflect more accurately the altruistic conviction of
Reb David'l of Lelow, who told Rabbi Yitzhak of Vorki:

> Everyone in their innermost heart, even when they don't know it, actu-
> ally wants to do good to other human beings. So everyone who works,
> as a shoemaker or tailor or baker or whatever who serves others, on
> the inside he doesn't do this work in order to make money, but in order
> to do good to his fellow human being — even though he does receive
> money for his trouble, but this is just secondary and unimportant, but
> the inner meaning of his work is that he wants to do good and show
> kindness to his fellow human being.[22]

As the chart below attests, Francis' economic choice of nonappropriation and his demand that the brothers witness to the world another kind of *oikonomía,* the "fraternal economy" offers a way of life that envisions the inbreaking of God's Economic Trinity coming on earth more closely to that which is in heaven.

The fraternal economy in a global economy dominated by the U.S. brand of capitalism:

Oikonomía	Global Capitalism	Economic Theory	Global Poverty	Francis' Vision	Fraternal Economy
Persons	Market share	Competing persons	Marginalization	Where brothers are	Subsidiarity
Relations	Manipulation	Wealth creation	Dependency in wealth distribution	Let them confidently	Solidarity
Resources	Profit: bottom line	Scarce resources	Basic needs	Make known needs	Sustainability

A unique way that this economy would be realized among the brothers, as well as the manner in which they went about seeking alms, would be based on trust. Francis made it clear that, if and when the friars were unable to work or get the support they needed from their work, they should "go seeking alms with confidence." Later in the same chapter 6 he writes: "Wherever the brothers may be and meet one another . . . let each one confidently make known his need to the other."

While I have discussed the notion of "confidence" that was connected with the way the brothers were to entrust their needs to each other, it is interesting that Francis would use the same word, "confidence," in describing how the brothers should interact with their benefactors when they could not find ways to meet their own needs.

Resisting the Ways of Entitlement

A key reason Francis rejected money can be found in the way he saw it take the place of human relationships. His insight remains true today.

In *The Money Culture,* social pundit Michael Lewis argues that what has transpired in the post–World War II world of the United States is that we have moved from being a people of acquisitiveness to become "an entire culture based on entitlement." This has created an "Americanism" wherein the common good has been replaced by a commonplace expectation of individual enrichment even if this is at the expense of other people and the planet itself. In other words, the "American Dream" of freedom and justice for all has become dominated by a kind of liberty that has become equated with entitlement. This has led Herbert Stein, former chair of the President's Council of Economic Advisers in 1972–74, to ask in a 1996 column in the *Wall Street Journal:* "Would it make any difference if instead of 'American dream' we said 'feeling of entitlement to being enriched by the efforts of others'?"

"Entitlements" are not only those programs that, in 2006, constituted 84 cents of every dollar the government spends every day in the form of programs such as Medicare, Medicaid, and Social Security. They also include thirteen thousand projects in 2006 costing $67 billion that are called "earmarks" that are put into the U.S. budget by politicians at the behest of corporate interests.[23] Unlike "entitlements" in other countries, people's rights to these benefits also include the right not to pay for them in the form of taxes. Indeed, another entitlement, especially for the rich, is tax breaks.

What in 2005 represented 84 cents on the dollar, in 1995 represented 61 percent of the federal budget. This dynamic occurred in some part because of the control of those very rich people who have made sure their taxes would be cut, which otherwise would have paid for some of these entitlements. As a result they now receive an even greater amount than those ordinarily identified with "welfare." In 2005, an editorial in *Business Week* declared that the "U.S. entitlement society has run up against a wall." Despite the fact that most citizens may be told of the collision-course that this represents, they were unwilling, the editorial declared, to "ax their own entitlements." Given this resistance to share their resources to promote the common good, the editorial asked (already in 1995!):

> Do they have the grit to return to a 19th century society where local neighbors and churches, and not government, provide social safety nets? We're not betting on it. Will country clubbers be as eager to lose their municipal-bond tax break (which is, after all, an entitlement) as they are to cut the earned income tax credit for the working poor? We're not counting on it. Will corporate managers, so happy to cut government spending on Medicare and food stamps, be as willing to see their tax subsidies chopped? Frankly we doubt it. Just take a look at the current negotiations over the tax bill in Congress, where an army of special interests writes government favors for themselves. Rich and poor, business and labor are all still hooked on entitlements.[24]

Indeed, rich and poor, business and labor as well as clerics and religious congregations of women and men, have all moved more and more into a sense of entitlement that stresses what is due one's self without thinking sufficiently for others — in the present as well as the future.

Entitlement and its ideology, once meant to offer a stop-gap effort to meet people's immediate needs, has become addictive. It is the new "right" that defines all other rights; it is the inevitable consequence of an individualistic culture. Somehow having whatever I desire becomes my birthright. I have found such thinking in my own attitudes of expectation of having what I "deserve" when I give talks or when I am asked for help. The attitude can easily infect a once-poor kid from the ghetto who has athletic abilities to such a degree that it can be exploited in a commercial for Reebok I saw recently. Picturing an African American playing basketball, it stated:

> A jump shot can get you
>   a shoe deal;
>   a super model;
>   a big house;
>   fancy cars;
>   a bunch of yes men;
>   a Swiss bank account.
> But few of these *things*
>   can get you a jump shot.

Solidarity with People Who Are Poor

When Francis wrote that, if the brothers did not make enough to live on from their work, they should be prepared to go begging for alms from door to door with their gospel of peace, he added that the whole attitude they should have as they lived in the world should be that of being "pilgrims and strangers":

Let the brothers not make anything their own, neither house, nor place, nor anything at all. As pilgrims and strangers in this world, serving the Lord in poverty and humility, let them go seeking alms with confidence, and they should not be ashamed because, for our sakes, our Lord made Himself poor in this world. This is that sublime height of most exalted poverty, which has made you, my most beloved brothers, heirs and kings of the Kingdom of Heaven, poor in temporal things but exalted in virtue. Let this be your portion which leads into the land of the living. Giving yourselves totally to this, beloved brothers, never seek anything else under heaven for the name of our Lord Jesus Christ.[25]

I find the attitude of being a "pilgrim and stranger in this world" is more an attitudinal stance rather than a geographic phenomenon. It begins with the notion of "surrender" insofar as it invites us to leave received ways of thinking in a way that finds us identified in compassion with those who are different from ourselves, i.e., those who are poor. It invites us to "catch" or embrace another way of living in the world, in solidarity with those who are the poor.

In an "Apostolic Exhortation" to members of Religious Congregations, including us Franciscans, Pope Paul VI clearly outlined an approach to the vow of poverty that is honest and relevant to the situation of poverty as we truly find it being experienced by those who are poor today. It offers all Christians a way to return to a truly "evangelical" way of responding to Jesus' invitation to the young man of the Gospels to "be perfect" (Matt. 19:21).

In *Evangelica Testificatio,* the pope noted that the disparity between the rich and the poor manifest on a global scale, especially "in a world experiencing the full flood of development," demanded a new way of responding to the "persistence of poverty stricken masses and individuals." He declared that this situation constitutes a pressing call for "a conversion of minds and attitudes," in other words, a global transformation that would bring about a truly evangelical way of life. He stated that the reality of such poverty and the plight of the poor challenges us to undergo a deep conversion of heart. "You hear rising up, more pressing than ever, from their personal distress and collective misery, 'the cry of the poor,'" he wrote, using this image of the "cry of the poor" from Old Testament texts such as Psalm 9:13, Job 34:28, and Proverbs 21:13. Recalling that the scriptures show how God continually intervened on behalf of the poor, the pope notes that it was exactly "in order to respond to their appeal as God's privileged ones that Christ came, even going as far as to identify with them." This is shown in New Testament texts such as Luke 4:18, 6:20, and the Matthean text that links true discipleship with bringing about justice in the way that the hungry are fed, the naked clothed, and other core needs are met by those with the resources to do so (Matt. 25:35–40).[26]

Noting that the way Jesus identified with the poor stood in marked contrast to some religious who resorted to violence in response to the exploitation of the poor, he then offered a two-point program of conversion. It outlines a contemporary way to be honest about our "vow" of poverty based on our solidarity with those who are truly poor in economic ways. After asking how the "cry of the poor" might echo in our lives, he said:

"That cry must, first of all, bar you from whatever would be a compromise with any form of social injustice." This statement makes it quite clear that, globally speaking, a definite connection exists between poverty and injustice; the "cry of the poor" demands that we separate ourselves (i.e., "withdraw") from all forms of violence that bring about the situation of poverty in, among, and around us. This involves challenges to unjust social structures. Second, the pope declared, the reality of global poverty (i.e., poverty at all levels of the world) demands that we inform others about its negative impacts in a way that invites people to evangelical penance: "It obliges you also to awaken consciences to the drama of misery and to the demands of social justice made by the Gospel and the Church."[27]

One of the problems in "awakening consciences to the drama of misery and to the demands of social justice made by the Gospel and the Church" centers on the fact that the one group best-equipped to do this — the most exploited group of the middle class — still believes that it truly benefits from the existing economic ordering, even as we have shown earlier that the rich are getting richer not on the backs of the poor, but their own middle class. Nonetheless, they still find themselves wedded to the old adage: "If you play by the rules and work hard, you will succeed." However, they are unaware that the rules have been changed gradually by those who will truly benefit from them, at their expense. Yet they still believe that they would be disadvantaged by any change. Edward M. Welch, in "The Church Was Right about Capitalism," noted the problem in a short article in the Jesuit weekly *America*. He concluded: "One does not get rich by taking money from the poor. They do not have much money to take. You get wealthy by taking from the middle class. Perhaps taking from the poor is more of a sin, but the problem will never be dealt with until the majority in the middle realize that they too are being victimized."[28]

In Francis' mind the ministry of the community to the poor was based on a conviction that, as long as anyone was poor, God's reign had not yet touched the hearts of the rich. The pope's challenge about having "no compromise" with any form of social injustice in order to bring "good news to the poor," combined with embracing a way of raising people's awareness about this injustice and its impact on the poor is daunting. It demands a way of preaching that challenges preachers and, indeed, all believers to make others aware of the poverty among them in a way that will work for its eradication and brings about greater liberty and justice for all.

As he pointed out the demand for all religious to have no compromise with any form of social injustice and to awaken the consciences of others to the plight of those who are poor, Pope Paul VI went a step further. He insisted that, while all religious are called to do the above two things if they will allow the "cry of the poor" to echo in their hearts, he noted that this same situation might "lead some of you to join the poor in their situation and to share their bitter cares." He also noted that this might also demand some institutional restructuring that would redirect "some of their works" toward "the good of the poor."

Finally, in a world obsessed with getting ever more creature comforts, he noted that those who dedicate themselves to a more public witness to the Gospel way of life must use the goods of the earth in a way that sets limits: "to what is required for the fulfillment of the functions to which you are called," rather than the opposite. This witness, he opined, would "give proof" to the world that "authentic poverty" was being taken seriously in our daily lives.[29]

Poverty as Personal: The Way of Simplicity

One time, after giving a talk on Francis' approach to poverty (which included many of the thoughts found in this chapter) a retreatant challenged me. "Mike," she said, "I was very surprised and quite disappointed that, in your reflections on poverty, you never talked about simplicity. Wasn't simplicity very much part of Francis' life?"

I responded more defensively (and, therefore, reactively and unreflectively) than I anticipated: "Francis really didn't talk about simplicity very much in the way we understand it today," I said. "So that's why I didn't talk about it."

Although I knew that Francis' approach to poverty was more on the side of austerity than simplicity, the minute I returned to my room I went to "The Sources." While I was right about Francis' understanding of poverty as austerity rather than simplicity in our received sense today, I discovered I was quite wrong in saying he did not really speak about simplicity in any significant way. Indeed he did. However, his notion was quite different from the "simple living" notions that have given rise to the voluntary simplicity movement, "downsizing," and even very successful magazines that invoke the name.

The most common meaning for "being simple" (*simplex*) employed by Francis was connected to other Latin words that need no translation: *imbecillis* and *idiota*. He ranked himself in such a category. He was unlettered and unschooled; as such he was "simple." In his *Testament* he also referred to himself as "simple" in the same breath as being "infirm."[30] However, beyond this notion it is clear that Francis' approach to poverty as "nonappropria-tion" contained a definite connection to simplicity insofar as simplicity is the virtue of being free of whatever might compromise our core commitments. It also included the notion of being "subject to all."[31] As such simplicity is the virtue that invites us to distinguish our needs from our wants in a way that submits us to the claims of those around us. Simplicity demands hearts that are pure and clear regarding what we really need that is determined by our solidarity with those whose basic needs still are not met. It shows that we are consciously aware and concerned about remaining connected in our lifestyle with the style of life of those whose basic needs cry to be addressed.

At its heart simplicity involves the simplifying of our lives from our wants to meeting our real needs. Simplicity is about being pure of heart regarding who we really are and what we really need. Simplicity involves a kind of con-scious connectedness to everyone and everything in the cosmos that results in a passion for nonviolent ways of relating and bringing about change — in our own lives, among others, and in our institutions.

Francis cut to the core of simplicity when he wrote that the brothers should be able to relate to each other in such a way that they can confi-dently make known "their needs." In examining those "needs," he insisted that they should remain very simple and uncomplicated. Refusing to accept money — which he believed cluttered people's hearts and compromised the spirit of prayer and devotion, to which every temporal consideration should be subordinate — he saw payment for work as that which would meet the friar's "temporal needs." The outline for this way of life followed the path of simple living.

Unlike our own era, in Francis' time a clear connection existed between poverty and simplicity when they were applied to the economy. Thus, by his embrace of a radical poverty defined by manual labor (living on the equiva-lent of the minimum wage), Francis and his followers would put themselves in conscious solidarity with the *minores* of that world. Yet today, such a clear connection between poverty and simplicity no longer exists, in good part because poverty is no longer recognized as having any value.

Given the above reflections, a contemporary approach to simplicity is critical for those embracing "poverty" by vow. It becomes the sine qua non for those who have the kind of economic security that is identified with having basic needs as well as reasonable wants ensured. At the same time it has become recognized as the one virtue necessary if we are to find a way to live justly in a creative and contemporary way of "doing penance" in our world today. In a way, using the noun "simple," as Francis used it, means to live our lives in an uncluttered way.[32] In the words of the Franciscan Richard

Rohr, such simplicity, modeled on the pattern of Francis, will go a long way in transforming our anxious world. He writes:

> Simplicity of lifestyle might be, after all, the most radical form of social justice possible. It is a nonpretentious way of simply living outside of the whole system of greed, consumption and injustice. Simplicity is clearly going to have to be part of any kind of reconstruction. Any rebuilding must move toward a more modest sense of self. The grandiose self is like a fragile but giant balloon bouncing around a room, and often demanding more inflation to avoid the inevitable. In the postmodern world, people set themselves up to be offended and to be addictive by their false sense of entitlement. Yet the only real entitlement is from God. When "your name is written in heaven," then all other titles are superfluous and even burdensome.[33]

Living simply involves a turning from a life defined by self-centered materialism to other-oriented simplicity in a way that ensures our basic sustainability and solidarity with creation and all its residents. This involves recognizing simplicity as sufficiency and sustainability in a world of disparity that is ideologically justified by the notion of entitlement. The embrace of such sufficiency and sustainability rather than abundance and affluence demands a clear choice. In the words of Stephen Hand:

> Choosing simplicity . . . does not make anyone good or righteous or — God forbid — better than your neighbor. It simply is a conscious effort to try not to contribute to the idolatry of materialism that sustains a world of wars and keeps us running helter skelter for all the things we must inevitably surrender when it is time for God to call us. "Living simply so that others may simply live" is the beginning, not the end, of a radical spiritual life. It does not require us to be canonized saints, but only caring persons.[34]

At the end of the day, perhaps Francis' words themselves show how simplicity and poverty lived authentically will "put to shame" everything else that masks selfishness and egoism in our own "stories" as well as the violence at the heart of so much of the materialism and militarism in our "culture's story" as well as in too much of the clericalism and legalism in our "church's story." When we become "simple, humble, and pure,"[35] the "Gospel story," pure and holy in its simplicity, may be able to be proclaimed again. As he wrote in A Salutation of the Virtues:

Hail, Queen Wisdom!
May the Lord protect You,
with Your Sister, holy pure Simplicity! . . .
Pure holy Simplicity confounds
all *the wisdom of this world*
and the wisdom of the body.
Holy Poverty confounds
the desire for riches, greed,
and the cares of this world.
Holy Humility confounds pride,
all people who are in the world
and all that is in the world.[36]

TEN

Enduring in Peace

May the Lord bless you and keep you
May He show His face to you and be merciful to you.
May He turn His countenance to you and give you peace.
May the Lord bless you, Brother Leo.[1]
                    —The Blessing of Francis for Brother Leo

Francis' Call for Peace in the Midst of Violence

Arnoldo Fortini, the former mayor of Assisi, who wrote a socio-historical biography of Francis some years ago, wrote of thirteenth-century Italy: "War was a condition of life for every city...It was also the way to wealth and commercial expansion. Any means were acceptable to subjugate other cities."[2] Those wars between the cities (which mirrored the wars between pope and emperor), were replicated within the cities as well.

Francis grew up in one such city: Assisi. It had used such conflicts to its own advantage, especially in the way it played off its allegiance between the pope and the emperor. For the first years of his life, Francis was a subject of the emperor under his local overlord, Duke Conrad of Urslingen. According to Donald Spoto, his "primary responsibility was to ensure that the nobility supported the emperor in a society in which peace had no meaning and war was both a habit and a dominating passion."[3]

Some time after his election as pope, Innocent III (1194–1216) demanded that Assisi come under his jurisdiction. For some unknown reason Conrad complied. While Conrad was on his way to make formal obeisance to the pope's legate, the citizens of Assisi, led by the merchants, who were no longer willing to serve its nobles as *minores,* besieged and razed Rocco Maggiori. Being a teenager, albeit a very young seventeen, Francis, it can be surmised, would have joined his father in the sacking of "The Rock."

Undoubtedly, such divisions between pope and emperor, as well as those between Perugia and Assisi (which found Francis also engaged in battle in 1202), the nobles and the merchants, the city-dwellers and indentured peasants as well as the division in and among them, became a key reason for Francis' efforts to be a peacemaker. Such divisions, represented in these "symmetrical opposites," Stanislaus da Campagnola writes, set the context "against which Francis struggled in his efforts to make peace, as well as in his efforts toward a leveling based on equality and fraternity. He tried to reconcile the two groups, at least socially, to have them live peacefully together in the cities."[4]

In his classic *The Soul's Journey into God,* St. Bonaventure highlights peace as central to the way his predecessor, as Minister of the Fraternity, proclaimed the Gospel. In his prologue, after praying "through the intercession of blessed Francis, our leader and father," that *"the eyes* of our soul" (i.e., the reader) might be enlightened "to guide our feet in the way of that peace which surpasses all understanding" (cf. Eph. 1:18; Luke 1:79; Phil. 4:7), he explains:

> This is the peace proclaimed and given to us by our Lord Jesus Christ and preached again and again by our father Francis.
>
> At the beginning and end of every sermon he announced peace; in every greeting he wished for peace; in every contemplation he sighed for ecstatic peace like a citizen of that Jerusalem of which that Man of Peace says, *who was peaceable with those who hated peace: Pray for the peace of Jerusalem* (Ps. 119:7; 121:6).
>
> For he knew that the throne of Solomon would not stand except in peace, since it is written: *In peace is his place and his abode in Sion.* (Ps. 75:3).[5]

The Need for a Franciscan Approach to Peace in Our Times

When I began writing this chapter, the print and electronic media were filled with stories of some U.S. soldiers captured, tortured, and killed by enemy combatants in Iraq. One word described it all: they were "brutalized." How little things have changed, I thought. "In the time of St. Francis, the people laughed at the agonies of enemies who were tortured and killed," Fortini writes. "They bragged with crude vulgarity about the things they had done to the women of the conquered cities. They made games of inflicting slow tormenting agonies. They shed blood now in arrogant wholesale slaughter, now with delicacy. Revenge — the vendetta — became a fixed idea."[6]

In his book *A Terrible Love of War,* James Hillman, a philosopher and Jungian psychologist, makes a strong case that shows violence and war are perennial, not accidental, ways of life. They are part of our personal, communal, and collective psyches. He even sees war as a "religion" insofar as it makes ultimate claim on our faith and imagination. He writes:

> I base the statement "war is normal" on two factors... its *constancy* throughout history and its *ubiquity* over the globe. These two factors require another more basic: *acceptability*. Wars could not happen unless there were those willing to let them happen. Conscripts, slaves, indentured soldiers, unwilling draftees to the contrary, there are always masses ready to answer the call to arms, to join up, get in the fight. There are always leaders rushing to take the plunge. Every nation has its hawks. Moreover, resisters, dissenters, pacifists, objectors, and deserters rarely are able to bring war to a halt. The saying, "Someday they'll give a war and no will come" remains a fond wish. War drives everything else off the front page.[7]

When our culture's story is skewed by Americanism and economism and sustained by militarism, Hillman's insights can't be easily discredited.

According to the 2005 "Human Security Report," the number of intra-state and inter-state conflicts has decreased dramatically since 1946; extra-state conflicts (colonial wars) have disappeared. However, in an article in the *New York Times Magazine,* which charted the decline, James Traub asked: "Since the cold war, the earth has become more peaceful. Why doesn't it feel that way?"[8] As he develops the article it becomes clear that this feeling is quite unique to people living in the United States. He says that "for all the talk of 'globalized' threats, the American experience of the world is becoming less, not more, similar to that of our allies and trading partners. Our world has become more dangerous; theirs, with some important exceptions, less so."[9]

In the effort to feel more secure, U.S. citizens were willing to have their government increase its military spending more and more, especially after September 11, 2001. Despite the fact that total global military expenditure in 2005 reached over $1 trillion dollars, a 3.4 percent increase since 2004, the biggest spender was the United States. It accounted for 80 percent of the increase in 2005. At the same time it joined Russia as the biggest seller of arms across the world.[10] The reason for such a way of addressing conflicts among people and the violence that so often results was the same that Fortini explains to justify the militarism embedded in the patterns and psyche of the people of Francis' day, including those who called themselves Christian: "They could not even imagine a faith that was not sustained by military skill."[11]

When the United States experienced its first invasion from the skies, on September 11, 2001, people's initial shock gave way to cries of vendetta and revenge. I was in New York that day. Shortly after returning to Milwaukee, still deeply saddened and quite overwhelmed by the act of terrorism and the reaction of so many Christians seeking revenge, I got up on September 19 to read the *Milwaukee Journal Sentinel*. On its front page was an iconic picture of the still smoldering area. The caption read: "Huge cranes work to clear the wreckage of one of the World Trade Center towers Tuesday in New York as operations — still characterized as rescue, not recovery — continue one week after the terrorist attack that destroyed the landmark twin towers."

The pain of that violence continued as I turned the pages. There on one of the next pages my pain turned to promise when my eyes fell on a box featuring a picture of St. Francis with his stigmatized hands extended down and outward from his stigmatized side. The text read:

Peace Prayer of St. Francis

Lord
Make us instruments of Your peace.
Where there is hatred, let us sow love;
Where there is injury, pardon;
Where there is doubt, faith;
Where there is despair, hope;
Where there is darkness, light;
And where there is sadness, joy.
Grant that we many not so much seek
To be consoled as to console,
To be understood as to understand,
To be loved as to love.
For it is in giving that we receive,
It is in pardoning that we are pardoned
And it is in dying that we are born to eternal life.
Amen.

Capuchin Franciscans
Province of St. Joseph

The Province of St. Joseph of the Capuchin Franciscan Order is my province, my group of Franciscan brothers. Even though we knew Francis never wrote this prayer (which came to light only in the last century),[12] we knew it was a popular prayer that would speak to the reality we were experiencing. It was our attempt to try to help our fellow citizens and partners in faith think differently about what we were experiencing. It was an effort to invite people to another way of imagining how we might more appropriately respond to the violence done to us in the name of God.

We are part of a nation whose annual defense spending triples that of the combined outlay of its enemies, including the "Axis of Evil" (Iraq, Iran, and North Korea) as well as former adversaries like Russia and China and a few others as well (Cuba, Sudan, and Syria). As such, the words of Fortini describing the character of the world in which Francis of Assisi felt called — wherein they "could not even imagine a faith that was not sustained by military skill" — invites us to look to him for an alternative imagination.[13]

Francis' Way of Proclaiming the Gospel of Peace

It has been said that the first reason all sides in wars use to justify their stance is the attitude that makes their opponents diabolical enemies or inimical.[14] The word "enemy" (*in* + *amicus* = no friend) means one who is not a friend. By not only befriending everyone but also calling everyone and everything "brother" and "sister," Francis was able to create a new way of peace based on relations of respect rather than dynamics of dissension.

In his effort to bring about a kind of "cosmic *shalom*," Francis tried to imagine a world that would be defined by reconciliation and peace rather than violence and war. He was convinced that he had been directly led by God to embrace this path in a world that could imagine no other way but military might. Thus he wrote in his *Testament*: "The Lord revealed a greeting to me that we should say: '*May the Lord give you peace.*'"[15]

The private revelation Francis received had its origin in divine revelation itself. Luke's Gospel portrays Jesus sending his first disciples into the world with one simple message — peace: "Go on your way ... Whatever house you enter, first say, 'peace to this house!' And if anyone is there who shares in peace, your peace will rest on that person, but if not, it will return to you" (Lk. 10:3, 5–6).

Upon being joined by Bernard of Quintavalle, Celano describes it as his "embracing the *delegation of peace.*"[16] When the numbers joining grew to eight, Francis "called them all to himself and told them many things about *the kingdom of God*," in the model of Jesus. Then he "separated them into four groups of two each. 'Go, my dear brothers,' he said to them, '*two by two* through different parts of the world, *announcing peace* to the people and *penance for the remission of sins.* Be *patient in trials,* confident that the Lord will fulfill His plan and promise.' "[17]

It is quite likely that these words[18] were contained in the *Protoregula,* or Primitive Rule, which he gathered from different sayings in scripture and presented as the way of life for the fraternity, as they presented themselves in 1209 for approval by Pope Innocent III. The same words are found in the subsequent Earlier Rule of 1221 and the approved Later Rule of 1223.

Thomas of Celano, Francis' first biographer, describes the approach Francis took when greeting people with peace and their initial reaction to it in two different ways. The first was positive; the second was confusion and even ridicule. Whatever the response, Francis urged his brothers to be "children of peace," as *The Assisi Compilation* notes.[19] However, it also notes that, while there may have been some initial negativity toward the greeting of peace, in time, because of the way they became "children of peace," they were able to turn the hearts of others toward peace as well. In this sense Celano writes:

> In all of his preaching, before he presented the word of God to the assembly, he prayed for peace saying: *"May the Lord give you peace."* He always proclaimed this to men and women, to those he met and to those who met him. Accordingly, many *who hated peace* along with salvation, *with the Lord's* help wholeheartedly embraced peace. They became themselves *children of peace.*[20]

Leonhard Lehmann writes: "The peace that he proclaimed and promoted was not an unrealistic pacifism. It made great demands on both speaker and hearers. Francis himself intervened in civil conflicts in Arezzo, Perugia, Bologna, and Assisi. His customary greeting: 'the Lord give you His peace!' was implemented with positive action."[21] In the process, Julian of Speyer notes: "he brought to true peace many who had previously lived at odds with Christ and far from salvation."[22]

The way Celano notes Francis uniting peace and salvation in this passage has definite overtones of the biblical notion of *shalom,* the vision of a totally new social order bringing about the transformation of all creation. We find it also in his greeting to Brother Leo, which opened this chapter, and in his greeting of "health [salvation] and peace" to The Rulers of the World.[23] This is encapsulated in Isaiah's vision of a new creation brought about when God's reign rules on earth. The sign of this "Peaceable Kindom" will be revealed when the wolf shall live with the lamb, the leopard shall lie down with the kid, the calf and the lion and the fatling together, and a little child shall lead them (Isa. 11:6). Francis may never have known the word *shalom,* but he did know that peace involved the reconciliation of enemies, starting with the need to do war within one's own members. Consequently the way to proclaim peace to the world included having peace within one's self and if the peace proclaimed to the world was meant to bring about the "kindom of God," Francis knew from his prayer, that to live in peace — for himself and everyone and everything in creation — was a foretaste of the salvation that constituted the messianic reign.

Even though Francis embraced poverty as the way of life for his brothers, as they went on their journey as "pilgrims and strangers" in this world, the evangelical message they were told to proclaim was "peace." Peace, therefore, was the vision of the Gospel of the Reign (*Shalom*) of God they were to announce. Consequently, as the secular Franciscans have discovered with the Franciscan expert, Ilia Delio, O.S.F., it can be said of the Franciscan way of life: "To be a 'peacemaker' is at the heart of its charism."[24] Despite this statement from Delio, it has been a source of continual amazement to me (as well as some degree of consternation) that we have so many experts in Franciscanism stressing its charism almost singularly with poverty without at least a comparable stress on peace as also at the "heart of its charism."

When one examines the evangelical basis for my position in Luke and Matthew, it becomes clear that the "take nothing for your journey" was the means to the evangelical proclamation to all households the message of peace (Matt. 10:9–14), especially since peace was the public message that Francis said should be given by the friars to others even as they themselves would ensure that they would place no obstacle to that peace in the way they dealt with possessions. In my mind, poverty is the way we "surrender to"; it is the means to the "catch" of the public evangelical proclamation of peace to all.

In this sense, I find it quite surprising, if not unbelievable, that one of the greatest Franciscan scholars, the Capuchin Octavian Schmucki, would write in the 1990s: "As far as I know, no one has done an in-depth study of the Gospel concept of peace which inspired the life and activity of St. Francis."[25] One of the reasons why this may not have been done is that many Franciscan scholars were locked into a historically supported way of thinking about the charism that linked it almost exclusively to poverty. However, as I have contended for many years and noted above, while poverty may have been the means Francis chose for his brothers to live *their lives*, it was the proclamation of penance, or countercultural living, that he proclaimed which would result in peace *in the world*. Indeed, I could even argue that he said the brothers should not have possessions because it would mean they would "need arms for our protection." Poverty is the disarming way that must be embraced if peace will be realized at all levels of our world's various *oikías*. This "poverty as the means to the end of peace" should be recognized as the true charism of the Order.[26]

One of the things that is intriguing about Francis' approach to peace at different levels, is that it reflects an inclusive rather than a restrictive approach. Rather than promoting a stance that says: before we can speak to others about peace we must be peace-filled ourselves, Francis took an integrative approach: promoting peace involves all levels at all times. Furthermore, it is something that is ongoing and must be continually developed. Thus we read in the early account of Francis simply called *The Anonymous of Perugia:* "As you announce peace with your mouth, make sure that you have greater peace in your hearts; thus no one will be provoked to anger or scandal because of you. Let everyone be drawn to peace and kindness through your peace and gentleness."[27] It's not a matter of "first you" and "then you"; it's "as you" preach peace to others make sure "you" are cultivating it in yourselves. With this in mind we can probe more deeply how Francis viewed peace at the various levels of our world.

The Franciscan Way to Personal Peace

Achieving inner peace or, as Francis described it, "peace in your hearts," has been a key goal of all great spiritualities. With such peace in our hearts, Francis believed, we would be able to witness to it more effectively. He explained: "Let no one be provoked to anger or scandal through you, but may everyone be drawn to peace, kindness, and harmony through your gentleness. For we have been called to this: to heal the wounded, bind up the broken, and recall the erring. In fact, many who seem to us to be members of the devil will yet be disciples of Christ."[28]

From Francis' perspective, a Franciscan spirituality begins in poverty. Here one moves to increasing nonappropriation of anything so that "nothing" can disturb. It is nurtured in contemplative prayer and developing a contemplative stance toward everyone and everything in the world. It is witnessed in one's untiring work to overcome violence through reconciling enemies as a way of promoting peace. This is the goal Franciscans must try to achieve in the world. The great manifestation of a Franciscan way of making peace with one's self is the character of becoming a person who is "disarmed" and "disarming."

First of all, to make peace with one's self demands two parallel dynamics. The one is represented in the refusal to try to control anyone; this is what Francis meant when he told "the brothers not [to] make anything their own, neither house, nor place, nor anything at all."[29] But they were to give up their very wills insofar as they would make no claims on anyone or anything. Not only did they give up the need to control; the way they did this brought them great joy. As *The Anonymous of Perugia* says of them: "They were constantly rejoicing, for they had nothing that could disturb them."[30]

Besides giving up these forms of trying to be in control, the second side of the coin called "being at peace with one's self" came from Francis' way of accepting himself for who he was, despite his admittedly extreme violence to his body. He believed that all people were made by God as "very good" and, therefore, blessed. No one was any better than anyone else, whether a leper or a lord. Thus he wrote in his 19th Admonition: "Blessed is the servant who does not consider himself any better when he is praised and exalted by people than when he is considered worthless, simple, and looked down upon, for what a person is before God, that he is and no more."[31] This latter part of the Admonition about who we are before God and nobody else and nothing more, was something Francis continually said, according to St. Bonaventure.[32]

Another way of achieving peace within one's self comes in a way that is related to nonappropriation. It involves the ways we strive to preserve peace in our minds and heart. This was made clear in Francis' Admonition for "Peacemakers." He quoted the Beatitude of Jesus in Matthew's Gospel (Matt. 5:9): *"Blessed are the peacemakers, for they shall be called the children of God,"* and then elaborated: "Those people are truly peacemakers who, regardless of what they suffer in this world, preserve peace of spirit and body out of love of our Lord Jesus Christ."[33] Preserving peace of mind and peace in one's heart demands letting go, or not "appropriating" anything that might disturb that peace. On the one hand, while it can involve material things, it can also be other "stuff" we cling to, such as hurts, grudges, and resentments. On the other hand, it involves developing a contemplative stance that centers us in the fact of God's presence grounding all reality.

A third way of maintaining peace in our hearts is characterized by the way we relate to others: to be free of whatever negative force may undermine our peace and our relationships. From this perspective Francis wrote: "I counsel, admonish and exhort my brothers in the Lord Jesus Christ not to quarrel or argue or judge others when they go about in the world; but let them be meek, peaceful, modest, gentle, and humble, speaking courteously to everyone, as is becoming... Into whatever house they enter, let them first say: 'Peace be to this house!' "[34]

If the above efforts are developed in order to cultivate peace within one's "house," then, no matter what kind of obstacle may be placed on one's path, the person's peace will remain "at home." A way of remaining "at home" with one's self and, from that space, offering a home for everyone and everything, I have discovered, is in the actual use of Francis' greeting which he noted in his *Testament*. Therein he declared that God had inspired him to use it as a greeting to all whom both he and his followers would meet: "May the Lord give you peace."

If Buddhists approach others from a grounding in "mindfulness" and Hindus acknowledge the divine in each other by bowing to each other and saying "namaste" ("the divine in me recognizes the divine in you"), it follows that the divinely ordained saying given Francis, accompanied by appropriate breathing in and out, might do much for ourselves if we use it to articulate the basic stance we take toward everyone and everything in creation, including our enemies. Wishing the enemy "peace" becomes a prayer that envisions the possibility of at-one-ment or the restoration of relationships that once divided us from other people. The more I am mindful of the text and say it, the more connected I find myself becoming with all God's creatures.

The Franciscan Way to Communal Peace: Reconciliation

The *Legend of the Three Companions* tells us that, in the way Francis announced the good news of the peace of God's reign, "by his salutary admonitions, [he] brought to true peace many who had previously lived at odds with Christ and far from salvation."[35]

We saw in the previous chapter that Francis' vision of a peaceable community involved a dynamic wherein the friars' basic needs could be met. "Wherever" they would be (i.e., in whatever relationship they would create), the relationships among the brothers were to be grounded in the trust that those needs would be met. This invited the brothers to find ways to affirm each other and, from that affirmation, find ways to nonviolently correct each other. Such a pattern of relating would create among themselves an oasis of peace in the midst of the desert of violence.

Only if they would not be able to meet those needs among themselves by their work should they seek to have them met by others beyond the fraternity. However, even here, they should go as proclaimers of peace. In begging "alms from door to door," Francis said that the "Lord revealed a greeting to me that we should say: '*May the Lord give you peace.*' "[36]

Another dimension of Francis' effort to bring about peace among warring parties is found in the way he sought to reconcile the two key players in Assisi's power structure: the *podestà* (mayor) and the bishop. Toward the end of his life, after he had already finished the Canticle of Creation, the bishop excommunicated the *podestà*. In retaliation, the *podestà* decreed that no citizen could transact any business with the bishop — taking away his ability to function economically. As a result, *The Assisi Compilation* says: "they thoroughly hated each other." It notes that, although he was "very ill, blessed Francis was moved by pity for them, especially since there was no one, religious or secular, who was intervening for peace and harmony between them."[37] Consequently he added a special strophe to his Canticle. It read:

> Praised be You, my Lord,
> through those who give pardon for Your love,
> and bear infirmity and tribulation.
> Blessed are those who endure in peace
> for by You, Most High, shall they be crowned.[38]

Francis then had one of his companions go to the *podestà* and have him go to the bishop's palace "with the city's magistrates and bring with him as many others as he can." Once assembled, he told the brother he should sing the Canticle of Creation, saying: "I trust in the Lord that He will humble their heart and they will make peace with each other and return to their earlier friendship and love."[39]

Upon hearing the Canticle sung with this addition, we read:

And immediately the *podestà* stood up and, folding his arms and hands with great devotion, he listened intently, even with tears, as if to the Gospel of the Lord. For he had a great faith and devotion toward blessed Francis.

When the *Praises of the Lord* were ended, the *podestà* said to everyone: "I tell you the truth, not only do I forgive the lord bishop, whom I must have as my lord, but I would even forgive one who killed my brother or my son." And so he cast himself at the lord bishop's feet, telling him: "Look, I am ready to make amends to you for everything as it pleases you, for the love of our Lord Jesus Christ and of his servant, blessed Francis."

Taking him by the hands, the bishop stood up and said to him, "Because of my office humility is expected of me, but because I am naturally prone to anger, you must forgive me." And so, with great kindness and love they embraced and kissed each other.[40]

Reconciliation demands repentance on the part of one and forgiveness on the part of the other in conflicts. *The Anonymous of Perugia* recounts how this would come about when a brother might say something that might "possibly give offense to another." Upon realizing that this had created a conflict "his conscience reproached him so much that he could find no peace until he confessed his fault" in a way that would bring about reconciliation between them.[41] However, the kind of reconciliation that was achieved between the bishop and the *podestà* was amazing insofar as it was mutual in the way both repented of their actions and both forgave each other. As such it serves as a way of reconciliation in the "culture's story" as well as the "church's story" that needs ever more practitioners.

A reconciliation that is truly "Franciscan" does not mean capitulation in the face of any dynamics that are connected to institutional forms of injustice rather than God's ways. Clare's witness to this kind of reconciliation in the face of ecclesiastical decrees that she could not accept is an example of this. As her Franciscan movement grew, it encountered a key obstacle to a peaceful serene life because of structured dynamics, coming from the leaders in the institutional church, with which she could not agree; hence she was not able to be reconciled with her opponents in Rome. This involved her conviction that God had inspired her to live, as did Francis, by the "Privilege of Poverty," i.e., the community was not to hold property. In her resistance to efforts by Rome to have it be otherwise, she acted in a truly Franciscan way because of three convictions: her belief that she had been inspired to her way of life and Rule by God, her abiding support from Francis during his life, and, most of all, by her own conscience which, Francis had said in his own Rule, was to be primary. In her article on "Franciscan Reconciliation," Joan Mueller, O.S.F., writes:

> St. Clare's struggle to obtain approval for her rule illustrates the Franciscan challenge to be true to one's call while remaining within the institutional church. Clare's ability to discern the time to negotiate and the time to accept institutional decisions illustrates the Franciscan gift of dancing with the other in a way that allows one to remain true to oneself and also true to the relationship with the other. One learns this dance not by attempting to outpower the partner, but by respecting the other while remaining true to one's vocational identity.[42]

Continuing the notion of the "dance" in our efforts to be reconcilers, one of the finest approaches to this critical task, I believe, is found in the article by the Duns Scotus expert Mary Beth Ingham, C.S.J.: "Presence, Poise and Praxis: The Three-fold Challenge for Reconcilers Today." She argues that, especially in times of fragmentation and distraction, we need to find ways to "force ourselves to pay attention to what is going on around us [that] strip our energy and leave us exhausted. On the contrary we need to develop ways of being present to reality and enter our relationships fully engaged,"[43] our affections and emotions, especially our desires related to happiness and justice, properly ordered. Such a kind of presence invites us to a kind of "readiness" in the way we present ourselves to others.

With such readiness we can be poised: being attentive and listening to everything around us. When this happens, Ingham writes: "I am like the dancer or the athlete. I am poised, ready to act, to execute the move or the play. The poise I refer to here is not the social grace of poise, that is the ability of 'keeping one's cool' in social settings, although this might be a consequence of the attitude. I refer rather to an internal point, sometimes called the still point, or the 'the zone' as athletes say."[44]

Grounded in a way of presence that brings us such a poise, we can get involved in the praxis or action for which the presence and poise have prepared us. Having found a way to harmonize our desires for happiness as well as for justice, we can be present to others in conflict, poised in that presence, as agents of good. As a result, we find ourselves present to others in a way that contributes to the greater reconciliation and harmony of the world itself. In Ingham's words, "Every act of praxis is a moment that has been prepared 'from the foundation of the world.' Every moment that has gone before has been leading up to this moment. At this moment, we are fully free, fully rational, and fully human. All reality awaits our choice."[45]

The Franciscan Way to Peace in the Midst of the World's Violence

All wars arise because of unresolved conflicts arising from a sense of unequal power relationships or property rights. Francis felt called to bring about a new order of peace that would be ushered in when people embraced the Gospel. As Octavian Schmucki writes:

> The Gospel was the inspiration for life, and life itself gave the Gospel new meaning. The revolutionary character and inventiveness of action for peace that was required by Christ in foregoing every form of violence, was highlighted against the background of the age. Francis imposed this requirement on all his friars as a universal rule of conduct.[46]

The Archdeacon Thomas of Spalato tells a case in point about an incident in Bologna on August 15, 1220. He saw Francis in front of the public palace preaching before "almost the entire city." However, "many a seigniorial family [was] torn apart until then by old, cruel, and furious hatreds even to the point of assassinations."

Throughout his discourse "he spoke of the duty of putting an end to hatreds and of arranging a new treaty of peace." Despite the fact that he "did not have an attractive face" and "was wearing a ragged habit," the result of his divinely inspired preaching was that "his words brought back peace" to many of the warring groups.[47]

When we examine the dynamics that lead to war and conflict between so many groups and parties in world, we find similar dynamics at play. They were at play in Francis' initial approach to Islam as well. He had inherited a certain cultural ideology, sustained by his faith, that made him and his religion right(eous) and Islam wrong and not right(eous). As a result the "infidel" had to be converted in order to be saved; even if this would involve killing. So deep was this culturally inherited notion in the mind-set of Francis that, originally, he was unable to see the ideological violence in the Crusades themselves. As Fareed Munir notes: "Although most of these concepts were not based in reality, having no foundation whatsoever, they were inherently part of the crusade ideology. As a result, they were transmitted from one generation to another through the channels of canon law and theology."[48] However, deeper than canon law or theology, the key to much of the conflict between Christianity and Islam was economic: the underlying goal was not so much the conversion of Islam but the reclaiming of the Holy *Land*. The massacre of Moslems was justified in order to reclaim this piece of property. The rationale? This land had been traveled by Jesus, the Prince of Peace.

As a result of this blindness, Francis was much like St. Paul. The latter may have had the vision of the new order in which there would be "no longer Jew or Greek, there is no longer slave or free, there is no longer male and female" because all were equally "one in Christ Jesus" (Gal. 3:27). However, given his own cultural blinders, he never was able to imagine and promote a world wherein women and men, slave and free could be as equal as he insisted Jew and Greek must be. Similarly, Francis may have sought to have his order become a new order of equals in a way that would create a nonviolent alternative to the violence endemic in his world; yet he seems to have been unable to recognize, acknowledge, and challenge the violence inherent in the Crusades. Despite this possible blind spot, even here, we find that he did move from a violence-based approach to Islam to a respectful way of dialoging with it. In this he again went deeper into the conversion process as outlined in the "surrender/catch" metaphor of Kurt Wolff, especially in the way he risked being hurt, suspended his received notions about Moslems, became totally involved with the sultan, and identified with him and his beliefs in a way that brought about a change in his own life that resulted in the "pertinence of everything."

When Francis was five or six years old, on October 2, 1187, Saladin conquered Jerusalem, ending the Christian control of the Holy Land that had been in place since the vicious slaughter of Jews and Muslims alike that occurred in 1099 when the crusaders conquered that area. Saladin's victory elicited the call for a Third Crusade by Pope Gregory VIII. Basically it was a failure. The next Crusade, the Fourth, called by Innocent III the same year he was elected pope (1198), also ended in failure.

Around 1212 Francis departed for Syria wanting to preach penance and belief in Christ to the Moslems; he did this apart from any support from Christian forces connected to a crusade. However, a serious storm kept him and a companion from getting there. Not long after this (c. 1213?), Celano writes, he attempted to preach the Gospel to "Miramamolin and his retinue" in Morocco. However, he took sick and, again, was forced to return home without having encountered Islam directly.[49]

In April 1213 Innocent III called for a Fifth Crusade; it was to begin in 1217. To ensure its success he decided that he would lay a proper foundation for it as well as direct it. Part of the foundation involved calling the Fourth Lateran Council, which would prepare the episcopal leaders from "the world" to mobilize their people in support of it. It seems Francis participated in this council but, while he embraced declarations coming from the council dealing with religious matters, nowhere can it be found that he worked to implement its decrees related to the crusade.

Instead he sent missionaries to Morocco on May 26, 1219, knowing they might become martyred (which occurred January 12, 1220). Determined himself to be a martyr, on June 24, Francis tried again to go to Syria. He arrived to find fierce fighting between the Christians and the Moslems who were in close quarters. The sultan, according to St. Bonaventure's account, had decreed that anyone who brought him the head of a Christian should be rewarded with a gold piece.[50]

Undaunted and unafraid of the bounty that would be on their heads, Francis and another brother set out to meet Sultan Malik al-Kamil, in 1221, still seemingly desirous of martyrdom. Previously, at the height of one particularly critical offensive, this same sultan had offered peace to the crusaders at least five times. All these offers were refused by the legate of Innocent III, Cardinal Pelagius.

First Celano describes how Francis finally came into the presence of Malik al-Kamil in graphic terms:

Before he reached the sultan, he was captured by soldiers, insulted and beaten, but was not afraid. He did not flinch at threats of torture nor was he shaken by death threats. Although he was ill-treated by many with a hostile spirit and a harsh attitude, he was received very graciously by the sultan. The sultan honored him as much as he could, offering him many gifts, trying to turn his mind to worldly riches. But when he saw that he resolutely scorned all these things like dung, the sultan was overflowing with admiration and recognized him as a man unlike any other. He was moved by his words *and listened to him very willingly.*[51]

As is clear from the story, Francis went absolutely convinced of the righteousness of his position. Without concern for what the sultan believed, and moving from some common ground to his goal of inviting him to embrace the Gospel, it seemed, from Celano's note that "in all this, however, the Lord did not *fulfill his* desire."[52] He was more intent on becoming a martyr, and did not respect the faith of the sultan, and, indeed, interpreted his solid faith in Allah as lack of faith in God.

In time it appears Francis had second thoughts about how he had reacted and how he responded initially when he heard about the deaths of the friars in Morocco as to how he should approach Islam's leaders. Building on his actual encounter with the sultan, it seems he began to embrace the various dynamics in the "surrender/catch" model of Wolff. Indeed, he found himself surrendering a militaristic way of dealing with Islam for a "spiritual" way.

Whether or not he discovered that the friars had been well treated by their audience until they berated them for being infidels to such a point that they reacted violently, killing them, or whether he realized that the sultan had refused to accept conversion for conscience reasons, it becomes clear Francis changed his approach as the years went by. This occurred in two main ways.

First of all, although Francis was unable to convert the sultan, it turned out that the sultan possibly converted Francis — not to his religion but to a religious practice that edified Francis: the five-times daily call to worship as announced in the *sâlat.* Thus he would write in his Letter to the Rulers of the People that they all should "foster such honor to the Lord among the people entrusted to you that every evening an announcement may be made by a messenger or some other sign that praise and thanksgiving may be given by all people to the all-powerful Lord God."[53]

Second, it seems that Francis learned that the brothers who went to Morocco went more as chaplains on a crusade and, therefore, linked to material and military interests rather than purely spiritual ones. For this reason, when he wrote his Earlier Rule (May 1221), while he did refer to the biblical quote about being sent like sheep among wolves and the need to be as prudent as serpents and simple as doves (Matt. 10:16) and also believed that people who consciously rejected Jesus as Savior of the world did so at their possible peril, he nevertheless insisted that the brothers go "spiritually" to Islam and other "unbelievers" in one of two ways:

> One way is not to engage in arguments or disputes but to be subject *to every human creature for God's sake* and to acknowledge that they are Christians. The other way is to announce the Word of God, when they see it pleases the Lord, in order that [unbelievers] may believe in almighty God, the Father, the Son and the Holy Spirit, the Creator of all, the Son, the Redeemer and Savior, and be baptized and become Christians because *no one can enter the kingdom of God without being reborn of water and the Holy Spirit.*[54]

It seems that, on the whole, Francis was more converted to Islam than the sultan was to Christianity. Or, at least, Francis found himself converted because of his encounter with the sultan. There, Fareed Munir, writes, Francis "was impressed by what he witnessed and learned firsthand about the Muslims. He was impressed so much that his subsequent Rule went against the religious protocol of his day, a mission idea that emphasized the crusade ideology that Muslims were served best with violence and war rather than the love of God."[55] Indeed, as Jan Hoeberichts writes in his *Francis and Islam,* "God had gone among the Saracens before him and had been the source of much that was good and beautiful. And where people had warned him of a 'wolf,' 'a cruel beast,' Francis met a friend."[56] The *in-amicus* was now another brother.[57]

The notion of the sultan being a beast or a "wolf" brings us to another image of the enemy that has become one of the most beloved of all stories about Francis.

The Franciscan Way of Ensuring We Will Live in Peace with Our Planet

As was the case with much hagiography in the Middle Ages, which typically presented holy people as being able to commune with nature, Celano and other biographers of Francis portrayed him not just communing with animals but also communicating with them.

According to Celano, the first time Francis realized he was able to communicate with animals — as well as other animate and inanimate creatures —
came at Bevegna, in the Spoleto valley. There a very great number of birds of
different types had congregated. Having "very great fervor and great tender-
ness toward lower and irrational creatures," Francis greeted them with the
same greeting he had given humans: "The Lord give you peace." Surprised
that "the birds did not rise in flight, as they usually do," he began to preach
to them of their Creator's concern and love for them. After he blessed them,
they flew away.

However, having realized he had become one with them, not by nature
but by grace, Celano notes: "After the birds had listened so reverently to the
word of God, he began to accuse himself of negligence because he had not
preached to them before. From that day on, he carefully exhorted all birds,
all animals, all reptiles, and also insensible creatures, to praise and love the
Creator, because daily, invoking the name of the Savior, he observed their
obedience in his own experience."[58]

Probably the best-known story of Francis' connectedness to animals relates to the story that the Sisters in the Milwaukee suburb wanted to hear, as
I noted in the preface. It can be found in the *Fioretti* ("Little Flowers") and,
as such, may be just a flowery gloss and may actually never have happened.

In short, in the vicinity of Gubbio a wolf roamed with rabid hunger. It
not only destroyed other animals but "devoured men and women, keeping
all the citizens in such danger and terror that when they went outside the
town, they went armed and guarded as if they had to advance toward deadly
battles." Despite their efforts they could not prevail. Consequently "hardly
anyone dared to go outside the city gate."

One day, while visiting Gubbio, "Francis decided to go out to meet that
wolf," accompanied by a brother and armed only with the sign of the cross.
The story continues:

> Suddenly that terrifying wolf, jaws wide open, rushed at St. Francis.
> St. Francis confronted the wolf with the sign of the cross, restrained
> it by the power of God away from himself and from his companion,
> stopped it in its tracks and closed those savage gaping jaws. Finally
> he called the wolf to himself: "Come here, Brother Wolf. On behalf of
> Christ I order you not to harm me or anyone else."

At that the wolf immediately lay at his feet, "like a lamb, not a wolf."
Then Francis told him of the terrible things it had done. "But," he added,
"Brother Wolf, I want to make peace between you and them, so that they no

longer will be harmed by you, and they will dismiss all your past offenses, and both men and dogs will no longer pursue you."

When the wolf gestured its agreement, Francis spoke again: "Brother Wolf, since you want to make this pact, I promise you that as long as you live I will have your needs constantly provided for by the people of this city, so that you will never again suffer hunger, because I know that, whatever evil you do, you do because of the frenzy of hunger."[59] The conclusion of the story, as in all good stories, is that "everyone lived happily ever after!"

Whether or not the story is authentic, it does indicate a tale that speaks of the wholistic way Francis *did realize* that the basic needs of everyone as well as *everything* in creation must be met if we are to have global peace among ourselves as well as with Mother Earth. The insight we get about the need to meet basic needs if peace is going to be established in communities at all levels is wonderfully described in the story of Francis and the wolf of Gubbio.[60]

As we learn from the wolf and people of Gubbio, all violence comes from the lack of needs being met or conflict over people's perception of their needs. When we look at Mother Earth, we find that she too has not had her basic need for harmonious relationships realized; consequently and unconsciously she has been forced to do violence to everyone and everything.

In the "Francis and the Wolf of Gubbio" story, we find a new way of addressing conflicts in order to bring about peace at all levels. In the words of Stanislaus da Campagnola, this was "socially significant." In the way that Francis persuaded both the people and the wolf to make a peace treaty that involved the wolf giving up his violence in exchange for the people obliging themselves to provide for his basic needs, including food and security or "physical safety," he writes, the result was not " 'unconditional surrender,' without any guarantees or provisions"; rather, it was a "win/win" solution, "with advantages for both parties":

> It shows the moderation and prudence of Francis's remarkable arbitration, in an age when armed clashes and political struggles nearly always ended with banishment and confiscation of goods for the defeated minority, and hardly ever with the search for a more difficult and conciliatory balance among the diverse social groups of the city.[61]

Early in this chapter I noted that the famous "Peace Prayer of St. Francis" was not only never written by Francis, but came to light only in the last part of the nineteenth century. However, in his 27th Admonition, Francis does have a real "Peace Prayer" that can serve as a conclusion of the thoughts I have developed herein regarding what will bring about an "enduring peace."

Where there is charity and wisdom,
   there is neither fear nor ignorance.
Where there is patience and humility,
   there is neither anger nor disturbance.
Where there is poverty with joy,
   there is neither greed nor avarice.
Where there is rest and meditation,
   there is neither anxiety nor restlessness.
Where there is the fear of the Lord to guard an entrance,
   there the enemy cannot have a place to enter.
Where there is a heart full of mercy and discernment,
   there is neither excess nor hardness of heart.[62]

ELEVEN

Joy

The Reason for
the Compelling Appeal of Francis

I slept and dreamt that life was joy.
I woke and I saw that life was service.
I acted and behold, service was joy.[1]
— Bengali poet, Rabindranath Tagore

The Perverse Joy Coming from
Witnessing Others' Pain

While finishing this book in late January 2007, I happened to be in Miami. At that time stories appeared in the media about plans underway, at the suggestion of Miami's city commissioner, Tomas Regalado, a Cuban-American, to throw a party in the Orange Bowl when Fidel Castro, the president/dictator of Cuba, should die.

When I heard this news item I was saddened that people could rejoice at the death of anyone, including their enemies. Relief would be understandable, but to actually rejoice at the death of one's enemy hardly seemed appropriate for people who identify themselves as Christian.

My surprise at this news led me to think of a parallel situation: the shock registered by many U.S. citizens when it was alleged that news of the attacks of September 11, 2001, was greeted by some people in the occupied West Bank territory with dancing in the streets.

Rejoicing at the pain of others, whether they be considered atheists or infidels, not only goes against the grain of the God who does not rejoice in the death of anyone, but it furthermore belies the kind of evangelical love that refuses to rejoice in what is wrong (1 Cor. 13:6). This manner of rejoicing perpetuates violence; as such it is sinful rather than a fruit of the Spirit. In moral theology it is called *delectatio morosa* or morose delectation. The

Germans call it *Schadenfreude:* "malicious joy at a person's misfortunes; malignity; grim enjoyment of a person's discomfiture."[2] We're all neurologically inclined to Schadenfreude and the desire for revenge, which it often includes, notes Jena McGregor in a 2007 cover issue on "Revenge" in *BusinessWeek*.[3]

While we might initially guffaw when someone slips on a banana peel, something deeply violent in our individual and collective psyche seems evident when such rejoicing is actually planned. While it might be understood, if not justified, when such rejoicing erupts spontaneously, as seems to have been the case in the alleged dancing among some Palestinians, it is something else when civic leaders actually *plan* to execute a party in the Orange Bowl to celebrate the death of someone. When this kind of celebration is planned by public officials, it is little wonder many people might be confused about the nature and meaning of authentic joy. Here again, Francis of Assisi can become a model for us — the embodiment of an alternative joy that is finally free of all forms of control and violence, all wrongdoing and injustice.

What Scientists Are Discovering about Joy

Also, as I was finishing this book, *The Economist* featured a cover article dedicated to "Happiness (and How to Measure It)," complete with a picture of a man in a suit jumping for joy. In the ensuing article, "Economics Discovers Its Feelings," *The Economist* noted: "In general, the economic arbiters of taste recommend 'experiences' over commodities, pastimes over knick-knacks, doing over having."[4] Then it editorialized that many among its readers might be looking for joy in the places unable to produce it: "To find the market system wanting because it does not bring joy as well as growth is to place too heavy a burden on it. Capitalism can make you well off. And it also leaves you free to be as unhappy as you choose. To ask any more of it would be asking too much."[5]

Long before this point was repeated by *The Economist*, the same wisdom was evident to St. Francis and his followers. They discovered that only the "sacred exchange" represented by commerce with God would be able to generate in their lives a deeply felt sense of joy. This joy would not come from any "works of the flesh," as Paul noted to the church at Galatia; it could only be produced as a fruit of the Spirit at work in them (Gal. 5:22). Because Francis spent his life trying to be led by this Spirit via the way he sought to surrender everything, including his own ego and its will, it's little wonder that this fruit of the Spirit would become one of his key attributes.

Saints are joyful people. "Why are you always smiling?" St. Degalus, one of the many Irish saints, was once asked. "Because no one can take God away from me," was his simple response. Happiness, Kurt Wolff writes, is "one of the characteristics of surrender"[6] so evident in the life of the saints.[7]

And yet if saints are joyful people, you would never know it from looking at the statues or the stained glass windows that appear in most Catholic churches. Even pictures of Francis rarely show him to be joy-filled. Yet this is a key characteristic of his compelling appeal to people throughout the ages. In fact, when you look at the difference between saints being people who may edify and people whom we want to emulate, I would bet the chief difference lies in their joy.

As Francis understood it, joy should characterize the way the brothers related to each other. Such joy, grounded in a spirit of nonappropriation and nonentitlement, would offer a welcoming invitation to others to join the community. Thus he wrote in the Earlier Rule:

Wherever the brothers may be, either in hermitages or other places, let them be careful not to make any place their own or contend with anyone for it. Whoever comes to them, friend or foe, thief or robber, let him be received with kindness.

Wherever the brothers may be and in whatever place they meet, they should respect spiritually and attentively one another, and *honor one another without complaining.* Let them be careful not to appear outwardly as sad and gloomy hypocrites but show themselves *joyful,* cheerful and consistently gracious *in the Lord.*[8]

So much did Francis believe in the need for joy to characterize the relationships the brothers had that, when he himself experienced his "Great Temptation" and went into a two-year depression upon his return from Egypt, he withdrew from the brothers, neither eating with them nor talking with them, "especially since he could not be his usual cheerful [i.e., joyful] self."[9] Because he could not evidence joy to his brothers, it seems that Francis "withdrew." It was not a healthy way to address the problem; nonetheless, as we saw in chapter 6, however unhealthy his withdrawal may have been at first, his experience of the scriptures at work in him ultimately freed him of this temptation to despair.

If we don't discover much about joy from the way many "saints" are depicted, we *are* at least learning much about the characteristics of joy from science. Indeed, in the last decade, hardly a year goes by without the publication of some scientific study concerning the desire for happiness and the search for an elusive joy.

Since the mid-1980s University of Illinois psychologist Edward Diener worked on the development of a "Satisfaction with Life Scale." Diener discovered that, once people's basic needs are met, other things often thought to be the source of happiness do not bring it about. These include such disparate things as money and youth, education and even living in sunny climes like California. However, what did score high on people's life-satisfaction lists related to family and friends and the quality of relationships.

In 2002 Martin E. P. Seligman, a former president of the American Psychological Association, wrote a best-selling book: *Authentic Happiness*. In the book he noted that the three components most important in bringing about people's happiness involved engagement with friends and family, a sense of meaning or purpose that involved being dedicated to a greater good, and the pursuit of pleasure. However, to the surprise of many, he argued that the "pursuit of pleasure" came well after the ways of engagement and meaning.[10] In its "Health Section," September 16, 2002, *Newsweek* featured the book and the findings of Seligman. I found two of Seligman's findings particularly intriguing.

First, Seligman was quoted as arguing that people can move into deeper happiness by examining their negative assumptions, savoring positive experiences, and managing their natural yearning for more. He noted: "Desire, as the Buddha understood, is infinite, but our capacity for pleasure is not. By adapting to ever richer indulgences, we only narrow our options for pleasing ourselves. Restraint may yield higher returns."[11] In other words, when we dedicate our lives to surrendering to some higher reality, some power greater than our own "fleshly" desires, we just might "catch" the Ultimate Object of our hearts' desire — that Source for which our hearts were ultimately made. When this Source is identified with Jesus Christ and we see ourselves actually wanting to "give up" or surrender to everything in order to follow this Jesus Christ, it is little wonder that something powerful happens in our hearts when we hear a classic piece like *Jesu, Joy of Our Desiring*. This led me to think that the early Franciscan approach to the countercultural way of life which then was called the "life of penance" was hundreds of years before its time! It made me recall various passages from the Gospel and the early lives of Francis. The Gospel passage about "finding" the treasure of great price talks about the finder being filled with "joy" at the find (Matt. 13:44). *The Anonymous of Perugia* speaks of the "great joy" that filled the first followers of Francis "as if they had just acquired an immense treasure."[12] Or this passage from Celano's *Life of St. Francis,* recalling the place the brothers first stayed upon their return from Rome, where they had their evangelical way of life approved by the pope:

They had great joy, because they saw nothing that could give them empty or carnal delight. There, they began to have commerce with holy poverty. Greatly consoled in their lack of all *things of the world,* they resolved to adhere to the way they were in that place always and everywhere. Only divine consolation delighted them, having put aside all *their cares* about earthly things. They decided and resolved that even if buffeted by tribulations and driven by temptations they would not withdraw *from its embrace.*[13]

The second thing that intrigued me as I thought about Seligman's work was another one of his findings: authentic happiness is not so much about maximizing utility or managing our moods; rather it involves outgrowing our obsessive concern with ourselves, our thoughts, our feelings, and our desires. Again, Francis intuited what psychologists have only come to accept: "letting go" brings about greater health. Thus, in his 10th Admonition he notes that the greatest enemy we face is our own body, since it is through our bodies that we sin. Therefore, he wrote: *"Blessed is the servant,* then, who always holds captive the enemy delivered into his power and wisely safeguards himself from him; because, as long as he does this, no other enemy visible or invisible will be able to harm him."[14]

In December 2004 I received my monthly *AARP Bulletin.* The title of an article caught my eye: "Feeling Joy." It featured an interview with Kay Redfield Jamison, author of *Exuberance: The Passion for Life.*[15] Her description of exuberance seemed closest to the "joy" that Francis exhibited and that seemed so compelling to people than what the experts were saying about the "science" of happiness. In the AARP interview Jamison stated:

Exuberance as applied to human nature and temperament means a copious abundance of joy and energy. It means a high-energy state, both physical and psychological. It's optimism, a passion for life that is unrestrained and irrepressible. Exuberant people have an intrinsic desire to stay engaged with the world. Extroverted, talkative, their love of life is palpable and can be catching to others who aren't naturally inclined to be exuberant. Many great personalities... "infected" or infused others with their own vast reservoirs of enthusiasm.[16]

Certainly, as I read Jamison's description of "exuberance," I felt she was close to describing the contagious character of Francis' joy.

Three years after the earlier *Newsweek* feature, *Time* magazine took up the theme as well. Its cover featured a big, round, yellow smiley face in the middle of spiraling atoms of more, but smaller smiley faces. In this, its third annual "Mind and Body" series, *Time* devoted several articles to "The Science of Happiness."[17] The issue began by highlighting Martin Seligman's work, but also noted that the field was growing rapidly.

Given the ever expanding science related to the dynamics promoting happiness, it would not be long before advertisers and others in the market economy would find a way to exploit this through goods and services. Thus I would read about the efforts of economists and advertisers to discover the characteristics of happiness and joy that they might be exploited for commercial purposes.

The January 10, 2005, issue of the *Financial Times* carried a story that grabbed my attention: "The 'Dismal Science' Turns Its Attention to Happiness." It noted that, while "economic output as measured by GDP has risen steeply in recent decades in the developed economies," people there "have not been getting significantly happier." This created a problem for economists as well as policy-makers. "If the link between GDP and happiness no longer exists," they have discovered, "one of the key objectives of government policy in keeping GDP on an upward trajectory is called into question. This is partly why economists have increasingly turned their attention to the study of happiness, once exclusively the preserve of psychology."[18]

For its part, in the "Pursuits" section of the weekend edition of the *Wall Street Journal,* March 18–19, 2006, the cover article featured an old-time cash register with smiley faces on each key while products and opportunities were the pop-ups. The title of the article described the way happiness and joy were already being exploited by the marketers: "Happiness, Inc." The subtitle of the lead article stated: "Science is exploring the roots of joy — and companies are putting the findings to work." Noting the work of people already mentioned above (i.e., Martin Seligman and Ed Diener), as well as others in "The Smile Squad" of "happiness researchers," the article noted:

> Companies spend billions of dollars every year on surveys and focus groups in the quest to figure out what makes consumers tick. Now there's a new weapon in the arsenal: the emerging field of scientific research into what makes people happy. The conclusions are being applied to everything from deciding the right color for washing machines to putting a price on spray paint.
>
> After decades spent focusing on the psyche's dark side, university scientists are churning out findings on what causes joyful emotions. The research is probing the pleasure quotient of buying a pet or shopping at a bookstore — in some cases, literally putting a price on happiness.[19]

Joy: The Meeting of Surrender and Catch

This book has used throughout a key insight from the sociology of knowledge, the phenomenological approach to "cognitive knowing" developed by Kurt H. Wolff: "surrender and catch." I have used it because its expression is exemplified almost perfectly in the original embrace between Francis Bernardone and the leper in 1207. This inaugurated a change in his life — even in his body and its senses — to become transformed, "a new creation," through his constant "surrendering to" the way he perceived and engaged everything afterward. Since the key passage has not been used since chapter 5, I will repeat it here. The opening sentences of Francis' *Testament,* which he wrote not long before his death, describe the experience: "The Lord gave me, Brother Francis, thus to begin doing penance in this way: for when I was in sin, it seemed too bitter for me to see lepers. And the Lord Himself led me among them and *I showed mercy* to them. And when I left them, what had seemed bitter to me was turned into sweetness of soul and body. And afterward I delayed a little and left the world."[20]

Being "in sin," for Francis meant having embraced the negative patterns of the "world." Somehow Francis became open to the never-ending promptings of the Spirit (called "grace") who always invites us (calls us) to move from sin to grace. This opening found himself ready to give up his culturally defined ego to be consciously connected to "the Lord's own *Self.*" This opening found him embracing that which was most despicable in himself, the social leper that he had now recognized in himself. It found him experiencing the depths of God's mercy. This was compassion at its peak: solidarity with the ultimate victim of society's violence and rejecting ways. It was an experience of true and pure, unconditional love. This found him changed, not only in his very being, his soul; his body too was transformed by this divine encounter. In his very flesh he got a glimpse of being united not only with God but with all humanity, especially in that which his "world" most rejected. This began the process of him seeking to "surrender to" in a way that would have him "leaving the world" to the point that he would not only become one with everyone and everything in creation; his own body itself would be transformed into the very sign of Christ's crucifixion and resurrection.

Although Francis does not use the word "joy" to describe the leper-experience of surrender/catch that overcame his whole being, soul and body, with his thinking, feeling, and consequent behavior, the notion of having his former repulsion "turned into sweetness of soul and body" is another image for "joy." Grounded in this joy, Francis became changed in both soul and body.

The notion of "joy" in Francis' life is further illuminated by C. S. Lewis' classic work, *Surprised by Joy*. Lewis described joy in words that also found their expression and realization in Francis' embrace of the leper. For Lewis joy is:

> an unsatisfied desire which is itself more desirable than any other satisfaction. I call it Joy, which is here a technical term and must be sharply distinguished both from Happiness and from Pleasure. Joy (in my sense) has indeed one characteristic, and one only, in common with them; the fact that anyone who has experienced it will want it again. Apart from that, and considered only in its quality, it might almost equally well be called a particular kind of unhappiness or grief. But then it is a kind of want. I doubt whether anyone who has tasted it would ever, if both were in his power, exchange it for all the pleasures in the world. But then Joy is never in our power and pleasure often is.[21]

When Lewis talks about being unwilling to exchange the "taste" of the new experience of the "catch" that brought Francis such a sense of sweetness in his soul as well as his body, the fact that it would never be given up "for all the pleasures in the world," is clear from Francis' last words in the opening paragraph: "And afterward I delayed a little and left the world." In "leaving the world," Francis exchanged those things that once delighted him into a new kind of desire; his surrender of a previous way of living was turned into the catch of another way of being present in the world: through joy. Lewis goes on to describe its surprising ways with great clarity. Possibly because he had something of this experience of joy when he was young, it contains all the more power when we consider that Francis had the leper experience when he was twenty-six:

> This desire, even when there is no hope of possible satisfaction, continues to be prized, and even to be preferred to anything else in the world, by those who have once felt it. This hunger is better than any other fullness; this poverty better than all other wealth. And thus it comes about, that if the desire is long absent, it may itself be desired, and that new desiring becomes a new instance of the original desire, though the subject may not at once recognize the fact and thus cries out for his lost youth of soul at the very moment in which he is being rejuvenated. This sounds complicated, but it is simple when we live it. "Oh to feel as I did then!" we cry; not noticing that even while we say the words the very feeling whose loss we lament is rising again in all its old bitter-sweetness.[22]

Hope and Resistance,
Praise and Gratitude

Francis' personality was always engaging. He was enthusiastic about life. His enthusiasm enabled him, even as a teenager, to be engaged with others. His way of relating energized them and gave them delight even before his "conversion." But, as with so many others considered saints, "grace built on nature." The joy that defined Francis' core personality, under the cultivation of his sense of being connected with God, came to be a core characteristic of his compelling witness to others. Joy, along with freedom, according to Robert Ellsberg, "became hallmarks of his spirituality, along with his constant tendency to turn the values of the world on their head."[23] If Wolff writes that surrender in itself arises from a sense of crisis and that its process evidences an effort "to change the world lest we all perish,"[24] joy becomes the universal sign that this world's ways, based on false desires, have already been conquered.

His natural gregarious nature, especially after the visitation he experienced at Spoleto, became a key characteristic of his way of relating for the rest of his life. After the Spoleto experience, when he felt the call to leave the trappings of war and material things, beginning to sense that God had something important in store for him, Celano writes: "He was filled with such great joy that, failing to restrain himself in the face of his happiness, he carelessly mentioned something to others," making his compatriots wonder what kind of love had smitten him.[25]

"At times, as we saw with our own eyes," Thomas of Celano writes, "he would pick up a stick from the ground and putting it over his left arm, would draw across it, as across a violin, a little bow bent by means of a string, and going through the motions of playing, he would sing in French about his Lord."[26] This joy was infectious among his followers.

As Francis evolved in his spirituality, met with popes and bishops, presided at Chapters, worked to resolve conflicts, and experienced unbelievable bodily suffering as well as psychological loss as he watched his movement become institutionalized, it seems (except possibly during his "Great Temptation") the underlying sense of joy never left him.

The uniqueness of the way wherein Francis resisted the sin of his world frustrated those who were equally concerned about its wrongdoing. What made Francis unique compared to so many others who preached "penance" was the joyful way he influenced people to change their hearts to let the reign of God's love take over in their lives and the rejoicing that spontaneously arose when it happened.

When Francis considered God's inbreaking in human history, especially in the scriptural stories of God's visitations to various people, he discovered it was accompanied, on their part, by one of two reactions: fear or joy. Francis chose to cultivate prayerfully his sense of the fire of the divine presence in his heart in a way that erupted in joy. Here words attributed to Pope John Paul II ring true, especially when we consider the way Christ enkindled hope and joy among those he encountered: "Christ came to bring joy; joy to children, joy to parents, joy to families and friends, joy to workers and scholars, joy to the sick and elderly, joy to all humanity. In a true sense joy is the keynote message of Christianity, and the recurring motif of the Gospels."[27]

If the experience of either fear or joy accompanied the inbreaking of the reign of God in one's life, joy is at the heart of the Gospel because it is grounded in hope in the "good news" of what is being promised. Francis found it in Gabriel's visit to Mary, at the announcement to the shepherds, and, above all, in many of the visitations to the disciples by the Risen Christ. Such joy is a sign of resurrection hope; as such it transforms all that previously has been darkness and depression. This fact reminds me of the saying attributed to Henri Nouwen: "I have never met a hopeful person who was depressed or a joyful person who lost hope."

Ultimately, true joy is a pure fruit of the Holy Spirit; therefore it is also a gift. Joy is the "catch" or "embrace" of the "surrender." It is the reward to those whose longing for another is intense, intentional, and directed. However, like any fruit, it needs to be cultivated. Francis knew how this could be done: by overcoming fears, anxieties, and anything that might lead to depression, without running from them either. "If the servant of God," Francis would say, "as may happen, is disturbed in any way, he should rise immediately to pray and he should remain in the presence of the heavenly Father until he restores unto him the joy of salvation."[28] In other words, one is able to overcome obstacles and oppression that seem to overwhelm when we are reminded where true salvation and liberation rest.

Grounding in hope energizes us to resist whatever form of injustice undermines the happiness and joy of others, wherever they may be. The more our care and compassion is extended beyond our own boundaries, the deeper and broader our joy will be — and the more we may find ourselves facing opposition. But even then, the joy does not fade. In this I am reminded of the banner that hangs in Queen's House, a retreat center in Saskatoon, Saskatchewan, that I have often seen: "Those who have finally learned to love find themselves absurdly happy, totally involved, tragically vulnerable (yet protected), and always in trouble."

Like Jesus, Francis was "always in trouble" in the way he embodied in his own life the troubles and sufferings, the worries and concerns of people around him. In inviting such people to find understanding and healing in his presence he empowered them into deeper experiences of salvation and peace.

In her book *Possessing the Secret of Joy,* Alice Walker tells the story of Tashi, a woman of the Olinka tribe. She has returned to Africa to submit herself to a scarification and infibulation (clitoridectomy) ritual practiced on women for centuries. The initiation ritual almost kills her. She sets out to challenge this tradition. In the process she discovers that she has found a new meaning in her life. Her resistance itself enables her to possess the secret of joy.[29]

If the life of "penance" was Francis' ultimate challenge to the "culture of death" that had once nurtured him, joy in that resistance was its characteristic.

The more I have probed the nature of joy, I find it to be something that cannot be calculated and commercialized; it has to be cultivated. And two factors that contribute to this cultivation are *gratitude* and *praise.*

The *Time* article noted above about the "science of happiness" highlighted the findings of a University of California (Riverside) psychologist, Sonja Lyobomirsky. She and her colleagues discovered that we experience deeper levels of happiness when we develop a life around gratitude that involves things like keeping a "gratitude journal" and making "gratitude visits" to thank people who have helped us over the years.[30]

On the one hand, in many ways all of Francis' writings can be considered a "gratitude journal." On the other, whenever he would visit a church, with the prayer he invited all his brothers to repeat, he was making a "gratitude visit." However, when we want to find a clear example of how Francis' thanks and gratitude were able to reach a crescendo, we need look no further than to the paean of appreciation that characterizes the extended last paragraphs of his Earlier Rule. The whole of chapter 23 can be considered one extended prayer of Thanksgiving. It closes with this wonderful prayer:

> Wherever we are, in every place, at every hour
> at every time of the day, every day and continually,
> let all of us truly and humbly believe, hold in our heart and
>   love,
> honor, adore, serve, praise and bless, glorify and exalt, magnify
>   and give thanks
> to the Most High and Supreme Eternal God Trinity and Unity,
> *Father, Son and Holy Spirit,*

Creator of all, Savior of all who believe and hope in Him and
    love Him, Who,
Without beginning and end, is unchangeable, invisible,
    indescribable, ineffable,
incomprehensible, unfathomable, blessed, praiseworthy,
    glorious, exalted,
sublime, most high, gentle, lovable, delightful, and totally
    desirable above all else
for ever. Amen.[31]

The Franciscan scripture scholar Michael Guinan notes that in the Bible "praise is the most characteristic response to the blessings of God in creation." It is not surprising, then, that in his life and writings that "Francis's favorite response to the goodness of God is praise."[32]

As I noted in chapter 4, when Francis considered God as his "Father," the image he used more than any other was that of God being "good." Praise is the natural response to the experience of another's goodness. Thus, as in the prayer found in chapter 23 of the Earlier Rule, gratitude and thanksgiving, praise and glory were Francis' natural response to God's abiding goodness in his life and throughout creation. God's greatness elicits our gratefulness.

Gratitude and praise are two sides of the coin of faith; if one believes that the ultimate source of all that is in creation and, therefore, all that is good, is God, one can only give praise and thanksgiving for such a good God. This sense of gratitude and praise at the fact that we have come to a point in our lives where God is all that matters is captured in the triumphal chorus found in the fourth movement of Ludwig von Beethoven's famous Ninth Symphony. He wrote this in order to offer a fitting musical expression for Friedrich Schiller's original *Ode an die Freuder,* which we know as the "Ode to Joy." However, the real source of such joy is elsewhere; this is articulated clearly in the well-known story recounted below allegedly told by Francis to Brother Leo about what constitutes "Perfect Joy" (or, as the original word *vera* means, "true" or "authentic" joy, not one that is *perfecta*).

Authentic Joy:
The "Catch" from a Life of Surrender

There is a saying that "joy is contagious." If this is so it is no wonder that the world of Francis' day "caught" what he had in such great numbers. It was precisely the infectiousness of his joy that made people embrace his "way of penance" when so many other preachers had failed to capture their imagination. Indeed, "one of the reasons for the great response" to the evangelical message of conversion preached by Francis and the brothers, Prospero Rivi notes, is "that penitence was for him intimately connected with the theme of gladness and joy."[33] This was a rarity in those days (and still is in short supply in our own)!

One day Francis and Brother Leo were together at St. Mary's (the Portiuncula) outside Assisi's gates. Of a sudden, Francis said to Leo: "Write ...what true joy is." Writing instrument in hand, Leo transcribed Francis' conviction about the key dynamic that must take place in our lives if we are to be transformed into authentic joy:

> A messenger arrives and says that all the Masters [of the University] of Paris have entered the Order. Write: this isn't true joy! Or, that all the prelates, archbishops, and bishops beyond the mountains, as well as the king of France and the king of England [have entered the Order]. Write: this isn't true joy! Again, that my brothers have gone to the nonbelievers and converted all of them to the faith; again, that I have so much grace from God that I heal the sick and perform many miracles. I tell you true joy doesn't consist in any of these things.
>
> Then what is true joy?
>
> I return from Perugia and arrive here in the dead of night. It's winter time, muddy, and so cold that icicles have formed on the edges of my habit and keep striking my legs and blood flows from such wounds. Freezing, covered with mud and ice, I come to the gate and, after I've knocked and called for some time, a brother comes and asks: "Who are you?" "Brother Francis," I answer. "Go away!" he says. "This is not a decent hour to be wandering about! You may not come in!" When I insist, he replies; "Go away! You are simple and stupid! Don't come back to us again! There are many of us here like you — we don't need you!" I stand again at the door and say: "For the love of God, take me in tonight!" And he replies: "I will not! Go to the Crosiers' place and ask there!"
>
> I tell you this: If I had patience and did not become upset, true joy, as well as true virtue and the salvation of my soul, would consist in this.[34]

At one level, one might think that Francis called this experience a manifestation of "true joy" in a negative sense of being rejected as the "father" of the community by one of its sons, in the same way he had experienced with Bishop Guido in Assisi years before. However, as Jansen notes, "now it is much more painful. For it is no longer a son who goes his own way and is put out of the house by his father, but now he is himself the father who is shown the way to the door by his own sons in his own house."[35]

The reason that Francis considered his joy as authentic or perfected was that, when he realized he had experienced such total rejection from a member of the very community he had founded, without responding with any kind of hurt, rancor, or righteousness, it finally dawned on Francis that his "surrender" had moved to "catch": this meant nothing at all mattered any more but God. The fruit of his continual effort to "appropriate to himself nothing" had paid off; this expression of being crucified had turned to resurrection; his surrender had brought him the catch: God alone was all that mattered. He had experienced salvation in the depth of his soul; this found the "desires" connected to "the world" transformed and this transformation, this surrender to such desires resulted in the catch of pure joy. He could "rejoice at his find" because now all that ruled his body and soul was the "reign of God." He had become the Gospel he had preached.

Free of any tendency to be disturbed, he could rejoice in the fact that nothing mattered to him but God alone. This experience became enshrined in the classic phrase that has become embedded in the "Franciscan coat of arms." Here, with Francis' arm crossing that of the Crucified, we read the words: *Deus Meus et Omnia:* "My God and My All." As Robert Ellsberg notes: "He taught that unmerited suffering borne patiently for love of Christ was the path to 'perfect joy.'"[36] No cross (including depression about his body's problems or those in the Order, the church, or society), no suffering (whether physical or personal, relational or communal), no persecution (whether from his own brothers or society around him) now could separate him from the love of God that had been modeled in Jesus Christ Crucified. He had grasped in the depths of his heart, his whole being, indeed his body and soul experienced the truth of two passages Paul wrote to the Galatians as he urged them to free themselves of the "works of the flesh" to be grounded in that kind of love whose fruit is joy: "And the life I now live in the flesh I live by faith in the Son of God, who loved me and gave himself for me . . . For in Christ Jesus neither circumcision nor uncircumcision counts for anything; the only thing that counts is faith working through love" (Gal. 2:20b, 5:6).

If Francis was to experience suffering it now would be expressed in joy. This in itself became the cause of great rejoicing on his part: *nothing* now would separate him from God and God's love revealed in the laying down of his life in all his crosses and in the catch of the new life this promised. This is evident in the last section of the Earlier Rule. Here Francis urged his brothers:

With our whole heart, our whole soul, our whole mind, with our whole strength and fortitude, with our whole understanding, with all our powers, with every effort, every affection, every feeling, every desire and wish, let us all love *the Lord* God Who has given and gives to each one of us our whole body, our whole soul, and our whole life, Who has created, redeemed and will save us by His mercy alone, Who did and does everything good for us . . .

Therefore, let us desire nothing else, let us want nothing else, let nothing else please us and cause us delight except our Creator, Redeemer and Savior, the only true God, Who is the fullness of good, all good, every good, the true and supreme good, *Who alone is good,* merciful, gentle, delightful, and sweet, Who alone is holy, just, true, holy, and upright, Who alone is kind, innocent, clean, from Whom, *through* Whom and in Whom is all pardon, all grace, all glory of all penitents and just ones, of all the blessed rejoicing together in heaven.[37]

Spiritual writers would call this realization that came to Francis in his story describing "perfect joy" to be a model of the marriage between the *via negativa* and the *via positiva.*

In his reflections on the surrender of Jesus in his incarnation, crucifixion, and the Eucharist, over a period of time, through prayer and his self-discipline of "surrendering to," Francis joyfully came to embrace a way of nonpossessiveness at all levels, including those things that dealt with his own ego, image, and prestige. This became for him mystical union; it became expressed in his eager embrace of the Lady he called "Poverty."

In his commentary on "Perfect Joy," the Franciscan André Jansen shows that what Francis promoted for others, especially in his Admonitions, he had practiced himself. For instance, we read in Admonition 19: "Blessed is the servant who does not consider himself any better when he is praised and exalted by people than when he is considered worthless, simple, and looked down upon, for what a person is before God, that he is and no more."[38] Showing how the story of "Perfect Joy" exemplifies the way Francis put into practice his own Admonition, Jansen writes: "In reaction to such an extreme situation of misjudgment, one must lay himself open to it. Amid such misjudgment, if he can still preserve his heart from being disturbed, then that is a proof that he has not lost himself in the outside world, that is, in the eyes of his fellow men. This is the proof that he bears in himself an invulnerable core."[39]

The "invulnerable core" was his conscious connectedness to God. This grounding left nothing in the way between himself and his God. God was his all. When he discovered this — that God alone was all that mattered — he could do nothing but rejoice. He had become highly favored by this divine visitation.

Joy at the Approach of Sister Death

When Francis was almost at death's door and suffering physically the disintegration of his body and psychologically the disintegration of his dream as the Order began reverting to old patterns of monasticism, Francis added a phrase to his Canticle of Creation:

> Praised be You, my Lord, through our Sister Bodily Death,
> from whom no one living can escape...
> Blessed are those whom death will find in Your most holy will,
> for the second death shall do them no harm.[40]

Having written the final strophe of the Canticle, it seems somewhat out of place that, along with Sisters Moon and Water and Brothers Sun and Fire, we would have Francis refer to death itself as a "sister." How could this be?

In the way he welcomed death. It seems Francis found a way to become familial with it; hence death itself became a reality with which he could commune in fellowship. This seems clear from the wonderful (and extended) narration of events leading to Francis' death.

When his body was wracked in pain, and because of the extreme summer heat, Francis was brought to Bagnara in the cool mountains above Assisi. However the Assisians were fearful their rival, Perugia, would attempt to take him or get parts of his body or clothing, so it sent soldiers to bring him, under military escort, to the bishop's palace. There he could receive the kind of care he needed. The contradiction was so clear. Having promoted a way of life without property lest he and his followers would feel the need to take up arms to protect it, at the end of his life, to protect his body itself, it had to be brought to Assisi under armed guard.

Now, "laying gravely ill in the palace of the bishop of Assisi, in the days after he returned from Bagnara," *The Assisi Compilation* notes:

> The people of Assisi, fearing that the saint would die during the night without them knowing about it, and that the brothers would secretly take his body away and place it in another city, placed a vigilant guard each night around the palace's walls.
>
> Blessed Francis, although he was gravely ill, to comfort his soul and ward off discouragement in his severe and serious infirmities, often

asked his companions during the day to sing the *Praises of the Lord* which he had composed a long time before in his illness. He likewise had the *Praises* sung during the night for the edification of the guards who kept watch at night outside the palace.

When Brother Elias reflected that blessed Francis was so comforting himself and rejoicing in the Lord in such illness, one day he said to him: "Dearest brother, I am greatly consoled and edified by all the joy which you show for yourself and your companions in such affliction and infirmity. Although the people of this city venerate you as a saint in life and in death, nevertheless, because they firmly believe that you are near death due to your serious and incurable sickness, upon hearing praises of this sort being sung, they can think and say to themselves: "How can he show such joy when he is so near death? He should be thinking about death."

"Do you remember," blessed Francis said to him "when you saw the vision at Foligno and told me that it told you that I would live for only two years? Before you saw that vision, through the grace of the Holy Spirit, who suggests every good in the heart, and places it on the lips of his faithful, I often considered day and night my end. But from the time you saw that vision, each day I have been even more zealous reflecting on the day of my death."

He continued with great intensity of spirit: "Allow me to rejoice in the Lord, Brother, and to sing His praises in my infirmities, because, by the grace of the Holy Spirit, I am so closely united and joined with my Lord, that, through His mercy, I can well rejoice in the Most High Himself."[41]

Contrary to Elias' attitude toward dying (which merely reflected that of his "world" itself), Francis did not just choose to die joyfully; he had lived his life in such a way of surrender that he "caught" Sister Death in an embrace that could find him being nothing but joyful, since it meant his resurrection.

After awhile, Francis asked to be moved to the cradle of the Order, St. Mary of the Angels, his beloved Portiuncula. Assisi's leaders gave permission, as long as he was escorted by armed guards. Once there he received the various brothers wanting to say their "good byes." He also sent a message to his dear friend Clare and her sisters at San Damiano.

Shortly before his death, he was visited by an old friend, Lady Jacopa dei Settesoli, commonly known as Brother Jacoba. However, because Francis earlier had determined that the Portiuncula should be "off limits" to women, a brother asked what should be done about it. Using his own brand of *epikeía,* Francis declared that the law need not apply: "This command need not be observed in the case of this lady whose faith and devotion made her come here from so far away." She came with a special confection he loved to eat. However he was able to eat only a bit "since he was near death, and daily his body was becoming weaker on account of his illness."[42]

He broke bread with the brothers and then, on the evening of October 3, he asked that the Passion according to the Gospel of John be read. He then asked that he be stripped naked, as when he had been born, and laid on the ground. In a voice hardly audible he began praying Psalm 141 (in some Bibles, Psalm 142). He died as the brothers prayed its final verse:

> Bring me out of prison, so that I may give thanks to your name.
> The righteous will surround me, for you will deal bountifully with me.

His life task was given him from the cross of San Damiano when he heard its words: "Francis, don't you see that my house is being destroyed? Go, then, and rebuild it for me."[43] He had worked to create a world that reflected the Trinitarian household of God in his own *oikía* and his community's *oikonomía.* He preached the gospel of peace to the whole *oikoumēne* in a way that included the whole *oikología;* now he could return to the household of God and be welcomed into God's embrace. As *The Anonymous of Perugia* says so beautifully: "Because the servant of God, Francis, wanted to go to His *house* and *the dwelling place of His glory,* the Lord called him to Himself, and so he gloriously passed over to the Lord."[44]

TWELVE

Qualities of Franciscan Holiness and Sanctity

Francis' highest intention, chief desire, his uppermost purpose was to observe the holy Gospel in all things and through all things and, with perfect vigilance, with all zeal, with all the longing of his mind and all the fervor of his heart, "to follow the teaching and the footsteps of our Lord Jesus Christ."[1]
— Brother Thomas of Celano, *First Life of St. Francis*, 30.84.

Saintliness

In the introduction to this book I indicated that I would be developing "Francis' story" from its interaction with other key stories of his day and our own (the culture's story, the church's story, and to some extent, my own story). Now, in this concluding chapter, I would like to highlight key characteristics of Francis' type of sanctity — some of which account for his universal appeal, even though he may not be universally imitated.

In his classic *The Varieties of Religious Experience*, William James noted that the "collective name" for those who have developed "the ripe fruits of religion" is found in a character called "saintliness." He wrote, in an extended passage that still rings true when we consider the sanctity of Francis of Assisi:

The saintly character is the character for which spiritual emotions are the habitual center of the personal energy; and there is a certain composite photograph of universal saintliness, the same in all religions, of which the features can easily be traced.

They are these: —

1. A feeling of being in a wider life than that of this world's selfish little interests; and a conviction, not merely intellectual, but as it were sensible, of the existence of an Ideal Power. In Christian saintliness this

power is always personified as God; but abstract moral ideals, civic or patriotic utopias, or inner versions of holiness or right may also be felt as the true lords and enlargers of our life, in ways which I described in the lecture on the Reality of the Unseen.

2. A sense of the friendly continuity of the ideal power with our own life, and a willing self-surrender to its control.

3. An immense elation and freedom, as the outlines of confining selfhood melt down.

4. A shifting of the emotional center toward loving and harmonious affections, toward "yes, yes," and away from "no," where the claims of the non-ego are concerned.[2]

It is evident from an examination of many holy persons that their lives were characterized by these traits. It is especially clear that Francis exemplified these features — in his way of penance, his countercultural living, his surrender and embrace (or whatever else might be used to define his way of embracing and promoting the Gospel of the reign of God). As a result, his life has become an inspiration to millions throughout the centuries, including our own.

Rather than take the four points of William James and argue their relevance to Francis' life, I would like to accept them as "givens" and bring together the various threads of the previous chapters in a few characteristics that summarize what I believe to be the unique drawing power of Francis for every age. They point to some key elements that make Francis the "universal saint" that he has become.

Francis' Highest Intention, His Chief Desire, His Uppermost Purpose

Elaborating on William James' qualities of a saint, we might begin by saying that a saint is someone driven by a "highest *intention*," as Celano said of Francis above. Intention indicates a strong sense of direction or aim that is accompanied by a determination to achieve the object of one's desire. As Celano's reflection makes clear, this was Francis' goal in "observing the holy Gospel" and following "the teachings and footsteps of Jesus Christ." In many ways, this seems to be what Erich Rohr means when he summarizes the core Franciscan virtues around the notion of "attention": "In reality the so-called Franciscan virtues — poverty, humility, obedience, gratitude, holy joy, and genuine simplicity — do not stem from ascetic or moral zeal but from genuine 'attentiveness' (*aufmerksamkeit*) tied up with love for the Lord."[3]

As I was writing this book I came upon a volume called *The Power of Intention*. The title intrigued me because it talked not just about "intention," but also the "power" inherent in intentional living. When we bring intention into our lives our way of life becomes a force that can bring about change. Carlos Castaneda writes that intention is a force that exists in the universe as an invisible field of energy. He notes that people living from their source "beckon intent, it comes to them and sets up the path for attainment, which means that [they] always accomplish what they set out to do."[4]

In the spiritual life we talk about "purity of intention." This is what Francis had in his approach to his goal of living the Gospel. He was not going to let anything get in the way. He was single-minded, or, as we read in the Beatitudes, he was "pure of heart." We are pure of heart, Francis wrote, when we are not defined by the things the world offers but rather "seek those of heaven, and, with a clean heart and spirit, never cease adoring and seeing the Lord God living and true."[5]

Second, we find a characteristic present in all seekers as well as all saints in this world: desire. Indeed, as I noted in chapter 1, quoting Edith Wyschogrod (who believes we are more likely to become virtuous because of the example of virtuous people than because of debates about the notion of virtue), contemporary saintliness "is not a nostalgic return to premodern hagiography but a postmodern expression of excessive desire, a desire on behalf of the Other that seeks the cessation of another's suffering and the birth of another's joy."[6]

In his well-reviewed book *On Desire: Why We Want What We Want*, William Irvine argues for the existence in each human of a "secret life of desire" that is expressed in two different forms: a "terminal" desire revolves around an end in itself; "instrumental" desires are in the service of other desires.[7]

While corporations and advertisers have known how to capitalize on people's "terminal" desires for years, "the science of desire" has become so sophisticated that a whole new area of ethnography has emerged in anthropology departments, dedicated to "identifying what's missing in people's lives — the perfect cell phone, home appliance, or piece of furniture — and working with designers and engineers to help dream up products and services to fill those needs."[8]

When we turn to desire as it is manifest in a saint, it is not something that can be manipulated insofar as it involves a choice between many goods; with a saint the longing totally grounds the person; it finds the person totally centered with a "chief *desire.*" Human beings are creatures of many desires, some of them conflicting. Some of our desires involve our basic needs, such as the desire for acceptance, understanding, and love. Others deal with our drives, such as the longing for power, possessions, and prestige. Still others deal with our passions, especially those related to sex. Ultimately, however, our underlying desire is the longing to be identified intimately with the source of our very lives: the God who made us. This notion was captured in the famous saying of St. Augustine: "Our hearts were made for thee, O God, and our hearts will never rest until they rest in thee." Francis found *"how the Lord fulfilled his desire,"*[9] as Julian of Speyer wrote, and how this desire was concretized in his embrace of the Gospel. He said it so clearly and simply: "This is what I want," he said, "this is what I seek, this is what I desire with all my heart."[10]

In a market-based economy where meeting basic needs cannot be counted on to drive the economic engine, people's desires or wants must be manipulated. Thus, when we seek what our body desires rather than what our heart ultimately desires, we find ourselves running after false gods, abetted with all the skills of the advertising industry. In Matthew's Gospel Jesus said, "Where your treasure is, there your heart will be also" (Matt. 6:21). In this case our treasure is our "chief desire." If one's chief desire is oriented to mammon in its various forms, our lives will become the servants of such drives. We will be "given over to" those forms of power, wealth, reputation, and sex, and these will preoccupy us. They can even become addictive (see Matt. 6:24). There must be a choice between these basic needs and God, the one source who is able to ground all our desires.

When our treasure is not connected to "seeking first" the reign of God revealed in the Gospel, then, as Jesus warned, we will be endlessly worried about other drives (Matt. 6:25–32), whether related to survival and security, physical needs (what we will eat or drink), or style (what we will look like). As one translation has it: we will be "running" after such things like an addict. To keep from being "anxious" about survival and security and meeting such needs, we should first seek God's reign and live in right relation with everyone. Then, having all our needs grounded in our "chief desire," all the rest will be realized (see Matt. 6:33).

The character of our lives and the quality of our spirituality is determined by how we direct our desire. Ronald Rolheiser describes it well in words that perfectly apply to Francis of Assisi: "Whatever the expression, everyone is ultimately talking about the same thing — an unquenchable fire, a restlessness, a longing, a disquiet, a hunger, a loneliness, a gnawing nostalgia, a wildness that cannot be tamed, a congenital all-embracing ache that lies at the center of human experience and is the ultimate force that drives everything else."[11]

When Francis talked about having a *chief* desire he was referring to his "terminal" desire, his goal in life; it meant he wanted the Gospel and all that it involved to be his "bottom line." This meant subordinating all other desires to the ultimate desire.

As I consider how I might cultivate this kind of desire, I find two main ways. The first is to orient our "instrumental desires" toward our "terminal desire." The other is to cultivate what Francis of Assisi called the spirit of "prayer and devotion" to which all things must be subservient.[12]

It is said, "We become what we desire." That was certainly true for Francis: he became the living articulation of the living Gospel, which prompted him to exclaim, upon hearing it proclaimed, this is what "I desire with all my heart." The early biographers make it clear that his embodiment of the Gospel was so complete that he bore the very wounds of Christ Crucified in his body in the form of the stigmata.[13]

The second task is to cultivate a spirit of "prayer and devotion" that helps us organize and focus our desires toward our "terminal desire." If Francis urged his followers to maintain a spirit of prayer and devotion in whatever they did, we too will benefit immensely from learning how to "pray with desire," as James Keegan writes. "One of the reasons we do not hear God responding to our prayer is that we tend not to treat our desires and needs with the respect they deserve," he notes. "Often we do not pray faithfully with our desires."[14] When we take time to consciously seek God in prayer and to orient all other desires to our desire to pray, that desire in itself can become a form of prayer.

In the end, in a world where so many are seeking "a purpose-driven life," we find that Francis' "uppermost *purpose*," his bottom line, was simply "to observe the holy Gospel in all things and through all things." In this way the purpose of his life would be united with the divine project itself (commonly known as "God's will") or, as Julian of Speyer writes: "so that *every wish* of the Divine Purpose might be more perfectly *fulfilled* in him."[15]

I recently came across a book called simply *Purpose*. The subtitle especially intrigued me, given my ministry in the area of socially responsible investing. It noted that "purpose" is *The Starting Point of Great Companies*. The author, Nikos Mourkogiannis, argues that it has long been a subject of argument whether the best approach to running companies involves operational effectiveness and immediate financial returns in the form of profits or longer-term strategic positioning. He counters that neither motive should drive a company. Instead, what really matters is the purpose that energizes the leaders of a company and its employees. From his consulting experience with hundreds of chief executives he has become convinced that a leadership-driven grand purpose is what distinguishes great companies. He writes: "Purpose is your moral DNA. It's what you believe without having to think...It's the core energy, the element that fuels everything else, big and small."[16]

An interesting element of the book includes Mourkogiannis' delineation of purpose in such companies in four key areas. The first three might be expected: discovery (the *new*), excellence (the *intrinsically beautiful*) and altruism (the *helpful*). However, it is his fourth key characteristic of a purpose-driven executive that intrigued me most: heroism (the *effective*).[17] This latter notion echoed a thought that began this book. In the Introduction I described saints as hero/ines who reach mythic proportions. Truly, it seems, even with Mourkogiannis, when such figures "withdraw" from the crises around them that are not being addressed adequately by their peers, they return driven by a purpose that energizes their lives as well as the lives of those around them.

Francis' purpose came to be linked with God's purpose as revealed in Jesus' proclamation of the purpose or reign or rule of God. Through his experience of "surrender and catch" and his successive efforts to continually "surrender to," that purpose became like his "moral DNA," the energizing force in his life. In the process he became one of the clearest models of the Christ the world has experienced.

In the introduction I showed how we all are invited into the process of moving from the violence in, among, and around us in a way of "withdrawal" that parallels the strategy of Jesus and Francis. I noted how I came to this conclusion when I myself was asked about the "purpose" of my life and found myself saying: "I want to be the Christ," the one in whom the scriptures can find contemporary fulfillment. I am convinced, as Paul wrote to the Galatians, that this must be the ultimate purpose of every follower of Jesus today: to have Christ be formed in them (Gal. 4:19) and to have Christ become the form of their lives. This demands a wholehearted conversion to the Gospel of the Reign of God that eclipses and relativizes every other competing power and principality.

In 2003 and 2004, the *New York Times* list of best-selling books was dominated by Rick Warren's *The Purpose Driven Life*. It captured the imagination as well as the desires of millions of people. Built around forty chapters designed for group discussion, Warren capsulated "God's five purposes for life" around five notions contained in the Great Commandment of God and the Great Commission of Jesus:

1. "Love God with all your heart": You were planned for God's pleasure, so your purpose is to love God through *worship*.

2. "Love your neighbor as yourself": You were shaped for serving, so your purpose is to show love for others through *ministry*.

3. "Go and make disciples": You were made for a mission, so your purpose is to share God's message through *evangelism*.

4. "Baptize them into...": You were formed for God's family, so your purpose is to identify with his church through *fellowship*.

5. "Teach them to do all things...": You were created to become like Christ, so your purpose is to grow to maturity through *discipleship*.[18]

When we speak of the "uppermost purpose" of a saint, I can't help but recall the definition we learned from the *Baltimore Catechism* about our "purpose in life": it was "to know, love and serve God in this life and to be happy with him in the next." Despite the fact that I had the answer drilled into my head, I now think it may have satisfied a "belief" question, but it is only half true when I consider it from the perspective of a living faith.

In my mind, as I tried to show in the previous chapter, the drawing power of a saint like Francis derives from the fact that his grounding in God in *this* life, and not in any *far-off* life to come, marks him with an unmistakable joy.

These three characteristics of intention, desire, and purpose were geared to a wholehearted embrace of the Gospel. In other words, Francis of Assisi brought *passion* to his way of living the Gospel in a world that had thought it never could be done in such a way again. It is to this next dimension of living as a saint that we now turn.

Embracing a Gospel Way of Life with Passion and Enthusiasm

In his historical novel about Francis of Assisi, *The Passionate Troubadour*, Edward Hays argues that the real gift of Francis to the world is found in the way he lived life: "Assisi's little man in rags is more the patron of passion. He is a holy pyromaniac, eager to set our hearts madly ablaze with love for God, Christ, all humanity, and all creation."[19]

One of my purposes in writing this book has been to offer a compelling and imitable way of spirituality that might stand as an alternative or antidote to an approach that sees Catholicism chiefly as a matter of faith prescriptions, rather than faith proclamation or faith personalization. It was my hope to make Francis' embrace of the Gospel of the Reign of God serve as a compelling alternative story to the stories of our culture and our church, whether those are defined by the "left" or the "right." In this effort I have been motivated by the first challenge given the churches in the Book of Revelation — the call to be defined not just by our works, but to rekindle our "first love," the love that nurtured left Francis of Assisi in all the works he performed:

> I know your works, your toil and your patient endurance. I know that you cannot tolerate evildoers; you have tested those who claim to be apostles but are not, and have found them to be false. I also know that you are enduring patiently and bearing up for the sake of my name, and that you have not grown weary. But I have this against you, that you have abandoned the love you had at first. Remember then from what you have fallen; repent, and do the works you did at first (Rev. 2:2–5a).

The works of the early church did at first represent an embrace of the Gospel that linked faith and works, mercy and justice, prayer and service (see Acts 11:26). It was passionate. But over time that passion waned.

Saints are passionate not only because they are single-minded in their desires, intentions, and purpose in life but also because they are in tune with that God whose passion for us has been revealed in the redemptive Incarnation of the Beloved One. It has been in this loving enfleshment of God in us, which has been accomplished in the Spirit of Trinitarian Love, that we come to realize why God can have no favorites, only those invited into God's passionate embrace.

Because God is love, God cannot be anything but passion personified; however, because God's person is triadic, God's passionate love is totally inclusive in its embrace of its objects of love. Indeed, God is the Source of All Passion.

One of my favorite stories about Francis reportedly took place near the woods of St. Mary of the Angels, Francis' beloved Portiuncula. A lumberman heard wailing and went looking only to find Francis loudly weeping. He was concerned and asked Francis what had happened. And Francis replied, "Love is not loved."

Francis was so affected by his meditation on Jesus' gift of Love and of Life and so sensitive to the fact that humankind was not responding with appropriate gratitude that he could not contain his grief. Love was not loved. The story may not be true but its meaning is.

Francis was passionate about what God was passionate about: the Beloved One and the need to bring about the kind of Trinitarian Reign of God on earth that is in heaven. Consumed with wonder at God's tremendous self-giving love, as revealed in the Incarnation, the crucifixion, and the Eucharist, Francis identified in a special way with those whom the Beloved was passionate about: the sick, the poor, and the marginated ones of society.

This passion of Francis for the Gospel way of life was evident the first time he made a conscious effort to understand what God's word might be saying to him. This "good news" was Jesus Christ. The result of his surrender and catch was not that he just became a nonconformist, which he did, but that he was able to offer a compelling, creative, countercultural alternative to the prevailing patterns of his church and culture. And he did this with passion and enthusiasm.

Enthusiasm, as is reflected in the word's roots (*en-theos*, or being "in God"), is ultimately a matter of being consciously in contact with God.

A friend of mine, Joe Tye, whom I first met while challenging the death-dealing ways of the tobacco companies, has since become "America's Values Coach." I get his e-mails twice a week. In one of his "Spark Plugs" he highlighted enthusiasm. He featured a poll that he had made which showed that "97 out of 100 people believe they would be happier in their personal lives and more effective in their professional lives if they could just be consistently more enthusiastic." The four "cornerstones" of enthusiasm, according to Joe, are positivity, curiosity, spontaneity, and humor.[20] Joe doesn't just promote enthusiasm as his sixth "Core Action Value"; as "America's Values Coach," he lives it and invites a huge following to embrace it in their lives. In many ways he is a secular St. Francis. Enthusiasm radiated from Francis; it characterizes Joe Tye as well. If it characterized me as well, I would be a much more effective witness to the Gospel, I am convinced.

Contemporary Chivalry

There was something about Francis, even before his leper experience, that could be described as chivalrous. The very first story told about Francis in *The Anonymous of Perugia* recounts how Francis refused to give alms to a poor man who asked for help in the name of God. After sending him away, Francis "began to accuse himself of great rudeness, saying: 'If the poor man had asked in the name of a count or a powerful baron, you would have granted him his request. How much more should you have done this for the King of Kings and the Lord of all?'"[21] The original term for "great rudeness" (*magna rusticitas*) bespeaks an action that compromised against chivalry.

In her book on *The Passionate God,* Rosemary Haughton singles out Francis as an example of one who translated passion into a chivalrous stance toward everyone and everything in creation. After his conversion, she writes, when

> he became possibly the most extraordinary and radiant of all Christian saints, there was converted in and with him the "courtly love" in which he had soaked himself... About the year 1225 he composed the *Laudes Creaturam,* a poem written in Italian "Romance," full of that vernal and delicate vitality, of a passion both gentle and ardent, which is characteristic of the best of troubadour poetry.[22]

Fortini writes, "Chivalry never developed in Italy as it did in other nations. Far better known in Italy was the rule of chivalry of St. Francis of Assisi."[23] It would follow then, that the combination of Francis' experience of the Crusades and his trips to France with his father influenced him to transform the traditional way of knighthood into a positive way of serving the "Lord" rather than the "Servant." In Francis' day, Fortini reminds us:

> Chivalry required joy. It ranked as equal in importance with valour. "The knight," according to an ancient regulation, "must be joyous, because this is the life of warriors: happiness in the field and joy in the castle... The highest valour was deemed that silently practiced in the face of tribulations and sufferings... The poets of feudal chivalry, the troubadours of Provence, say that one does not talk of great anxieties, such as illness, unrequited love, defeat, dishonor, betrayal, death."[24]

Increasingly, in our violent world, we need an alternative way of nonviolence. But this cannot be another form of charge and countercharge; we need another approach that disarms. Whether it is a matter of conflicts in the church or the culture, opposing sides are all too adept at labeling their opponents and thus dismissing their message. We need to recover a sense of courtesy. In the midst of so much negativity, a recovery of the Franciscan imagination might be just what we need to turn our nation and church around. We need more of what Francis urged of his followers. According to the *Fioretti* Francis said that "courtesy is one of the qualities of God, who gives His sun and His rain to the just and unjust out of courtesy."[25] Inspired by such a God of Courtesy, those who would aspire to follow this Great Ruler should take this model to heart. Consequently, Francis declared: "Let them be careful not to appear outwardly as sad and gloomy hypocrites but show themselves *joyful,* cheerful and consistently gracious [courteous] *in the Lord.*"[26]

In our effort to challenge the ideologies that have become so core to our "culture's story" and our "religion's story," the joyful and positive way of

Francis, which invited his co-religionists and citizens to the "life of pen-ance" or a countercultural way, needs to be revitalized with meaning. "The testimony of many witnesses gives us the impression that Francis and his companions went about the countryside more like God's troubadours and jongleurs than as preachers of penance."[27] It was this positive approach that captured the hearts and minds of the people of his generation. I believe it will do the same in our own time, because it is ultimately grounded in the power of the Living God that we find in the Gospels themselves.

Years ago, when I read Mario von Galli's *Living Our Future: Francis of Assisi and the Church Tomorrow* I marveled that a Jesuit was able to capture the personality and power of Francis. The paragraph that caught my attention then still finds me returning to it. It is where he develops the notion of courtesy, or *cortesia*.

> The word *noblesse* better expresses what Francis realized as *cortesia*. Perhaps we must go further and say that everything we designate today as *solidarity* with the suffering and the oppressed corresponds to the *cortesia* of Francis, or, at the very least, does not run counter to it. I refer to real solidarity with those whose human dignity has been violated, so that we are prepared to share their lot and to fashion a community of established people for the purpose of initiating effective action and bringing about structural change.[28]

Ultimately, in considering the spiritual meaning of chivalry, we must acknowledge the importance of thanksgiving, appreciation, and gratitude, which always accompanied the stance of the knight before the *signeur*. These attitudes indicated that serving such a master was something positive rather than a burden. As such, they must also be considered in relation to the key qualities of "the saint." Indeed, if we would follow the thought of the eighteenth-century spiritual writer William Law, we would conclude that the triad of thanksgiving, appreciation, and gratitude are all that we need to be considered holy. He writes:

> Would you know him who is the greatest saint in the world? It is not he who prays most or fasts most; it is not he who gives most alms; but it is he who is always thankful to God, who receives everything as an instance of God's goodness and has a heart always ready to praise God for it.
>
> If anyone would tell you the shortest, surest way to all happiness and perfection, he must tell you to make a rule to thank and praise God for everything that happens to you. Whenever seeming calamity

happens to you, if you thank and praise God for it, it turns it into a blessing. Could you therefore work miracles, you could not do more for yourself than by this thankful spirit; it turns all that it touches into happiness.[29]

Having developed the notions of holiness that seemed so evident in Francis' life, I can think of no better way to conclude this chapter on his saintliness and the qualities of Franciscan holiness and sanctity than to return to a wonderful passage from G. K. Chesterton. His *St. Francis of Assisi* has gone through more reprintings, I believe, than any other book on Francis in the English language. In words that show the power of a new way of life that is available to all who are willing to enter the dynamics of surrender and catch that constituted Francis' original, life-changing conversion, he writes (with apologies for the exclusive language):

The transition from the good man to the saint is a sort of revolution; by which one for whom all things illustrate and illuminate God becomes one for whom God illustrates and illuminates all things. It is rather like the reversal whereby a lover might say at first sight that a lady looked like a flower, and say afterwards that all flowers reminded him of his lady. A saint and a poet standing by the same flower might seem to say the same thing; but indeed though they would both be telling the truth, they would be telling different truths. For one the joy of life is a *cause* of faith, for the other rather a *result* of faith. But one effect of the difference is that the sense of a divine dependence, which for the artist is like the brilliant Levin-blaze, for the saint is like the broad daylight. Being in some mystical sense on the other side of things, he sees things go forth from the divine as children going forth from a familiar and accepted home, instead of meeting them as they come out, as most of us do, upon the roads of the world. And it is the paradox that by this privilege he is more familiar, more free and fraternal, more carelessly hospitable than we. For us the elements are like heralds who tell us with trumpet and tabard that we are drawing near the city of a great king; but he hails them with an old familiarity that is almost an old frivolity. He calls them Brother Fire and Sister Water.[30]

I conclude this book as I began — by articulating the reason for writing it. In a world torn apart, whether by violence, materialism, or ideology, Francis' life offers us a nonviolent alternative. It is my hope that he will again offer the kind of inspiration for emulation that he has done throughout the centuries

since he once walked among us. Never satisfied with what he had done, realizing the need continually to be converted and to evidence that conversion
in deeds of justice, mercy and love, Francis would say to his followers words
that might still stimulate us to do more: " 'Let us begin, brothers, to serve
God. Let us begin,' he would say. 'And let us make progress, because up to
now we have made too little progress.' "[31]

Notes

Preface

1. 1LtF, 1.10, in FA:ED I, 42. For explanation of "FA:ED," see the following note.

2. The three-volume series *Francis of Assisi: Early Documents,* ed. Armstrong, Hellmann, and Short, cover "The Saint," "The Founder," and the "Prophet." As the definitive volumes, these are indispensable for any research on Francis. See Regis J. Armstrong, O.F.M.Cap., J. A. Wayne Hellmann, O.F.M.Conv., William J. Short, O.F.M., *Francis of Assisi: Early Documents,* 3 vols. (New York: New City Press, vol. 1, 1999; vol. 2, 2000; vol. 3, 2001). Hereafter noted as FA:ED. I have also been helped immeasurably by a separate volume published in 2002: *Index.*

3. Since much was written about Francis, almost from the beginning, scholars have developed an approach that highlights certain sources and diminishes the historical authenticity of others. For instance, *The First Life of St. Francis* was written by one of his contemporaries, Brother Thomas of Celano. He also wrote a follow-up: *The Remembrance of the Desire of a Soul.* Scholarship has shown it was written to make Francis more acceptable to officials in the Roman Church. Popular writings about Francis, such as the *Fioretti* (The Little Flowers), will be used only minimally, as they reflect the culturally conditioned approach to hagiography (biographies about holy people) that elevated them to the status of "super men" and "super women" — good for inspiration but not emulation.

4. A fine articulation on the "Sources" can be found in William R. Hugo, O.F.M.Cap., *Studying the Life of Francis of Assisi: A Beginner's Workbook* (Quincy, IL: Franciscan Press, 1996).

Introduction

1. 1C, 3.7, in FA:ED I, 188.

2. Joseph Campbell, in Joseph Campbell with Bill Moyers, *The Power of Myth* (New York: Doubleday, 1988), 15.

3. Ibid., 129.

4. Ibid., 136.

5. Leonardo Boff, *Saint Francis: A Model for Human Liberation,* trans. John W. Diercksmeier (Maryknoll, NY: Orbis, 2006), 18.

6. I have shown elsewhere that the "Matthew" of the Gospel may have had origins in the "tax collector" whom we discover in Matthew 9:9; however, since the version of the Gospel of Matthew we have today was written only in the 80s or 90s, beyond the expected life-span of males of that time, it is not likely that this "Matthew" is the author of the Gospel. See Michael H. Crosby, *House of Disciples: Church, Economics and Justice in Matthew* (Maryknoll, NY: Orbis, 1989; Eugene, OR: Wipf and Stock, 2004), 43–48.

7. Campbell, *The Power of Myth,* 136.

8. R. I. Moore, *The Formation of a Persecuting Society: Power and Deviance in Western Europe, 950–1250* (Oxford and New York: Blackwell, 1987), 5.

9. Decree noted in Arnoldo Fortini, *Francis of Assisi,* trans. Helen Moak (New York: Crossroad, 1985), 74.

10. Ibid., 56.

11. Ibid.

12. Ibid., 55.

13. Ibid., 54.

14. Ibid., 149.

15. 1C, 4.8, in FA:ED I, 188.

16. 1C, 3.6, in FA:ED I, 187.

17. Leonhard Lehmann, O.F.M.Cap., "Franciscan Global Spirituality," trans. Ignatius McCormick, O.F.M.Cap., *Greyfriars Review* 5, no. 3 (1991): 308.

18. Kurt H. Wolff, quoting one of his students, in Kurt H. Wolff, *Surrender and Catch: Experience and Inquiry Today,* Boston Studies in the Philosophy of Science 51 (Dordrecht, Holland, and Boston: D. Reidel, 1976), 291–92.

19. 1C, 27.71, in FA:ED I, 243.

20. 1C, 3.6, in FA:ED I, 187.

21. Meg Bortin, "Poll Finds Discord between the Muslim and Western Worlds," *New York Times,* June 23, 2006.

22. New York Times news service, "Global View of U.S. Worsens, Poll Shows," *New York Times,* January 23, 2007.

23. Peggy Noonan, "The Culture of Death," *Wall Street Journal,* April 22, 1999.

24. Alan Ehrenhalt, "A Culture of Corruption," Book Review of Matthew Continetti, *The K Street Gang, Wall Street Journal,* April 26, 2006.

25. Geogg Dyer, "Developing World Afflicted by 'Diseases of Affluence,'" *Financial Times,* October 31, 2005.

26. Daniel Akst, "In a Culture of Greed, How Bad Is an Affair?" *New York Times,* June 25, 2006.

27. Anna Bernasek, "Income Inequality, and Its Cost," *New York Times,* June 25, 2006.

28. Lawrence E. Mitchell, "The Tyranny of the Market," *BusinessWeek,* July 30, 2007. A "dangerous trend in American capitalism," Mitchell writes, is "short-term, rapid-fire finance." This reveals "an economy likely to self-destruct over the long haul," 90.

29. Noonan, "The Culture of Death."

30. Ibid.

31. Bob Herbert, "An American Obsession," *New York Times,* February 2, 2006.

32. U.S. Catholic Bishops, "When I Call for Help: A Pastoral Response to Domestic Violence against Women," 10th anniversary edition, November 12, 2002, *Origins* 32, no. 24 (2002): 400.

33. Ibid.

34. Camilo Macisse, O.C.D., "Violence in the Church," *The Tablet* (2003): 1.

35. Ibid., 7.

36. Kurt H. Wolff, "Toward Understanding the Radicalness of Surrender," *Sociological Analysis* 38, no. 4 (Winter 1977): 397.

37. Eleanor M. Godway, commenting on Wolff, "Faith *and* Knowledge in Crisis: Towards an Epistemology of the Cross," *Listening* 27, no. 2 (Spring 1992): 104.

38. I describe my realization, after more than twenty-five years of being a celibate, that God *does not* have such specific plans related to our life-choices to be single, married, priest, or celibate, in my book, *Rethinking Celibacy, Reclaiming the Church* (Eugene, OR: Wipf and Stock, 2003), 1ff.

39. 1C, 3.7 in FA:ED I, 188.

Chapter 1: Francis of Assisi

1. Solanus Casey, O.F.M.Cap., quoted in *Solanus Casey: The Official Account of a Virtuous American Life,* ed. Michael Crosby, O.F.M.Cap. (New York: Crossroad, 2000), 1.

2. Sue Shellenbarger, "Young People's Stories Offer Surprises on How They Define a Hero," *Wall Street Journal,* June 6, 2001.

3. Kurt H. Wolff, *Surrender and Catch: Experience and Inquiry Today,* Boston Studies in the Philosophy of Science, 51 (Dordrecht, Holland, and Boston: D. Reidel, 1976), 293. Here Wolff comments on the thoughts of one of his students.

4. I am thankful to Richard P. McBrien for these insights. See his *Lives of the Saints* (San Francisco: HarperCollins, 2001). See Dietrich Bonhoeffer, *The Cost of Discipleship,* rev. and unabridged ed. (New York: Macmillan, 1967).

5. Richard Rohr, O.F.M., "Foreword," in Markus Hofer, *Francis for Men: "Otherwise, We Need Weapons"* (Cincinnati: St. Anthony Messenger Press, 2003), vi.

6. Fareed Munir, Ph.D., "Islam and Franciscanism: Prophet Mohammad of Arabia and St. Francis of Assisi in the Spirituality of Mission," in Daniel Dwyer, O.F.M. and Hugh Hines, O.F.M., eds., "Islam and Franciscanism: A Dialogue 38," *Spirit and Life* 9 (2000): referring to an insight of Maulana Muhammad Ali, *The Religion of Islam: A Comprehensive Discussion of Its Sources, Principles and the Practices of Islam,* 3rd ed. (Lahore: Ripon Printing Press, 1971), 268.

7. Bishop Raymond A. Lucker, "St. Francis: Person of the Millennium," *The Cord* 50, no. 5 (2000): 215–17.

8. Lynn Townsend White, "The Historical Roots of Our Ecologic Crisis," *Science* (May 1967).

9. Michael D. Guinan, O.F.M., *The Franciscan Vision and the Gospel of John: The San Damiano Cross; Francis and John; Creation and John,* The Franciscan Heritage Series (St. Bonaventure, NY: Franciscan Institute, 2006), 39.

10. 1C, 3.119, FA:ED I, 289.

11. Leonhard Lehmann, O.F.M.Cap., "Franciscan Global Spirituality," trans. Ignatius McCormick, O.F.M.Cap., *Greyfriars Review* 5, no. 3 (1991): 305.

12. AP Prologue 2, FA:ED II, 34.

13. Elizabeth A. Johnson, *Friends of God and Prophets: A Feminist Theological Reading of the Communion of Saints* (New York: Continuum, 2003), 2.

14. Ibid.

15. Kenneth L. Woodward, *Making Saints: How the Catholic Church Determines Who Becomes a Saint, Who Doesn't, and Why* (New York: Simon and Schuster, 1990).

16. This is the image used in an article on Solanus Casey that accompanied a cover feature on him in *Our Sunday Visitor* 84, no. 26 (October 29, 1995). The image was taken from the movie *Forrest Gump,* because of Solanus' simplicity and innocence.

17. Solanus Casey, quoted in Michael H. Crosby, O.F.M.Cap., *Thank God Ahead of Time: The Life and Spirituality of Venerable Solanus Casey* (Quincy, IL: Franciscan Press, 2000), 299.

18. Lawrence Cunningham, *The Meaning of Saints* (New York: Harper & Row, 1980), 65.

19. Edith Wyschogrod, *Saints and Postmodernism: Revisioning Moral Philosophy* (Chicago: University of Chicago Press, 1990), xiii.

20. Ibid., xxii–xxiv.

21. Joan Chittister, O.S.B., *How Shall We Live? Because There Is a Monk in All of Us* (Erie, PA: Benetvision, 2006).

22. Ibid., 20.

23. Joseph Campbell, *The Inner Reaches of Outer Space: Metaphor as Myth and as Religion* (New York: Harper & Row, 1986), 69.

24. Emanuela Prinzivalli, "A Saint to Be Read: Francis of Assisi in the Hagiographic Sources," trans. Edward Hagman, O.F.M.Cap., *Greyfriars* Review 15, no. 3 (2001): 254.

25. Two exceptions are allowed and will also be used more extensively in this biography: *The Anonymous of Perugia* and *The Legend of the Three Companions.* Prinzivalli writes that these "must be linked to the *First Life* for two main reasons. Despite their significant differences with the *First Life,* they both have a chronological development that parallels the *First Life* and, second, "even though on certain important points they depend ideologically on the *First Life,* they also deliberately distance themselves from it and correct it on certain particular points." Ibid., 269.

26. Ibid., 264.

27. Ibid., 263.

28. 2LtF, 18, FA:ED I, 46.

29. Robert N. Bellah, Richard Madsen, William M. Sullivan, Ann Swidler, and Steven M. Tipton, *Habits of the Heart: Individualism and Commitment in American Life* (Berkeley and Los Angeles: University of California Press, 1985).

30. Kurt H. Wolff, "Presuppositions of the Sociology of Knowledge and a Task for It," Supplement, in Kurt H. Wolff, *Trying Sociology* (New York: John Wiley & Sons, 1974), 548.

31. Wolff, "Presuppositions," 549.

32. David Gelernter, "Americanism — and Its Enemies," *Commentary* 119, no. 1 (2005): 41.

33. Richard John Neuhaus, "Our American Babylon," *First Things* (December 2005): 26. Without discussing the downside of the metaphor, i.e., the "Babylonian Captivity" of the Catholic Church in the United States, as I do in this book and my other writings, Neuhaus does realize there is a problem. Setting his remarks in the context of the need for a new story to guide us in the church in the United States, he writes: "American theology has suffered from an ecclesiological deficit, leading to an ecclesiological substitution of America for the Church through time. Alongside this development, and weaving its way in and out of it, is a radical and vaulting individualism that would transcend the creaturely limits of time, space, tradition, authority, and obedience to received truth," 25.

34. Walter Brueggemann, *The Prophetic Imagination,* 2nd ed. (Minneapolis: Fortress, 2001), 28.

35. Donald Cozzens, *Sacred Silence: Denial and the Crisis in the Church* (Collegeville, MN: Liturgical Press, 2004), 118.

36. Cardinal Joseph Ratzinger, "Homily," April 18, 2005, *Origins* 34, no. 45 (2005): 720.

37. Wolff, *Surrender and Catch,* 32, 97. Wolff calls this process "surrendering to" (see pp. 103, 164) as well as focusing itself, 177; see also Wolff, "Toward Radicalism in Sociology and Every Day," in George Psathas, ed., *Phenomenological Sociology: Issues and Application* (New York: Wiley, 1973), 54.

38. Peter A. Campbell and Edwin M. McMahon, *Bio-Spirituality: Focusing as a Way to Grow* (Chicago: Loyola University Press, 1985), 56.

Chapter 2: Assisi and Francis

1. Morris L. West, *Shoes of the Fisherman* (New York: St. Martin's Press, 1990), 270.

2. Lester K. Little, *Religious Poverty and the Profit Economy in Medieval Europe* (Ithaca, NY: Cornell University Press, 1978), 24.

3. Alexander Murray, *Reason and Society in the Middle Ages* (Oxford: Clarendon Press, 1986), 60.

4. Lázaro Iriarte, O.F.M.Cap., "Francis of Assisi and the Evangelical Movement of His Time," trans. Edward Hagman, O.F.M.Cap., *Greyfriars Review* 12, no. 2 (1998): 169.

5. Kurt H. Wolff, *Surrender and Catch: Experience and Inquiry Today,* Boston Studies in the Philosophy of Science 51 (Dordrecht, Holland, and Boston: D. Reidel, 1976), 298.

6. Karen Armstrong interviewed by Peter Stanford, "Violence, Compassion and World Religions," *America,* October 16, 2006: 25.

7. Richard Rohr, O.F.M., "Thoughts on the Papacy: Container versus Contents," *Sojourners* website, April 22, 2005.

8. Wolff, *Surrender and Catch,* 33–34.

9. Robert J. Schreiter, *Reconciliation: Mission and Ministry in a Changing Social Order* (Maryknoll, NY: Orbis, 1992), 34.

10. Wolff, *Surrender and Catch,* 40–41.

11. Ibid., 43.

12. Sharon Daloz Parks, *The Critical Years: The Young Adult Search for a Faith to Live By* (San Francisco: Harper & Row, 1986), 12–13.

13. Ibid., 14.

14. Michael Lerner, *The Left Hand of God: Taking Back Our Country from the Religious Right* (New York: HarperCollins, 2006), 44.

15. Pope Benedict XVI, address to Swiss bishops, November 2006, in Zenit news service, December 7, 2006.

16. Bob Dixon, "Catholics Who Have Stopped Going to Mass," Summary Report, Research Project, Pastoral Projects Office, Australian Catholic Bishops Conference, October 2006, 13.

17. Francis A. Quinn, "A Looming Crisis of Faith," *America,* April 7, 2003, 14.

18. R. I. Moore, *The Formation of a Persecuting Society: Power and Deviance in Western Europe, 950–1250* (Oxford and New York: Blackwell, 1987), 23.

19. Ibid., 140.

20. Ibid., 146.

21. Arnoldo Fortini, *Francis of Assisi*, trans. Helen Moak (New York: Crossroad, 1985), 45–46. In a more nuanced perspective that has impact on our understanding of the stance of Francis, Michael Cusato writes: The term *minores* can have two meanings in Assisi of the early thirteenth century. It refers first and more specifically to the bourgeois class of merchants, the *homines populi*, who were defined in opposition to the *maiores* class of nobles and their families, also called the *boni homines* (the good men or, as the English might say, your 'betters'). The defining measure was the ownership of property: the latter class had a greater (*maior*) amount of lands and goods than did the former class who had less (*minor*) than they in their portfolio. The second, more generic meaning of the term refers to that mass of people who constituted the landless peasantry and the poor. The people of this class were more frequently referred to as *villani*, literally people of vile condition." Michael F. Cusato, O.F.M. "To Do Penance / *Facere poenitentiam*," *The Cord* 57, no. 1 (2007), ft. 23, 19.

22. Prospero Rivi, O.F.M.Cap., "Francis of Assisi and the Laity of His Time," trans. Heather Tolfree, *Greyfriars Review* 15 (2001): Supplement, 6. I am indebted to Rivi for my opening remarks.

23. Moore, *The Formation of a Persecuting Society,* 4.

24. Ibid., 5. For further discussion see 90ff.

25. Fortini, *Francis of Assisi,* 11.

26. Ibid., 45.

27. Ibid., 26.

28. Ronald Rolheiser, O.M.I., "Walking the Ambit," in *Secularity and the Gospel: Being Missionaries to Our Children,* ed. Ronald Rolheiser (New York: Crossroad, 2006), 20.

29. Fortini, *Francis of Assisi,* 166.

30. 1C, 1.1, FA:ED I, 183.

31. 1C, 4.8, FA:ED I, 188.

32. L3C, 2.5, FA:ED II, 70.

33. L3C, 2.6, FA:ED II, 71.

34. Julio Micó, "The Spirituality of St. Francis: Francis's Image of God," trans. Paul Barrett, O.F.M.Cap., *Greyfriars Review* 7, no. 2 (1993): 133.

35. Ibid., 139.

36. PrCr, FA:ED I, 40.

37. Anna Bernasek, "Income Inequality, and Its Cost," Economic View, *New York Times,* June 25, 2006.

38. "If the rich can influence political outcomes through lobbying activities or membership in special interest groups, then more inequality could lead to less redistribution rather than more," Edward L. Glaeser, quoted in Bernasek, "Income Inequality, and Its Cost."

39. Alan Ehrenhalt, "A Culture of Corruption," Book Review of Matthew Continetti, *The K Street Gang* (New York: Doubleday, 2006), in the *Wall Street Journal,* April 26, 2006.

40. Nolan McCarty, Keith Poole, and Howard Rosenthal, *Polarized America: The Dance of Ideology and Unequal Riches* (Cambridge, MA: MIT Press, 2006). Paul

Krugman comments on this in his column "Class War Politics," *New York Times,* June 19, 2006.

41. The numbers can be found in Bob Herbert, "Working for a Pittance," *New York Times,* July 3, 2006.

42. Clarence Page, "How Rich Do You Think You Are? Well, Here's the Truth," *Chicago Tribune,* January 19, 2003.

43. Robert B. Reich, "Don't Blame Wal-Mart," *New York Times,* March 1, 2005.

44. In 2005 57 percent of all Catholics interviewed vs. 65 percent of others in the United States supported the death penalty. This was down from 72 percent of Catholics in 1999. Cathy Lynn Grossman, "Catholics Come Together: Opposition to Death Penalty Unites," *USAToday,* November 8, 2005.

45. 1C, 1.2, FA:ED I, 184.

46. Marie Dennis, Cynthia Moe-Lobeda, Joseph Nangle, O.F.M., and Stuart Taylor, *St. Francis and the Foolishness of God* (Maryknoll, NY: Orbis, 1993), 37.

47. Stanislaus da Campagnola, "Francis of Assisi and the Social Problems of His Time," trans. Edward Hagman, O.F.M.Cap., *Greyfriars* Review 2, no. 1 (1988): 133.

48. Fortini, *Francis of Assisi,* 315.

49. Fenton Johnson, "Beyond Belief: A Skeptic Searches for an American Faith," *Harper's,* September 1998: 52.

Chapter 3: Francis' Approach to Change

1. L3C, 5.13, FA:ED II, 76. Words adjusted to popular version.

2. 1 C, 3.6, FA:ED I, 187.

3. 1 C, 3.7, FA:ED I, 188.

4. Michael H. Crosby, *"Do You Love Me?" Jesus Questions the Church* (Maryknoll, NY: Orbis, 2000), 209ff. My argument is developed from Raymond Brown.

5. ER 23.6, FA:ED I, 83. I am indebted to the Franciscan biblical scholar Michael Guinan for this insight. See Michael D. Guinan, O.F.M., *The Franciscan Vision and the Gospel of John: The San Damiano Cross; Francis and John; Creation and John* Franciscan Heritage Series 4 (St. Bonaventure, NY: Franciscan Institute, 2006), 21. In turn Guinan credits his insight to Norbert Nguyen-Van-Kanh, O.F.M., *The Teacher of His Heart: Jesus Christ in the Thought and Writings of St. Francis.* Franciscan Pathways Series (St. Bonaventure, NY: Franciscan Institute, 2003), 223.

6. Guinan, *The Franciscan Vision and the Gospel of John,* 41. I discovered Guinan's book after submitting my original manuscript to Orbis. However, his insights, along with those of Joseph Chinnici, the general editor, resonate with mine. In a wonderful summary, Guinan writes: "If Francis saw all of creation as God's HOUSE, then perhaps he saw us, everyone and everything in creation, as members of one family, children of the same God and brothers and sisters of each other. He called all creatures brother and sister, and he praised God FOR the good gifts which this family was to him.

"If Francis saw all of creation as God's TEMPLE, as the place where God's presence could be experienced and where we could respond in reverent worship, then perhaps he might call on all of his family to join him in his prayer so that God might be praised BY the whole chorus, just as we saw above in Psalm 138.

"If Francis saw all of creation as mediating the BODY of Christ to him, then he might praise God THROUGH all creatures" (41).

7. L3C, 5.13, FA:ED II, 76.

8. Ibid.

9. Michael Blastic, O.F.M., "Custodians of Franciscan Households," *Review for Religious* 65, no. 2 (2006): 123.

10. Sandra M. Schneiders, *The Revelatory Text: Interpreting the New Testament as Sacred Scripture* (San Francisco: HarperSanFrancisco, 1991), 153.

11. Joseph P. Chinnici, O.F.M., general editor, "General Editor's Introduction," in Guinan, *The Franciscan Vision and the Gospel of John*, vi.

12. Sharon Daloz Parks, "Home and Pilgrimage: Companion Metaphors for Personal and Social Transformation," *Soundings* 72, nos. 2–3 (1989): 299.

13. Ibid., 303.

14. Ibid., 312.

15. LR, 3.14, FA:ED I, 102; see ER, 14.2, FA:ED I, 73.

16. Test 23, FA:ED I, 126.

17. ER, 23.1, FA:ED I, 81–82.

18. Leonhard Lehmann, "Franciscan Global Spirituality," trans. Ignatius Mc-Cormick, O.F.M.Cap., *Greyfriars Review* 5, no. 3 (1991): 320.

19. The Jocist model of social analysis was the basis for Catholic Action in the middle part of the twentieth century. This model also finds an echo in Bernard Lonergan's notion of intellectual, moral, and religious conversion. I have discussed this in my earlier book on Jesus' Prayer: *Thy Will Be Done: Praying the Our Father as Subversive Activity* (Maryknoll, NY: Orbis, 1977), 197–211.

20. Kurt H. Wolff, *Surrender and Catch: Experience and Inquiry Today,* Boston Studies in the Philosophy of Science 51 (Dordrecht, Holland, and Boston: D. Reidel, 1976), 181.

21. For more on this see Vishnu Magee, *Archetype Design: House as Vehicle for Spirit* (Taos, NM: Archetype Design Publications, 1999). I am indebted to my confrere, Gary Keegstra, O.F.M.Cap., for leading me to this source.

22. Clare Cooper Marcus, *House as a Mirror of Self: Exploring the Deeper Meaning of Home* (Berkeley, CA: Conari Press, 1995).

23. ER, 22.27, FA:ED I, 80; 1Frg, 16, FA:ED I, 88.

24. St. Teresa of Avila, *Interior Castle,* trans. E. Allison Peers (Garden City, NY: Doubleday Image Books, 1961), 28.

25. St. John of the Cross, "The Dark Night," in Kieran Kavanaugh, O.C.D., and Otilio Rodriguez, O.C.D., trans, *The Collected Works of St. John of the Cross* (Washington, DC: ICS Publications, 1973), 295, 297.

26. Jessica Powers, "The House at Rest," in *Selected Poetry of Jessica Powers*, ed. Regina Siegfried, ASC, and Robert F. Morneau (Kansas City, MO: Sheed & Ward, 1991), 122.

27. LR, 6.7–89, FA:ED I, 103.

28. LJS v.31, FA:ED I, 390.

29. LR, 5.1–3, FA:ED I, 102–3.

30. LJS 1.1, FA:ED I, 370. Julian of Speyer narrates this event in 2.12, FA:ED I, 377.

31. Stanislaus da Campagnola, "Francis of Assisi and the Social Problems of His Time," trans. Edward Hagman, O.F.M.Cap., *Greyfriars Review* 2, no. 1 (1988): 137.

32. 1C, 28.76, FA:ED I, 247–48.

33. da Campagnola, "Francis of Assisi and the Social Problems of His Time," 137.

34. David Wessel, "In Poverty Tactics, An Old Debate: Who Is at Fault," *Wall Street Journal,* June 16, 2006.

35. Anjali Athavaley, "Ranks of Rich Grow, but at a Slower Pace; Interest Rates Cited," Reporting on World Wealth Report compiled by Merrill Lynch & Co. and Capgemini Group, *Wall Street Journal,* June 21, 2006.

36. Anna Bernasek, "Income Inequality, and Its Cost," Economic View, *New York Times,* June 25, 2006.

37. Joseph P. Chinnici, O.F.M., "Hierarchy, Power, and the Franciscan Family in the American Church: A Dialogue with St. Bonaventure," *The Cord* 54, no. 5 (2004): 222, 223.

38. Shantilai P. Bhagat, *Creation in Crisis: Responding to God's Covenant* (Elgin, IL: Brethren Press, 1990), 45.

39. H. Mislin, in H. Mislin and S. Latour, *Franziskus: Der ökumenisch-ökologische Revolutionär* (Berg/Bodman, 1982, Freiburg: J. Green, Bruder Franz, 1984), 121–23, in Lehmann, "Franciscan Global Spirituality," 323.

Chapter 4: Finding a Father to Believe In

1. L3C, 6.20, FA:ED II, 80.

2. Lester K. Little, *Religious Poverty and the Profit Economy in Medieval Europe* (Ithaca, NY: Cornell University Press, 1978), 14.

3. Ibid., 11.

4. 1C, 29.83, FA:ED I, 253.

5. 1C, 1.1, FA:ED I, 182.

6. 1C, 1.2, FA:ED I, 183.

7. L3C, 3.10, FA:ED II, 73.

8. L3C, 6.17, FA:ED II, 79.

9. L3C, 6.19, FA:ED II, 80.

10. L3C, 6.20, FA:ED II, 80.

11. Ronald Rolheiser, O.M.I., "Walking the Ambit," in *Secularity and the Gospel: Being Missionaries to Our Children,* ed. Ronald Rolheiser (New York: Crossroad, 2006), 20.

12. 1LtF 11, FA:ED I, 42; 2LtF 54, FA:ED I, 49.

13. 2LtF, 21, FA:ED I, 47.

14. Julio Micó, O.F.M.Cap., "The Spirituality of St. Francis: Francis's Image of God," trans. Paul Barrett, O.F.M.Cap., *Greyfriars Review* 7, no. 2 (1993): 144. For his part, Norbert Nguyên-Van-Khanh writes: "Francis' vivid awareness of the fatherhood of God was reinforced by the fact that he lacked the support of his earthly father. Having been mistreated by him since the first days of his conversion, Francis placed all his trust in the heavenly Father." Norbert Nguyên-Van-Khanh, O.F.M., *The Teacher of His Heart: Jesus Christ in the Thought and Writings of St. Francis,* trans. Ed Hagman, O.F.M.Cap. (St. Bonaventure, NY: Franciscan Institute, 1994), 134.

15. ER 1.4, 5, FA:ED I, 64; ER 22.34, FA:ED I, 80.

16. LR, 6.8, FA:ED I, 103.

17. LtL, 2, FA:ED I, 122.

18. 2C, 49, 137, FA:ED II, 336. For a fine elaboration on this see Robert Stewart, O.F.M., "Motherhood in God, Jesus, Francis, and the Franciscan Tradition," *The Cord* 52, no. 1 (2002): 3–17.

19. RH, 2, 8–10, FA:ED I, 61–62.

20. Nguyên-Van-Khanh, *The Teacher of His Heart,* 133.

21. Thaddée Matura, O.F.M., " 'My Holy Father!' God as Father in the Writings of St. Francis," trans. Cyprian Rosen, O.F.M.Cap., *Greyfriars Review* 1, no. 1 (1987): 106.

22. Ibid., 129.

23. Julian of Speyer summarizes the movement's expansiveness as follows: "He founded three Orders, the first of which he prized above all others by profession and habit, and which, as he had written in its Rule, he called the Order of Lesser Brothers. The Second Order, the Order of the Poor Ladies and virgins of the Lord, also mentioned above, likewise took its fruitful origin from him. The Third, also an order of considerable perfection, is called the Order of Penitents, which profitably brings together clerics and laity, virgins, unmarried, and married persons of both sexes" LJS 4.23, FA:ED I, 385.

24. Julio Micó, O.F.M.Cap., "The Spirituality of St. Francis: Brothers to All," quoting 1LtF 1.13, trans. Paul Barrett, O.F.M.Cap., *Greyfriars Review* 7, no. 1 (1993): 151.

25. ER, 22.27, FA:ED I, 80.

26. ER, 23.11, FA:ED I, 85–86.

27. Matura, "My Holy Father," 116.

28. Margaret Carney, O.S.F., "Naming the Earthquake: Franciscans and the Evangelical Life," *The Cord* 56, no. 2 (2006): 87.

29. Bruce J. Malina and Richard L. Rohrbaugh, *Social-Science Commentary on the Synoptic Gospels* (Minneapolis: Fortress, 1992), 159.

30. LJS 5.27, FA:ED I, 388.

31. Matura, "My Holy Father," 128, quoting 2LtF, 54.

32. ER, 22.33–34, FA:ED I, 80.

33. LR, 3, 5–6, FA:ED I, 65.

34. ER, 22, 28, FA:ED I, 80.

35. 2LtF, 21, FA:ED I, 47.

36. PrOF, 1–10, FA:ED I, 158–60.

37. 2LtF, 48–53, FA:ED I, 48–49. The text is almost word-for-word in 1LtF, 6–10, FA:ED I, 41–42.

38. 2C, 145.193, FA:ED II, 371.

39. AC 83, FA:ED II, 186.

40. 1C, 21.58, FA:ED I, 234.

41. CtC, 1–9, FA:ED I, 113–14. No good explanation has been given as to why some of the "Praised" words are italicized and others are not.

42. Micó, "Francis's Image of God," 141, quoting Admonition 18.2 and 2LtF, 61.

43. Ibid., 135.

44. 2LtF, 61–62, FA:ED I, 49–50.

45. Octavian Schmucki, O.F.M.Cap., "The 'Way of Life according to the Gospel' as It Was Discovered by St. Francis of Assisi," trans. Patrick Colbourne, O.F.M.Cap., *Greyfriars Review* 2, no. 3 (1988): 11.

46. ER, 17.17, FA:ED I, 76.

Chapter 5: How Francis Made Conversion Compelling

1. Test 1–3, FA:ED I, 124.

2. See Kurt H. Wolff, *Surrender and Catch: Experience and Inquiry Today,* Boston Studies in the Philosophy of Science 51 (Dordrecht, Holland, and Boston: D. Reidel, 1976), 298.

3. Prospero Rivi, O.F.M.Cap., "Francis of Assisi and the Laity of His Time," trans. Heather Tolfree, *Greyfriars Review* 15, Supplement (2001): 31–32.

4. Ibid., 32.

5. Ibid.

6. For further treatment on how Francis' "leper experience" is treated in key Franciscan sources, see Joseph Wood, O.F.M.Conv., "St. Francis's Conversion and His Encounter with the Leper as Related in the Sources," *The Cord* 53, no. 5 (2003): 226–38.

7. R. I. Moore, *The Formation of a Persecuting Society: Power and Deviance in Western Europe, 950–1250* (Oxford and New York: Blackwell, 1987), 58–59.

8. Ibid., 62.

9. Ibid., 79.

10. Arnoldo Fortini, *Francis of Assisi,* trans. Helen Moak (New York: Crossroad, 1985), 210–11.

11. Ibid., 211.

12. 1C, 7.17, FA:ED I, 195.

13. L3C, 4.11, FA:ED II, 74.

14. LJS 2.12, FA:ED I, 377.

15. 1C, 28.76, FA:ED I, 248; LJS 9.45, FA:ED I, 401.

16. Kurt H. Wolff, *Beyond the Sociology of Knowledge: An Introduction and a Development* (Lanham, MD: University Press of America, 1983), 265–66.

17. Kurt H. Wolff, "Toward Understanding the Radicalness of Surrender," *Sociological Analysis* 38, no. 4 (1977): 397.

18. Ibid., 398.

19. Ibid., 397.

20. Judith Feher, "On Surrender, Death, and the Sociology of Knowledge," *Human Studies* 7, no. 2 (1995): 216.

21. Kurt H. Wolff, "Surrender-and-Catch and Phenomenology," *Human Studies* 7, no. 2 (1984): 205.

22. Kurt H. Wolff, "Surrender to Morality as the Morality of Surrender," in Anna-Teresa Tymieniecka and Calvin O. Schrag, *Foundations of Morality, Human Rights, and the Human Sciences* (Dordrecht, Holland, and Boston: D. Reidel, 1983), 495.

23. Wolff, "Surrender-and-Catch and Phenomenology," 1.

24. Ibid., 377.

25. Kurt H. Wolff, "Presuppositions of the Sociology of Knowledge and a Task for It," Supplement, in Kurt H. Wolff, *Trying Sociology* (New York: John Wiley & Sons, 1974), 550.

26. Wolff, "Surrender-and-Catch and Phenomenology," 195.

27. Wolff, *Surrender and Catch,* 377.

28. Leo Tolstoy, quoted in Wolff, *Surrender and Catch,* 22.

29. See Feher, "On Surrender, Death, and the Sociology of Knowledge," 222.

30. Wolff, *Surrender and Catch,* 23.

31. Ibid.

32. William James, *The Varieties of Religious Experience: A Study in Human Nature* (New York: Modern Library, 1929), 422.

33. Eugene T. Gendlin, Ph.D., *Focusing* (New York: Bantam Books, 1981), 32. I am indebted to John Shea, O.S.A., who taught a course on "Focusing" I attended while writing this book. It helped me immeasurably in understanding the applicability of the *dynamic* involved in Francis' conversion for average persons serious about making changes in their lives.

34. While Wolff devotes a whole chapter to "Surrender and the Body," he admits that he did not know how his notion related to "catch." In my mind, Francis' own words show that he was changed in spirit *and* body. His very emotion of consolation seemed to have had a powerful impact on his bodily senses. This is reinforced by Thomas of Celano, who talks about Francis being changed in mind and body. See Wolff, *Surrender and Catch*, 179–213.

35. 1971 Synod of Bishops, "The Ministerial Priesthood," I, *Origins* 1 (1971): 378.

36. 1971 Synod of Bishops, "Justice in the World," III, 40 in Joseph Gremillion, presenter, *The Gospel of Peace and Justice* (Maryknoll, NY: Orbis, 1976), 522.

37. Wolff, *Surrender and Catch*, 39.

38. 1C, 3.7, FA:ED I, 188.

39. "The Deeds of Blessed Francis and His Companions," 1.20. Eng. trans. FA.ED III, 437.

40. Ilia Delio, O.S.F., *Franciscan Prayer* (Cincinnati: St. Anthony Messenger Press, 2004), 48.

41. Rivi, "Francis of Assisi and the Laity of His Time," 56.

Chapter 6: Becoming the Christ

1. Kurt H. Wolff, *Surrender and Catch: Experience and Inquiry Today* (Dordrecht, Holland, and Boston: D. Reidel, 1976) I, viii.

2. See ibid., 1.

3. Ibid. According to Wolff, in surrender "man is thrown back on what he really is, which is what he shares with mankind" (190). This is the "self," or the "I am" that is common to all humans made in the image of God (see 32).

4. This is the phraseology of the second oldest biography of Francis extant, written by a Franciscan, Julian of Speyer, between 1232 and 1235. See LJS 3.15, FA:ED I, 379.

5. Giovanni Iammarrone, O.F.M.Conv., "The Timeliness and Limitations of the Christology of John Duns Scotus for the Development of a Contemporary Theology of Christ," trans. Ignatius McCormick O.F.M.Cap., *Greyfriars Review* 7, no. 2 (1993): 235–36.

6. "St. Francis of Assisi, Later Admonition and Exhortation," in Ilia Delio, O.S.F., *Franciscan Prayer* (Cincinnati: St. Anthony Messenger Press, 2004), 99.

7. IC, 9.115 (The Second Book), FA:ED I, 283–84.

8. Iammarrone, "The Timeliness and Limitations of the Christology of John Duns Scotus for the Development of a Contemporary Theology of Christ," 231.

9. IC 30.84, FA:ED I, 254.

10. Wolff, *Surrender and Catch*, 172.

11. Octavian Schmucki, O.F.M.Cap., "The 'Way of Life according to the Gospel' as It Was Discovered by St. Francis of Assisi," trans. Patrick Colbourne, O.F.M.Cap., *Greyfriars Review* 2, no. 3 (1988): 19.

12. Wolff, *Surrender and Catch*, 20.

13. Ilia Delio, O.S.F., "Francis and the Humility of God," *The Cord* 51, no. 2 (2001): 61.

14. 1C, 30.84, FA:ED I, 255.

15. 1C, 30.85, FA:ED I, 255–56.

16. Wolff, *Surrender and Catch*, 22.

17. Iammarrone, "The Timeliness and Limitations of the Christology of John Duns Scotus for the Development of a Contemporary Theology of Christ," 230.

18. Wolff, *Surrender and Catch*, 23.

19. Ilia Delio, "Are We at Home in the Cosmos? A Franciscan Perspective," *New Theology Review* 18, no. 4 (November 2005): 35.

20. Eleanor M. Godway, "Faith *and* Knowledge in Crisis: Towards an Epistemology of the Cross," *Listening* 27, no. 2 (Spring 1992): 103.

21. Ibid., 106–7.

22. L3C 5.14, FA:ED II, 76.

23. Whether Francis had the stigmata has been debated almost from his death onward. My examination makes me believe he did have it. For more on the subject see André Vauchez, "The Stigmata of St. Francis and Its Medieval Detractors," trans. Edward Hagman, O.F.M.Cap., *Greyfriars Review* 13, no. 1 (1999): 61–89.

24. Thaddée Matura, "The Church in the Writings of St. Francis of Assisi," trans. Helen M. Eckrich, O.S.F., *Greyfriars Review* 12, no. 1 (1998): 21.

25. Test 4–5, FA:ED I, 124–25; see also AP 5.19, FA:ED II, 42; LJS 5.27, FA:ED I, 388.

26. Celano writes that after hearing the words of the Gospel and saying, "This is what I wish, this is what I see, this is what I long to do with all my heart," he made his own habit. "Immediately, *he took off the shoes from his feet,* put down the staff from his hands, and, satisfied with one tunic, exchanged his leather belt for a cord. After this, he made for himself a tunic showing the image of the cross, so that in it he would drive off every fantasy of the demons. He made it very rough, so that in it he might *crucify the flesh with its* vices and sins. He made it very poor and plain, a thing that the world would never covet." 1C, 9.22, FA:ED I, 202.

27. For a fine reflection on the meaning of the Tau cross, see Benet A. Fonck, O.F.M., "Called to Build a More Fraternal and Evangelical World," *The Cord* 52, no. 3 (2002): 114–17.

28. Adm 6, 1–3, FA:ED I, 131.

29. ER 22.32–35, FA:ED I, 80–81.

30. Leonhard Lehmann, O.F.M.Cap., "Franciscan Global Spirituality," trans. Ignatius McCormick, O.F.M.Cap., *Greyfriars Review* 5, no. 3 (1991): 318.

31. AC 63, FA:ED II, 165–66. William Short, O.F.M., one of the editors of FA:ED, believes that it was during this period of withdrawal that he spent time writing the Revised Rule and that the experiences of having it approved in 1223 combined with the Greccio celebration of the Creche led to him being able to be free of what he considers to be Francis' two years of depression. Another event that helped bring him out of his Dark Night was the experience of the stigmata itself. Conversation with Michael Crosby, February 1, 2007. My thanks to Bill for his help on this issue.

32. Grado Giovanni Merlo, "The Story of Brother Francis and the Order of Friars Minor," trans. Edward Hagman, O.F.M.Cap., *Greyfriars Review* 15, no. 1 (2001): 9. I am thankful to Ilia Delio for inviting me to deepen this perspective on Christ Crucified and for reminding me of Merlo.

33. L3C, 8.29, FA:ED II, 86.

34. Marie Dennis, Cynthia Moe-Lobeda, Joseph Nangle, O.F.M., and Stuart Taylor, *St. Francis and the Foolishness of God* (Maryknoll, NY: Orbis, 1993), 131.

35. Barbara E. Reid, O.P., "Telling the Terror of the Crucifixion," *The Bible Today* 44, no. 4 (2006): 228.

36. John Howard Yoder, *The Politics of Jesus* (Grand Rapids: Eerdmans, 1972), 46.

37. LtOrd 12–13, FA:ED I, 117.

38. Adm 1.16–18, FA:ED I, 129.

39. Jean Carroll McGowan, *Concelebration: Sign of the Unity of the Church* (New York, 1964), quoted in Robert F. Taft, "Is There Devotion to the Holy Eucharist in the Christian East?," *Worship* 80, no. 3 (2006): 216.

40. For more on this see William Hugo, Capuchin, "The Eucharistic Writings of Francis of Assisi," *The New Round Table* 41, no. 2 (1988): 62ff. Hugo also includes the Letter to Rulers of the Peoples as a Eucharistic letter. However, it seems to me, it is a significant part but not the main thrust.

41. Test 10, FA:ED I, 125.

42. 1LtCl 3, FA:ED I, 52; 2LtCl, 3, FA:ED I, 54.

43. Adm 1.16–22, FA:ED I, 129.

44. Adm 1.12, FA:ED I, 129.

45. LtOrd, 26–29, FA:ED I, 118.

46. LR, 9.1, FA:ED I, 104.

47. Test 26, FA:ED I, 126.

48. Test 9; Adm, 26; 2LtF, 33.

49. There was an earlier version (1LtCl), written before 1219, and a later version (2LtC), written around 1220. Pertinent passages inviting the clergy to conversion were 9, 10, and 14. In FA:ED I, 52–55.

50. Matura, "The Church in the Writings of St. Francis of Assisi," 25.

51. Test 6–10, FA:ED I, 125.

52. LR 7.1–3, FA:ED I, 103–4.

53. This "third way" that stood as an alternative to the "fight/flight" options that prevailed at the time of Jesus has been suggested as another way of interpreting Matthew 5:38–42 by Walter Wink, *The Powers That Be: Theology for a New Millennium* (New York: Doubleday, 1998), 98–111.

Chapter 7: The Gospel as Francis' Life-Project

1. Test 14, FA:ED I, 125.

2. Octavian Schmucki, O.F.M.Cap., "The 'Way of Life According to the Gospel' as It Was Discovered by St. Francis of Assisi," trans. Patrick Colbourne, O.F.M.Cap., *Greyfriars Review* 2, no. 3 (1998): 3.

3. L3C, 8.25, FA:ED II, 84. See also LJS 3.15, FA:ED I, 379.

4. LJS1.3, FA:ED I, 372.

5. Ibid., Thomas of Celano notes that "he was no deaf hearer of the Gospel; rather he committed everything he heard to his excellent memory and was careful to carry it out to the letter" (1C9.22, FA:ED I, 202).

6. L3C, 8.27. FA:ED II, 85.

7. 1C, 10.24, FA:ED I, 204.

8. AP 2.11, FA:ED II, 38.

9. The passage quoted by Thomas of Celano is not found verbatim in any of the Gospels; rather it is a compilation of Matt. 19:21 (which alone uses the word "perfect") and Luke 18:22 (which alone says that "all" must be sold).

10. This passage comes quite directly from Mark 3:8 and Luke 9:3.

11. This is the only one of the three times where the passage is almost verbatim in all three of the synoptic Gospels (Matt. 16:24, Mark 8:34, and Luke 9:23).

12. L3C, 8.29. FA:ED II, 86.

13. Test 14, FA:ED I, 125.

14. 1C, 12.29, FA:ED I, 207.

15. Test 14–15, FA:ED I, 125.

16. AP 7.31, FA:ED II, 48.

17. L3C, 12.48, FA:ED II, 96.

18. L3C, 12.51, FA:ED II, 98.

19. LR 12.4, FA:ED I, 106.

20. For more on a Franciscan way of dissent, see my *Can Religious Life Be Prophetic?* (New York: Crossroad, 2005), 145ff. Also Charles Finnegan, O.F.M., "Franciscans and the Church," *The Cord* 55, no. 5 (2005): 219–26.

21. LJS 4.23, FA:ED I, 384.

22. L3C, 14.57, FA:ED II, 101.

23. Schmucki, "The 'Way of Life According to the Gospel,' " 12.

24. 1C, 4.97, FA:ED I, 266.

25. 1C, 4.97, FA:ED I, 266.

26. Cardinal Joseph Ratzinger, "Evangelization Must Speak about God," Fourth General Congregation, European Synod of Bishops, December 2, 1991, in *L'Osservatore Romano,* Weekly Edition 50, December 16, 1991, 9.

27. Wes Howard-Brooke, *The Church before Christianity* (Maryknoll, NY: Orbis, 2001), 125.

28. Mattam Joseph, S.J., "The Our Father: The Revolutionary Prayer of Commitment to the Kingdom of God," *African Ecclesial Review* 35 (1993): 72.

29. Julio Micó, "The Spirituality of St. Francis: Brothers to All," trans. Paul Barrett, O.F.M.Cap., *Greyfriars Review* 8, no. 2 (1994): 151.

30. *Catechism of the Catholic Church,* rev. ed. (Washington DC: National Conference of Catholic Bishops, 2000), no. 2789.

31. Lester K. Little, *Religious Poverty and the Profit Economy in Medieval Europe* (Ithaca, NY: Cornell University Press, 1978), 134.

32. Ibid., 130.

33. 1C, 3.7, FA:ED I, 188.

34. 1C, 1.89, FA:ED I, 259–60. I am indebted to Schmucki for this insight.

35. Ratzinger, "Evangelization Must Speak about God."

36. John C. Haughey, "Church-ianity and Christ-ianity," *America,* May 24, 2004, 8.

Chapter 8: The Contagious Character That Created a Classless Community

1. LR 6.7–8, FA:ED I, 103.
2. Arnoldo Fortini, *Francis of Assisi,* trans. Helen Moak (New York: Continuum, 1981), 26.
3. 1C, 4.8, FA:ED I, 189.
4. Fortini, *Francis of Assisi,* 260.
5. Ibid.
6. Ibid., 315.
7. Leonhard Lehmann, O.F.M.Cap., "Franciscan Spirituality," trans. Ignatius McCormick, O.F.M.Cap., *Greyfriars Review* 5, no. 3 (1991): 310.
8. Stanislaus da Campagnola, "Francis of Assisi and the Social Problems of His Time," trans. Edward Hagman, O.F.M.Cap., *Greyfriars Review* 2, no. 1 (1988): 135.
9. Ibid., 137–38.
10. L3C, 12.46, FA:ED II, 95.
11. Julio Micó, "The Spirituality of St. Francis: Brothers to All," trans. Paul Barrett, O.F.M.Cap., *Greyfriars Review* 8, no. 2 (1994): 151.
12. 1C 15.38, FA:ED I, 217.
13. *The Rule of St. Benedict,* cc 21, 43, 63; also 69, 98–99, trans. Anthony C. Meisel and M. L. del Mastro (New York: Doubleday Image Books, 1975).
14. ER 6, FA:ED I, 68.
15. AC 49, FA:ED II, 148.
16. Micó, "The Spirituality of St. Francis," 149.
17. Ibid., 150.
18. See 1LtF 1.8–9, FA:ED I, 42. 2LtF 51–53.
19. Michael H. Crosby, *House of Disciples: Church, Economics, and Justice in Matthew* (Eugene, OR: Wipf and Stock, 2004 [Maryknoll, NY: Orbis, 1987]), 24–31. In his opening remarks about the connection among fraternity, religion, and order, when he talks about Francis' view of fraternity (the brothers in relationship or "fraternity," as well as the structured, organized relationships or "Fraternity"), Micó discusses it in light of the New Testament context: "In classical Rome, there were various kinds of association — of those who followed the same occupation or profession, or of those devoted to the same god, as well as burial societies which poor people joined to ensure a decent burial in a community cemetery. Any group of this kind was known as a *collegium, consortium* or *societas.*" Micó, "The Spirituality of St. Francis," 143. Later he notes that Francis adopted the notion of a *fraternitas* which made his "a group of equals who had come together for a common purpose," which, in his case, would be religious rather than secular (144).
20. Joseph P. Chinnici, O.F.M., general editor, "General Editor's Introduction," in Michael D. Guinan, O.F.M., *Franciscan Vision and the Gospel of John: The San Damiano Cross; Francis and John; Creation and John,* Franciscan Heritage Series 4 (St. Bonaventure, NY: Franciscan Institute, 2006), ix.
21. Ibid. (referring to Fortini, chapter 2), x.
22. Crosby, *House of Disciples,* 33.
23. Micó, "The Spirituality of St. Francis," 146.
24. Ibid., 145.
25. ER, 5.9–12, FA:ED I, 67.

26. LR, 10, 3, 1, FA:ED I, 105.

27. LR, 8.4, FA:ED I, 104.

28. LR, 6.7–8, FA:ED I, 103.

29. AP 6.26, FA:ED II, 46.

30. Sr. Mary Elizabeth Imler, C.S.J.O., "Brothers, and Not Just a Bunch of Friends," Retreat Notes given Conventual Franciscan Friars, 2005. Province of Our Lady of Consolation, 2006. No pagination.

31. I am indebted to my Capuchin Franciscan brother Julio Micó for this insight. See "The Spirituality of St. Francis," 154–57.

32. LR, 6.9, FA:ED I, 103.

33. LR, 4. 1–3, FA:ED I, 102.

34. ER, 9.1–13, FA:ED I, 72.

35. LR, 7.1–3, FA:ED I, 103–4.

36. Donald W. Winnicott, *The Maturational Process and the Facilitating Environment: Studies in the Theory of Emotional Development* (New York: International Universities Press, 1965).

37. LR, 3.10–11; FA:ED I, 102.

38. AC, 18, FA:ED II, 132–33.

39. 1C, 15.36, 37, FA:ED I, 215–17. Celano's reference to the "triple army of those being saved" has traditionally been interpreted to refer to the three groupings that identified with him: the Friars Minor, the Poor Ladies [founded by Clare of Assisi to parallel his group of brothers], and the Lay Penitents. Others have said it refers to the clergy, religious, and laity who identified with him.

40. 1C, 29.81, FA:ED I, 251.

41. Micó, "The Spirituality of St. Francis," 160.

42. 1C, 28.77, FA:ED I, 248.

43. David Wessel, "As Rich-Poor Gap Widens in the U.S., Class Mobility Stalls," Moving Up, First in a Series, *Wall Street Journal,* May 13, 2005.

44. Jessica E. Vascellaro, "Wage Winners and Losers," *Wall Street Journal,* September 13, 2005.

45. Bill Keller, ed., *Class Matters* (New York: Henry Holt/Times Books, 2006).

46. David Cay Johnston, "Richest Are Leaving Even the Rich Far Behind," *New York Times,* June 5, 2005.

47. Paul Krugman, "Losing Our Country," *New York Times,* June 25, 2005.

48. Wessel, "As Rich-Poor Gap Widens in the U.S., Class Mobility Stalls."

49. Paul Krugman, reflecting on Nolan McCarty, Keith Poole, and Howard Rosenthal, *Polarized America: The Dance of Ideology and Unequal Riches* (Cambridge, MA: MIT Press, 2006), in "Class War Politics," *New York Times,* June 19, 2006. President George W. Bush acknowledged the gap in early 2007 when he stated: "The fact is that income inequality is real; it's been rising for more than 25 years." Deborah Solomon, "Addressing Wealth Gap," *Wall Street Journal,* February 6, 2007.

50. Robert Guy Matthews, "Recovery Bypasses Many Americans," *Wall Street Journal,* August 31, 2005.

51. "Study Finds CEO Pay Has Soared Since 2001," *Wall Street Journal,* August 31, 2005.

52. Mark N. Naison, "Black Poverty's Human Face," *BusinessWeek,* September 19, 2005.

53. For more on this, see Paul Krugman, "Tragedy in Black and White," *New York Times*, September 19, 2005.

54. David Luhnow and John Lyons, "In Latin America, Rich-Poor Chasm Stifles Growth," Moving Up: Challenges to the American Dream, *Wall Street Journal*, July 18, 2005.

55. Horsey, in the *Seattle Post-Intelligencer*, June 14, 2006. The data to support the cartoon is found in studies by the World Bank. The United Nations Development Program's "Human Development Report 2003" showed that 1.2 billion people survive on less than $1 a day and 2.8 billion live on less than $2 (Jeff Madrick, "A Disappointing Report Card on the War on Poverty," *New York Times*, August 7, 2003). "The 2000 World Development Report found that average income in the 20 richest countries is 37 times the average in the 20 poorest nations — double the gap of 40 years ago" (James Cox, "Poor Nations Just Getting Poorer," *USAToday*, September 13, 2000).

Chapter 9: Nonpossessiveness

1. AP 3.17, FA:ED II, 41; see also L3C, 9.35, FA:ED II, 89.

2. Arnoldo Fortini, quoting Giuseppe Ferrari, *Francis of Assisi*, trans. Helen Moak (New York: Crossroad, 1985), 259.

3. Ibid., 146.

4. ER 7.14, FA:ED I, 69.

5. Michael F. Cusato, O.F.M., "To Do Penance / *Facere poenitentiam*," *The Cord* 57, no. 1 (2007): 19, 18.

6. LR, 6.1, FA:ED I, 103.

7. Lester K. Little, *Religious Poverty and the Profit Economy in Medieval Europe* (Ithaca, NY: Cornell University Press, 1978), 29.

8. Ibid., 16.

9. Ibid., 36.

10. Marbod, Archbishop of Rennes, "De Nummo," in Alexander Murray, *Reason and Society in the Middle Ages* (Oxford: Clarendon Press, 1985), 73.

11. Cusato, "To Do Penance," 14.

12. LR, 5, 1–2, FA:ED I, 103.

13. Michael Lerner, *The Left Hand of God: Taking Back Our Country from the Religious Right* (San Francisco: HarperSanFrancisco, 2006), 48.

14. Ibid., 49.

15. Leonhard Lehmann, quoting Hans Mislin and Sophie Latour, *Franziskus: Der ökumenisch-ökologische Revolutionär* (Berg-Bodman, 1982, Freiburg: J. Green, Bruder Franz, 1984), 89–90, in "Franciscan Global Spirituality," trans. Ignatius McCormick, O.F.M.Cap., *Greyfriars Review* 5, no. 3 (1991): 319.

16. Test 20–23, FA:ED I, 125–26.

17. LJS 1.1, FA:ED I, 370.

18. 1C, 10.24, FA:ED I, 204.

19. Adm, 2.1–5, FA:ED I, 129.

20. Ilia Delio, O.S.F., *Franciscan Prayer* (Cincinnati: St. Anthony Messenger Press, 2004), 83.

21. Adam Smith, *The Wealth of Nations*, ed. Edwin Cannan (New York: Modern Library, 1965), 14.

22. Reb David'l, quoted in Gedulat Mordechai ve Gedulat haTzadikkim, in Lerner, *The Left Hand of God,* 279.

23. Eamon Javers, "Inside the Hidden World of Earmarks: A *Business Week* Investigation Reveals How Company Spending on Lobbyists Can Pay Off," *Business Week,* September 17, 2007, 57. For more on how the corporations have influenced the present disparity, see Timothy P. Carney, *The Big Ripoff* (New York: Wiley, 2006).

24. "The De-Entitling of America," Editorial, *Business Week,* November 20, 2005.

25. LR, 6, 1–6, FA:ED I, 103.

26. Pope Paul VI, *Evangelica Testificatio,* 17, June 29, 1971 (Washington, D.C.: United States Catholic Conference Publications Office, 1971), 7.

27. Ibid., 18, 7.

28. Edward M. Welch, "The Church Was Right about Capitalism," *America,* December 1, 2003, 18.

29. Pope Paul VI, *Evangelica Testificatio,* 18.

30. Test 29, FA:ED I, 126.

31. Ibid. 18, FA:ED I, 125.

32. I use the notion taking off from Francis' insistence on living the Rule simply and purely. Test 39, FA:ED I, 127.

33. Richard Rohr, O.F.M., with John Bookser Feister, *Hope against Darkness: The Transforming Vision of Saint Francis in an Age of Anxiety* (Cincinnati: St. Anthony Messenger Press, 2001), 155–56.

34. Stephen Hand, "A Vow of Simplicity for Young and Old," *Traditional Catholic Reflections Reports,* June 21, 2006.

35. 2LtF 45, FA:ED I, 48.

36. SalV 1, 10–11, FA:ED I, 164, 165.

Chapter 10: Enduring in Peace

1. BlL 1–3, based on Num. 6:24–27, FA:ED I, 112.

2. Arnoldo Fortini, *Francis of Assisi,* trans. Helen Moak (New York: Crossroad, 1985), 53.

3. Donald Spoto, *Reluctant Saint: The Life of Francis of Assisi* (New York: Viking Compass, 2002), 2.

4. Stanislaus da Campagnola, "Francis of Assisi and the Social Problems of His Time," trans. Edward Hagman, O.F.M.Cap., *Greyfriars Review* 2, no. 1 (1988): 135.

5. St. Bonaventure, "The Soul's Journey into God," in *Bonaventure,* trans. with intro., Ewert Cousins, Classics in Western Spirituality (New York: Paulist, 1978), 53–54.

6. Fortini, *Francis of Assisi,* 55.

7. James Hillman, *A Terrible Love of War* (New York: Penguin Books, 2004), 22.

8. James Traub, "Wonderful World?" *New York Times Magazine,* March 19, 2006, 13.

9. Ibid., 14.

10. Stockholm International Peace Research Institute, *2006 Yearbook,* June 12, 2006. *www.sipri.org/contents/publications/yearbooks.html.*

11. Fortini, *Francis of Assisi,* 244.

12. A good examination of the origin and development of the so-called "Peace Prayer of St. Francis" can be found in *Greyfriars Review* 10, no. 3 (1996): especially 235–68.

13. Fortini, *Francis of Assisi,* 244.

14. The "diabolical enemy image" represents the first of a series of attitudes shared by both sides in a war that justifies the war's continuation. See Ralph K. White, *Nobody Wanted War: Misperception in Vietnam and Other Wars* (Garden City, NY: Doubleday Anchor Books, 1970).

15. Test 23, FA:ED I, 126.

16. 1C 10.24, FA:ED I, 203.

17. 1C 12.29, FA:ED I, 207.

18. Octavian Schmucki notes that, when Francis and the brothers actually did greet people with peace, it was not as Jesus said, i.e., "to this house," but when Francis, "whether meeting individuals or addressing a crowd, preferred to use the blessing of Aaron, 'The Lord ... give you [*tibi* or *vobis*] peace.'" Octavian Schmucki, O.F.M.Cap., "St. Francis of Assisi, Messenger of Peace in His Time," trans. Edward Hagman, O.F.M.Cap., *Greyfriars Review* 9, no. 2 (1995): 149.

19. AC 19, FA:ED II, 133; also 101, FA:ED II, 205.

20. 1C 10.23, FA:ED I, 203.

21. Leonhard Lehmann, "Franciscan Global Spirituality," trans. Ignatius Mc-Cormick, O.F.M.Cap., *Greyfriars Review* 5, no. 3 (1991): 322.

22. LJS 3.16, FA:ED I, 380.

23. LtR, FA:ED I, 58. I am indebted to Schmucki for this insight, 150.

24. Ilia Delio, O.S.F., "The Franciscan Path to Peace," *The Cord* 54, no. 6 (2004): 282.

25. Schmucki, "St. Francis of Assisi, Messenger of Peace in His Time," 148.

26. L3C, 9.35, FA:ED II, 89.

27. AP 8.38, FA:ED II, 52–53.

28. L3C, 14.58, FA:ED II, 102.

29. LR 6, 1, FA:ED I, 103.

30. AP 6.30, FA:ED II, 48.

31. Adm 19.1–2, FA:ED I, 135.

32. LMj 6.1, FA:ED II, 569.

33. Adm 15.1–2, FA:ED I, 134.

34. LR, 3.10–11, 13–14, FA:ED I, 102.

35. L3C 8.26, FA:ED II, 85.

36. Test 23, FA:ED I, 126.

37. AC 84, FA:ED II, 187.

38. CtC 10–11, FA:ED I, 114.

39. AC 84, FA:ED II, 187.

40. AC 84, FA:ED II, 187–88.

41. AP 6.27, FA:ED II, 46.

42. Joan Mueller, O.S.F., "Franciscan Reconciliation: The Struggle to Embrace Joy," *Greyfriars Review* 17, no. 1 (1998): 121.

43. Mary Beth Ingham, C.S.J., "Presence, Poise and Praxis: The Three-fold Challenge for Reconcilers Today," *The Cord* 53, no. 6 (2003): 304.

44. Ibid., 308.

45. Ibid., 314.

46. Octavian Schmucki, O.F.M.Cap., "The 'Way of Life according to the Gospel' as It Was Discovered by St. Francis of Assisi," trans. Patrick Colbourne, O.F.M.Cap., *Greyfriars Review* 2, no. 3 (1988): 14.

47. Thomas of Spalato, Latin text, in ibid., 157.

48. Fareed Munir, Ph.D., "Islam and Franciscanism: Prophet Mohammad of Arabia and St. Francis of Assisi in the Spirituality of Mission," *Spirit and Life* 9 (2000): 36.

49. 1C 56, FA:ED I,.

50. LMj 9.7, FA:ED II, 602.

51. 1 C 20.57, FA:ED I, 231; LJS 7.36, FA:ED I, 395.

52. 1 C 20.57, FA:ED I, 231.

53. LtR 7, FA:ED I, 58–59. I am thankful for the editors for this insight; however they themselves do not state whether they believe this link was the source for Francis' request that such praise be made.

54. ER 16.5–7, FA:ED I, 74.

55. Munir, "Islam and Franciscanism," 37.

56. Jan Hoeberichts, *Francis and Islam* (Quincy, IL: Franciscan Press, 1997), 70.

57. I am not as positive in my interpretation of Francis and Islam as some scholars. I agree regarding Francis' desire to make the *in + amicus* a friend as evangelical, and that he succeeded in this. Yet, I believe Francis was not quite so shocked at the insulting approach used by the friars in Morocco which resulted in their killings nor opposed "the efforts of the crusaders at Damietta" except in a *quite specific rejection* about the timing of a particular battle there (thus his opposition being termed "prophetic"). For an apparently broader interpretation see Michael Cusato, O.F.M., "To Do Penance / *Facere poenitentiam,*" *The Cord* 57, no. 1 (2007): 23.

58. 1C 21.58, FA:ED I, 234.

59. LFl, 23.1–20, FA:ED III, 482–83.

60. I follow the approach of Gaerard Pieter Freeman, "St. Francis and the Wolf of Gubbio: A Synchronous Interpretation of the Fioretti Chapter 21," trans. Fr. Timothy Gottschalk and Ignatius McCormick, *Greyfriars Review* 7, no. 3 (1993): 301–22. He writes that he has approached the text from the Fioretti using "the synchronous method" that will avoid the historical questions about the story's authenticity (302). Consequently, in an effort to find a meaning to the story that fits all ages, he stated: "I am not interested in finding out whether the event really took place. Neither do I get involved in the question of whether there were real wolves roaming about Gubbio in the thirteenth century. Nor am I concerned about who was the first to tell the story. The theory that the wolf was in fact a real live bandit, some banished citizen, or a robber baron is interesting, but I won't address it since the text offers no basis for these suppositions. I am not curious, either, about the variations of the stories as found in different manuscripts ... " (302–3).

61. da Campagnola, "Francis of Assisi and the Social Problems of His Time," 140.

62. Adm 27.1–2, FA:ED I, 136–37.

Chapter 11: Joy

1. Rabindranath Tagore was a Bengali poet. He received the Nobel Prize for Poetry.

2. "Schadenfreude," in Dr. Karl Wildhagen and Dr. Will Héraucourt, *English-German, German-English Dictionary in Two Volumes,* II (London: Allen & Unwin, 1957), 937.

3. Jena McGregor, "Sweet Revenge: The Power of Retribution, Spite, and Loathing in the World of Business," *BusinessWeek,* January 22, 2007, 67.

4. Unsigned article, "Economics Discovers Its Feelings," *The Economist,* December 23, 2006–January 5, 2007, 34.

5. "Happiness (and How to Measure It)," Editorial, *The Economist,* December 23, 2006–January 5, 2007, 13.

6. Kurt H. Wolff, *Surrender and Catch: Experience and Inquiry Today.* Boston Studies in the Philosophy of Science 51 (Dordrecht, Holland, and Boston: D. Reidel, 1976), 182.

7. For a fuller treatment of this theme, see Robert Ellsberg, *The Saints' Guide to Happiness* (New York: North Point Press, 2003). See, in particular, his treatment of St. Francis, pp. 23–35.

8. ER 7.13–16, FA:ED I, 69.

9. AC 63, FA:ED II, 165.

10. Martin E. P. Seligman, *Authentic Happiness* (New York: Free Press, 2002).

11. Geoffrey Cowley, "The Science of Happiness," building on the work of Seligman above, *Newsweek,* September 16, 2002.

12. AP 3.15, FA:ED II, 40.

13. 1C 14.35, FA:ED I, 214.

14. Adm 10.3–4, FA:ED I, 132.

15. Kay Redfield Jamison, *Exuberance: The Passion for Life* (New York: Knopf, 2004).

16. Kay Redfield Jamison, "Feeling Joy," Interview, *AARP Bulletin,* December 2004, 16.

17. Claudia Wallis, "The New Science of Happiness," Third annual mind and body issue, *Time,* January 17, 2005, A1–A8.

18. Scheherazade Daneshkhu, "The 'Dismal Science' Turns Its Attention to Happiness," *Financial Times,* January 10, 2005. Daneshkhu notes that scientists were working to develop a kind of "National Well-Being Account" that could be measured by certain characteristics.

19. Jeffrey Zaslow, "Happiness Inc.," Pursuits, *Wall Street Journal,* March 18–19, 2006, P1.

20. Test 1–3, FA:ED I, 124.

21. C. S. Lewis, *Surprised by Joy: The Shape of My Early Life* (New York: Harcourt Brace & Company Harvest Book, 1984), 17.

22. Ibid., 17–18.

23. Robert Ellsberg, "St. Francis of Assisi: Founder of the Friars Minor (1182–1226)," in Robert Ellsberg, *All Saints: Daily Reflections on Saints, Prophets, and Witnesses for Our Time* (New York: Crossroad, 1997), 433.

24. Wolff, *Surrender and Catch,* viii.

25. 1C 3.7, FA:ED I, 188.

26. Arnoldo Fortini, *Francis of Assisi,* trans. Helen Moak (New York: Crossroad, 1985), 382.

27. Pope John Paul II, by attribution, in *Christopher NewsNotes.*

28. Fortini, *Francis of Assisi,* 483.

29. Alice Walker, *Possessing the Secret of Joy* (New York: Pocket Books, 1993).

30. Sonja Lyobomirsky has discovered eight practical steps for growing in happiness: (1) count your blessings, (2) practice acts of kindness, (3) savor life's joys,

(4) thank a mentor, (5) learn to forgive, (6) invest time and energy in friends and family, (7) take care of your body, and (8) develop strategies for coping with stress and hardships. See Wallis, *Time,* January 17, 2005, A8–A9.

31. ER, 23.11, FA:ED I, 85–86.

32. Michael D. Guinan, O.F.M., *The Franciscan Vision and the Gospel of John: The San Damiano Cross; Francis and John; Creation and John* The Franciscan Heritage Series 4 (St. Bonaventure, NY: Franciscan Institute, 2006), 40.

33. Prospero Rivi, O.F.M.Cap., "Francis of Assisi and the Laity of His Time," trans. Heather Tolfree, *Greyfriars Review* 15 (2001): Supplement, 56.

34. TPJ, FA:ED I, 166–67.

35. André Jansen, O.F.M., "The Story of the True Joy: An Autobiographical Reading," *Greyfriars Review* 5, no 3 (1991): 385.

36. Ellsberg, *All Saints,* 433.

37. ER, 23, 8–9, FA:ED I, 84–85.

38. Adm 19.1–2, FA:ED I, 135.

39. Jansen, "The Story of the True Joy," 372.

40. CtC, 12–13, FA:ED 114.

41. AC 99, FA:ED II, 202–3.

42. AC, 8, FA:ED I, 122–23.

43. L3C, 5.13, FA:ED II, 76.

44. AP 12.47, FA:ED II, 58.

Chapter 12: Qualities of Franciscan Holiness and Sanctity

1. 1C 30.84, in Marion A. Habig, ed., *St. Francis of Assisi: Writings and Early Biographies* (Chicago: Franciscan Herald Press, 1972), 299. I have chosen this translation of Celano rather than that in FA:ED because it seems to fit more clearly the thrust of this book.

2. William James, *The Varieties of Religious Experience: A Study in Human Nature,* The Gifford Lectures, 1901–2 (New York: Modern Library, 1929), 266–67.

3. Erich Rohr, *Der Herr und Franziskus* (1965), in Mario von Galli, S.J., *Living Our Future: Francis of Assisi and the Church Tomorrow,* trans. Maureen Sullivan and John Drury (Chicago: Franciscan Herald Press, 1972), 203.

4. Carlos Castaneda, quoted in Wayne W. Dyer, *The Power of Intention: Learning to Co-Create Your World Your Way* (Carlsbad, CA: Hay House, 2004), 4.

5. Adm 16.2, FA:ED I, 134.

6. Edith Wyschogrod, *Saints and Postmodernism: Revisioning Moral Philosophy* (Chicago: University of Chicago Press, 1990), xxiv.

7. William B. Irvine, *On Desire: Why We Want What We Want* (Oxford and New York: Oxford University Press, 2005).

8. Spence E. Ante, with Cliff Edwards, "The Science of Desire," Managing, *BusinessWeek,* June 5, 2006, 99.

9. LJS 3.20, FA:ED I, 381.

10. 1C 9.22, FA:ED I, 201–2. See LMj 3.1, FA:ED II, 542.

11. Ronald Rolheiser, *The Holy Longing: The Search for a Christian Spirituality* (New York: Doubleday, 1999), 4.

12. LR 5.2, FA:ED I, 102, LtAnt, 2, FA:ED I, 107.

13. LJS 11.61, FA:ED I, 410; AP 12.46, FA:ED II, 58. Whether Francis received the stigmata was a matter of debate almost from the beginning. In his encyclical letter

on the death of St. Francis (October 1226), Elias of Cortona, the Minister General of the Order, allegedly wrote: "For a long time before his death, our Brother and Father Francis was visibly crucified; he bore on his body the five wounds, the genuine stigmata of Christ." This "letter" appears to have been a forgery written sometime after 1250. While there was a hagiographical effort to make Francis "another Christ," several groups, especially some Dominicans, resented the fact that the stigmata was identified with him. Opposition to the stigmata also depended on the situation. This "divinization" of Francis was generally accepted in the Franciscan Order. For a good study of this see André Vauchez, "The Stigmata of St. Francis and Its Medieval Detractors," trans. Edward Hagman, O.F.M.Cap., *Greyfriars Review* 13, no. 1 (1999): 61–89. For myself, it does not matter one way or another. The witness of his life, not something extraordinary like this, is what has inspired me to try to emulate him.

14. James M. Keegan, S.J., "Praying with Desire," *Human Development* 11, no. 3 (1990): 33.

15. LJS 11.59, FA:ED I, 409.

16. Nikos Mourkogiannis, *Purpose: The Starting Point of Great Companies* (New York: Palgrave Macmillan, 2006), 6–7.

17. Ibid., 17. Unfortunately, one of the companies cited by Mourkogiannis, ExxonMobil, is the very company my province and others challenged for ten years as its "moral DNA" seemed adamant about obfuscating the issue of global warming and the contribution made to it by the burning of its fossil fuels. This behavior seems far from "heroic," given the crisis we are facing related to global warming.

18. Rick Warren, *The Purpose Driven Life: What on Earth Am I Here For?* (Grand Rapids, MI: Zondervan, 2002), 306.

19. Edward Hays, *The Passionate Troubadour: A Medieval Novel about Francis of Assisi* (Notre Dame: Ave Maria/Forest of Peace Books, 2004), 6.

20. Joe Tye, Spark plug's Weekend Spark, June 15, 2006. For more on Joe Tye see *www.joetye.com.*

21. AP 1.4, FA:ED II, 35.

22. Rosemary Haughton, *The Passionate God* (New York: Paulist Press, 1981), 49.

23. Arnoldo Fortini, *Francis of Assisi,* trans. Helen Moak (New York: Crossroad, 1985), 11.

24. Ibid., 479.

25. LFl, 37, FA:ED III, 638.

26. ER, 7.16, FA:ED I, 69.

27. Leonhard Lehmann, O.F.M.Cap., "Franciscan Global Spirituality," trans. Ignatius McCormick, O.F.M.Cap., *Greyfriars Review* 5, no. 3 (1991): 315–16.

28. Mario von Galli, S.J., *Living Our Future: Francis of Assisi and the Church Tomorrow,* trans. Maureen Sullivan and John Drury (Chicago: Franciscan Herald Press, 1972), 205.

29. William Law, *A Serious Call to a Devout and Holy Life,* 1729. In *The Tablet* July 26, 2003.

30. G. K. Chesterton, *St. Francis of Assisi* (Garden City, NY: Doubleday Image Books, 1957), 76.

31. LJS 12.67, FA:ED I, 415.

Index